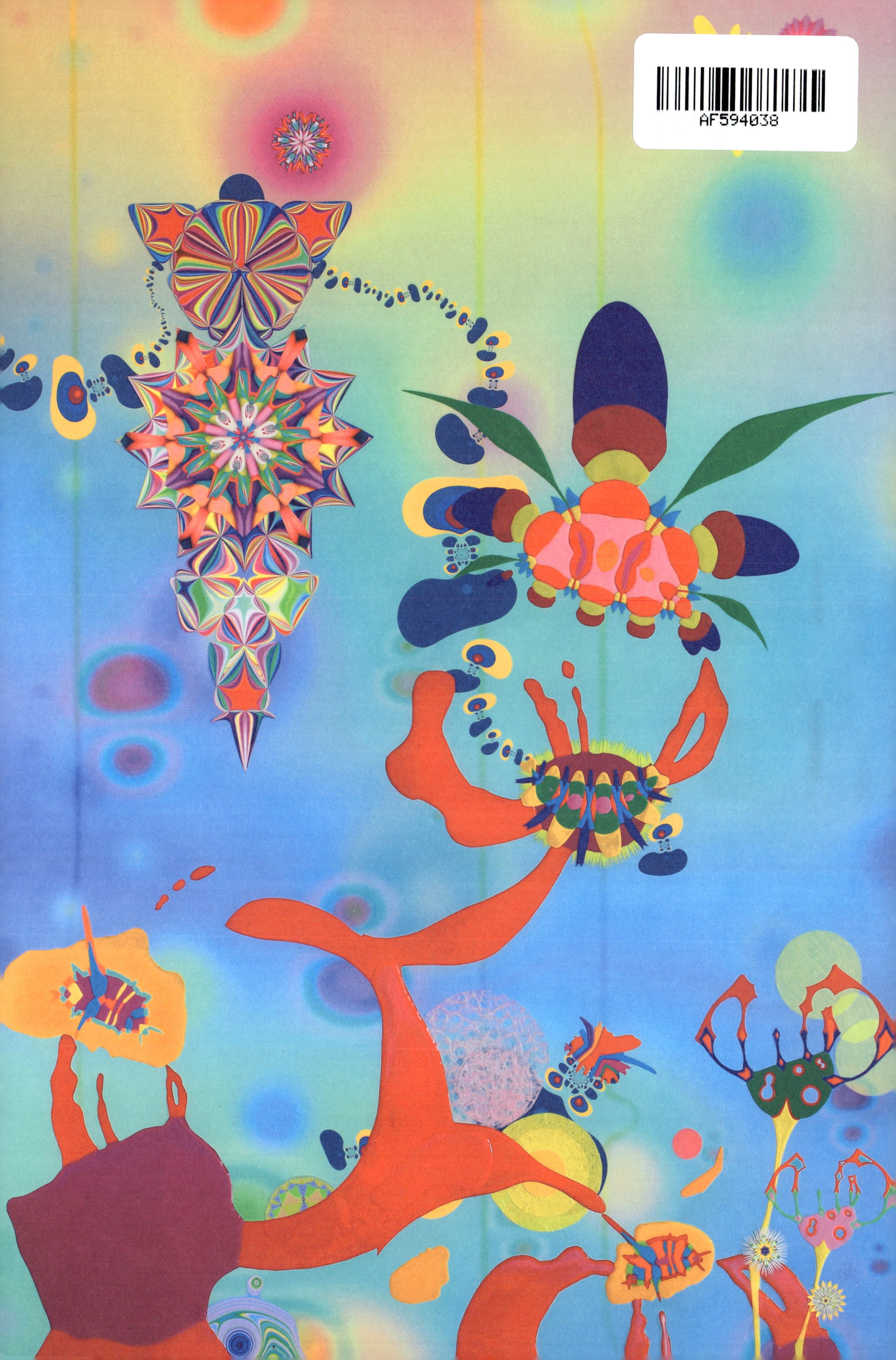
AF594038

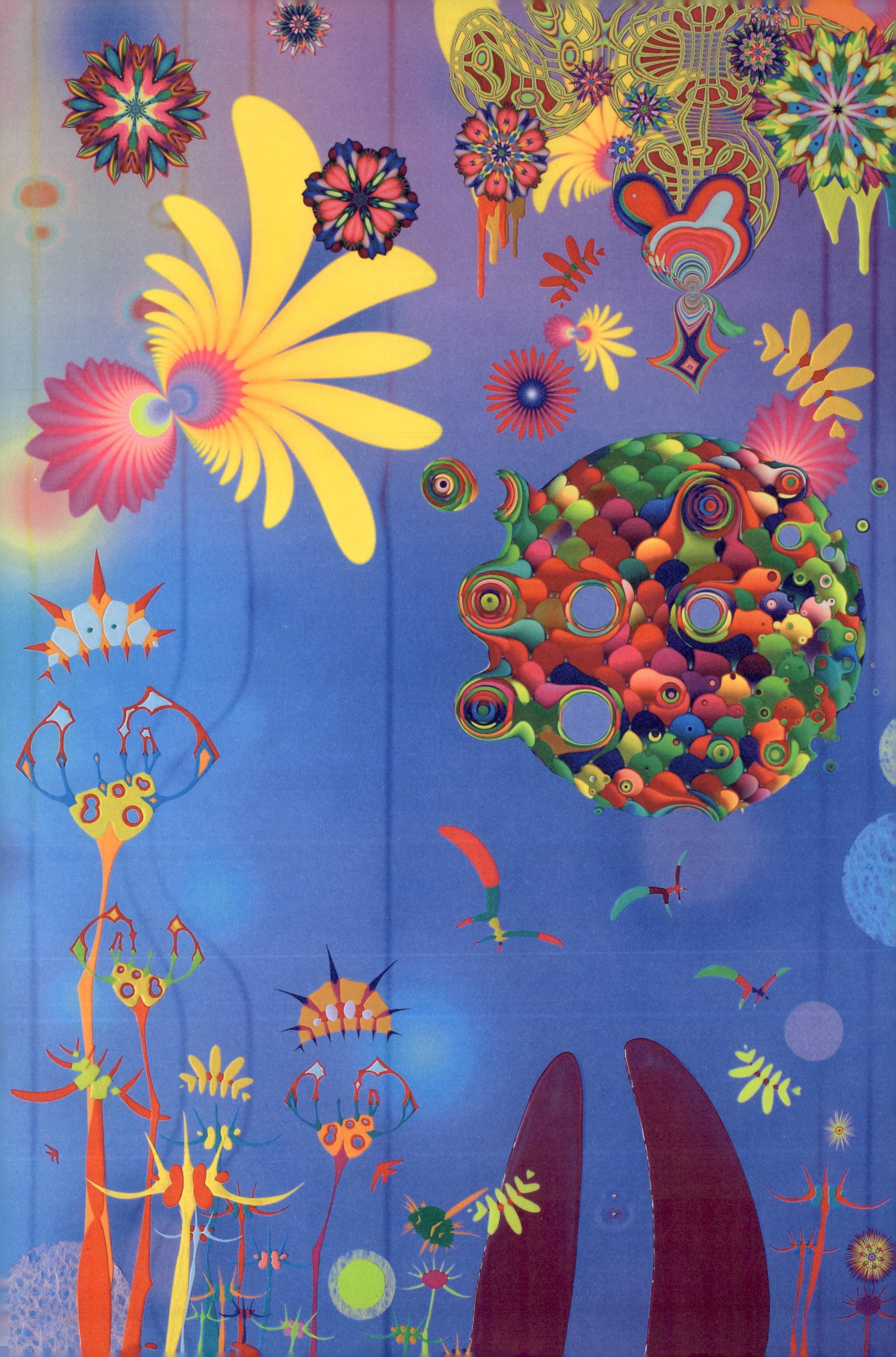

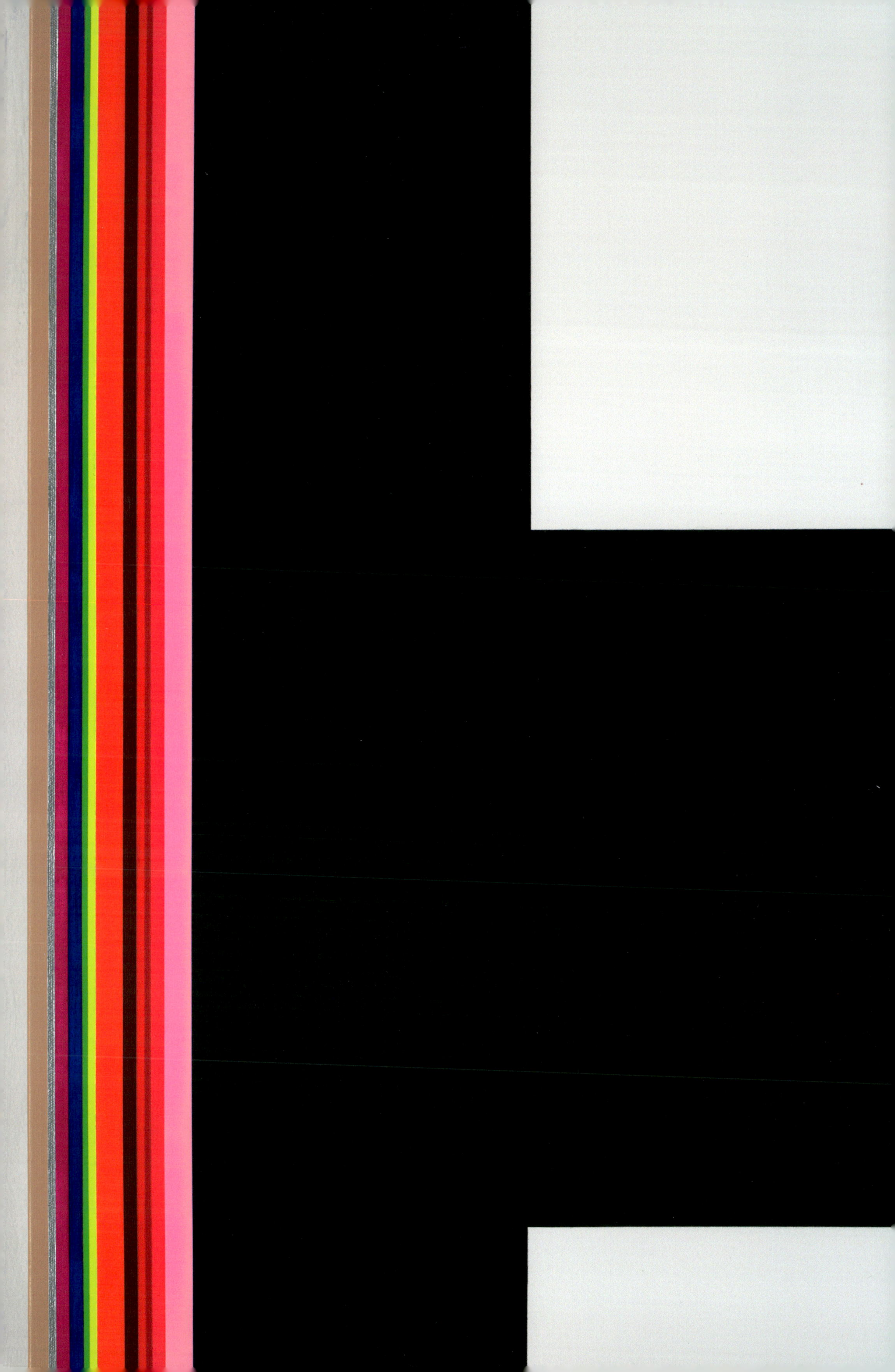

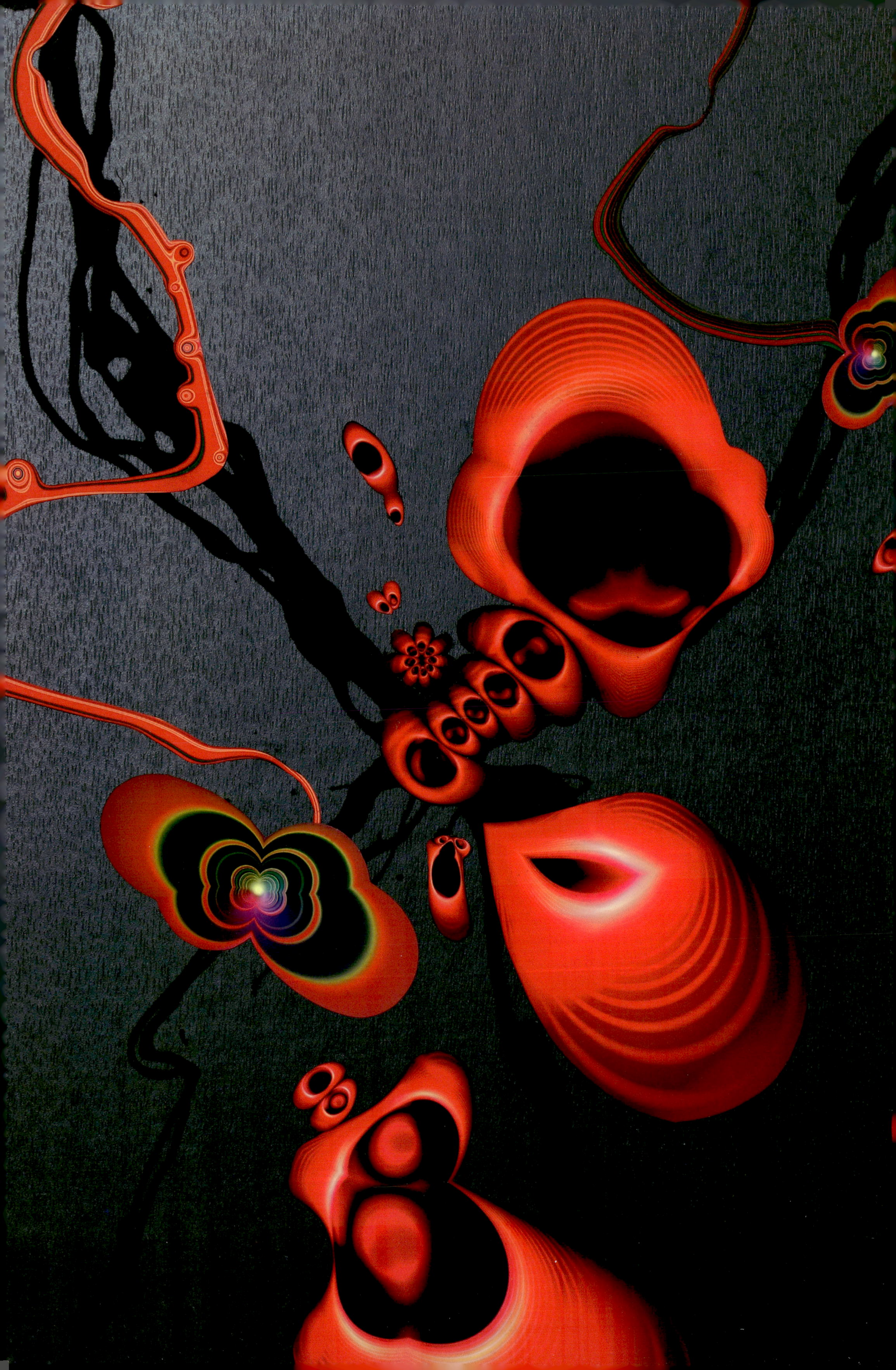

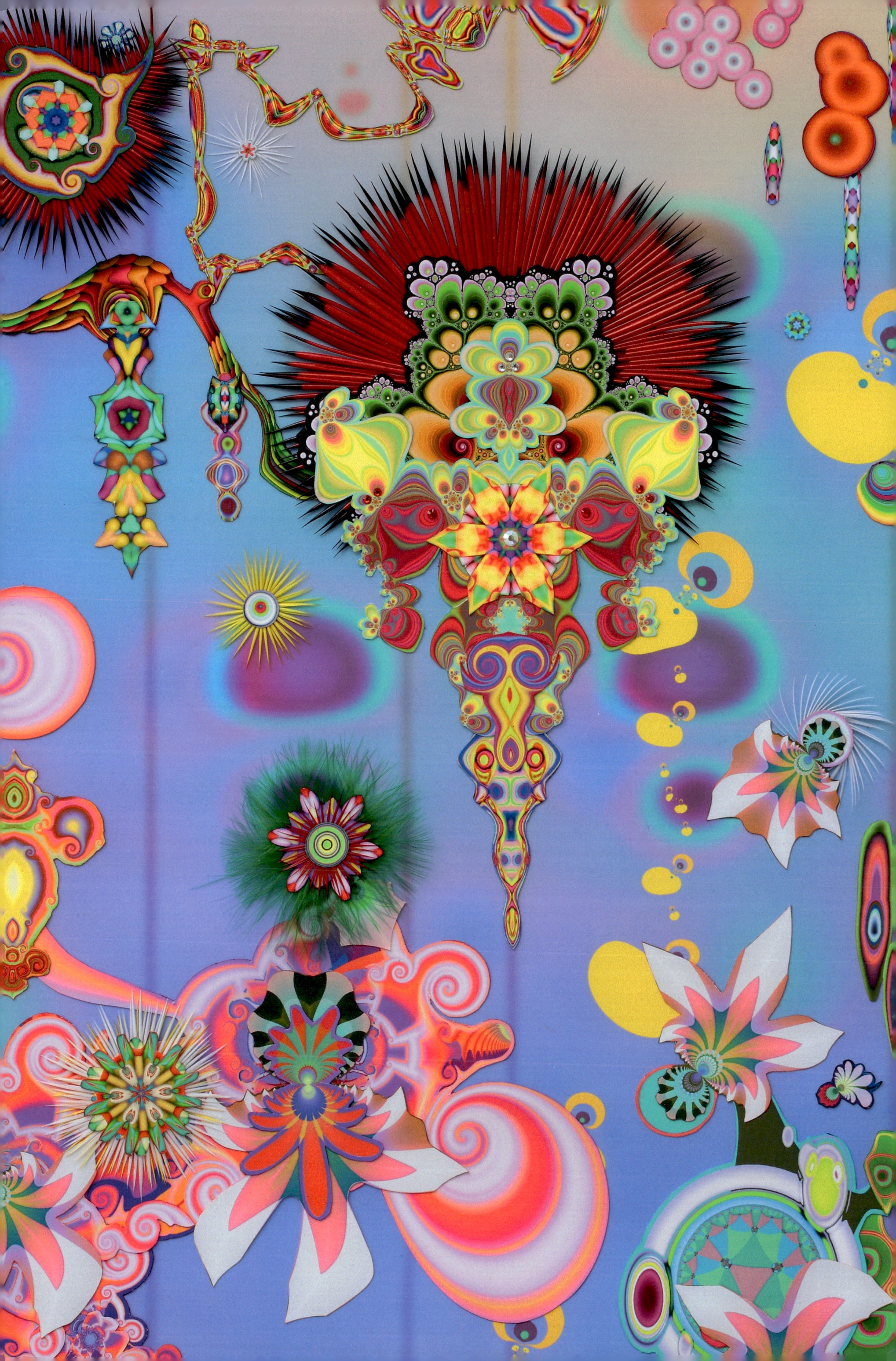

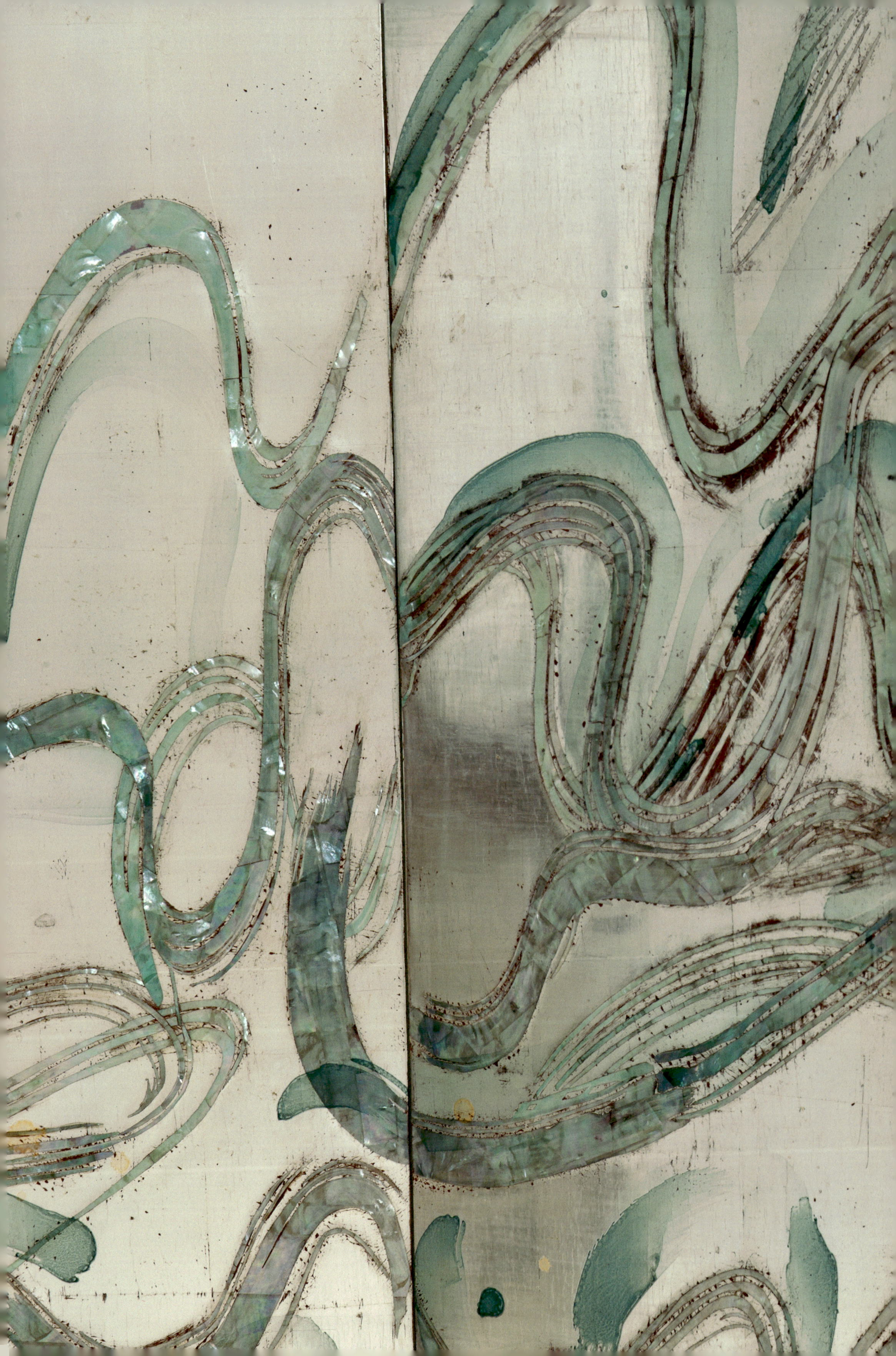

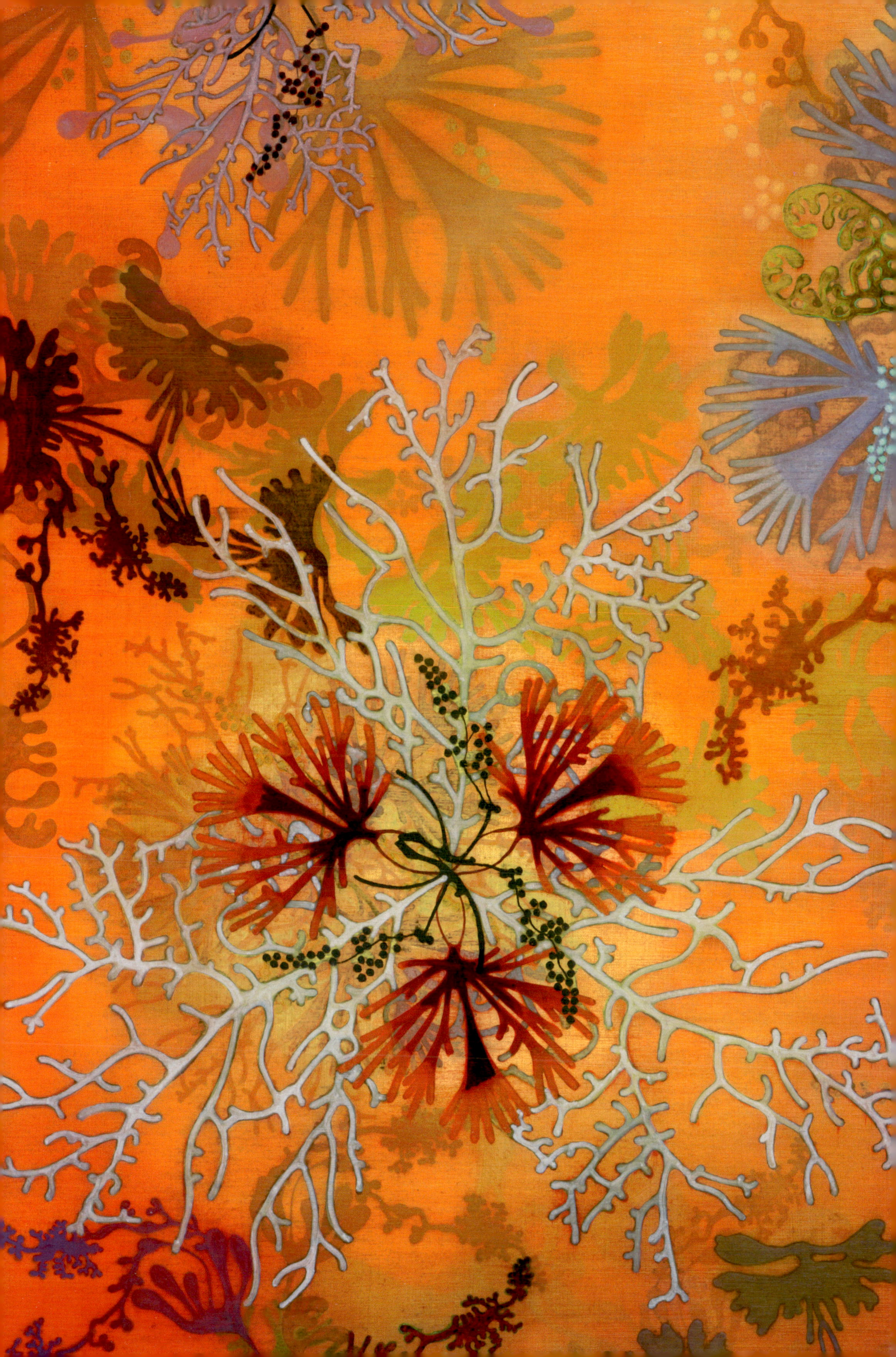

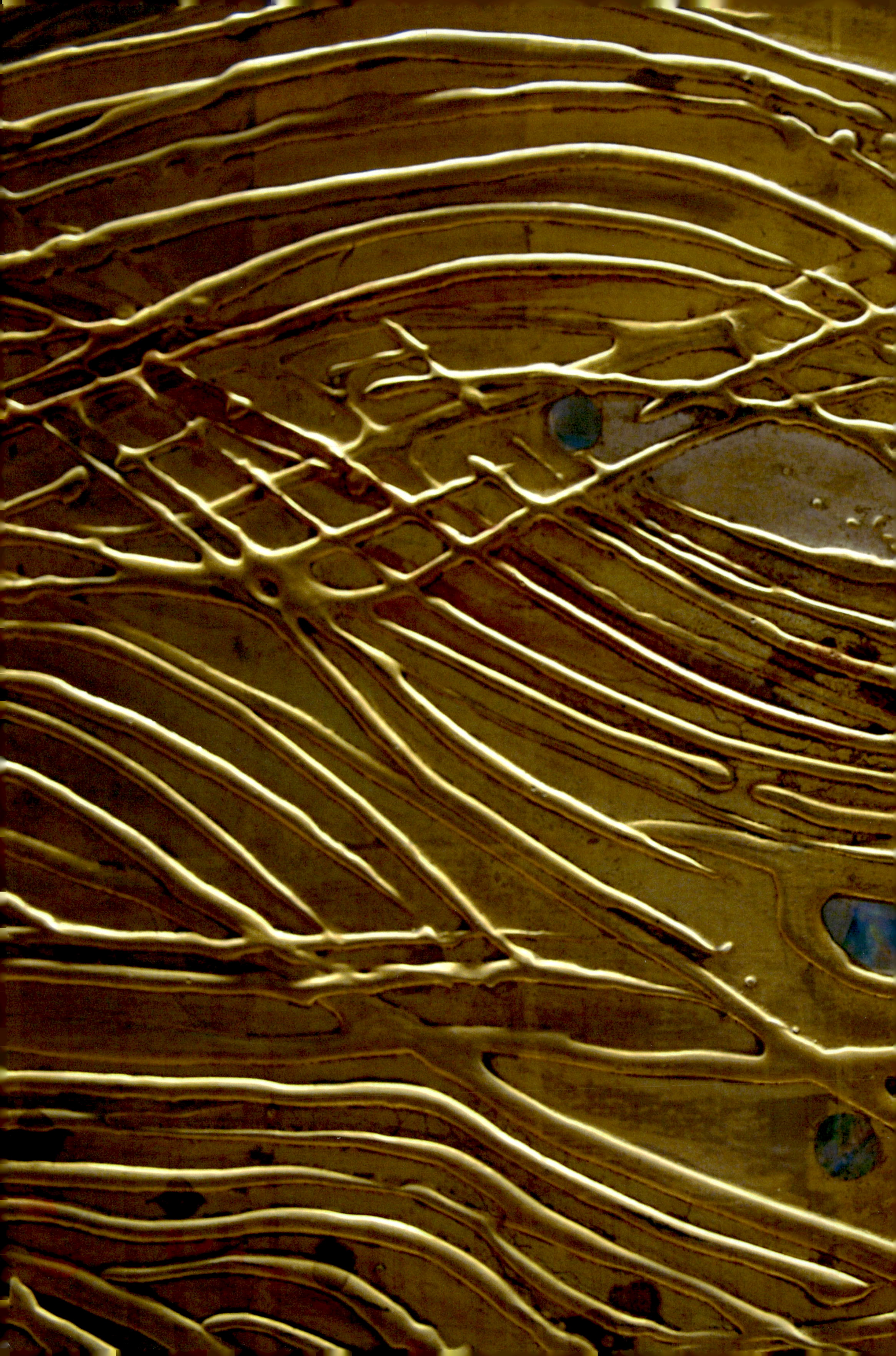

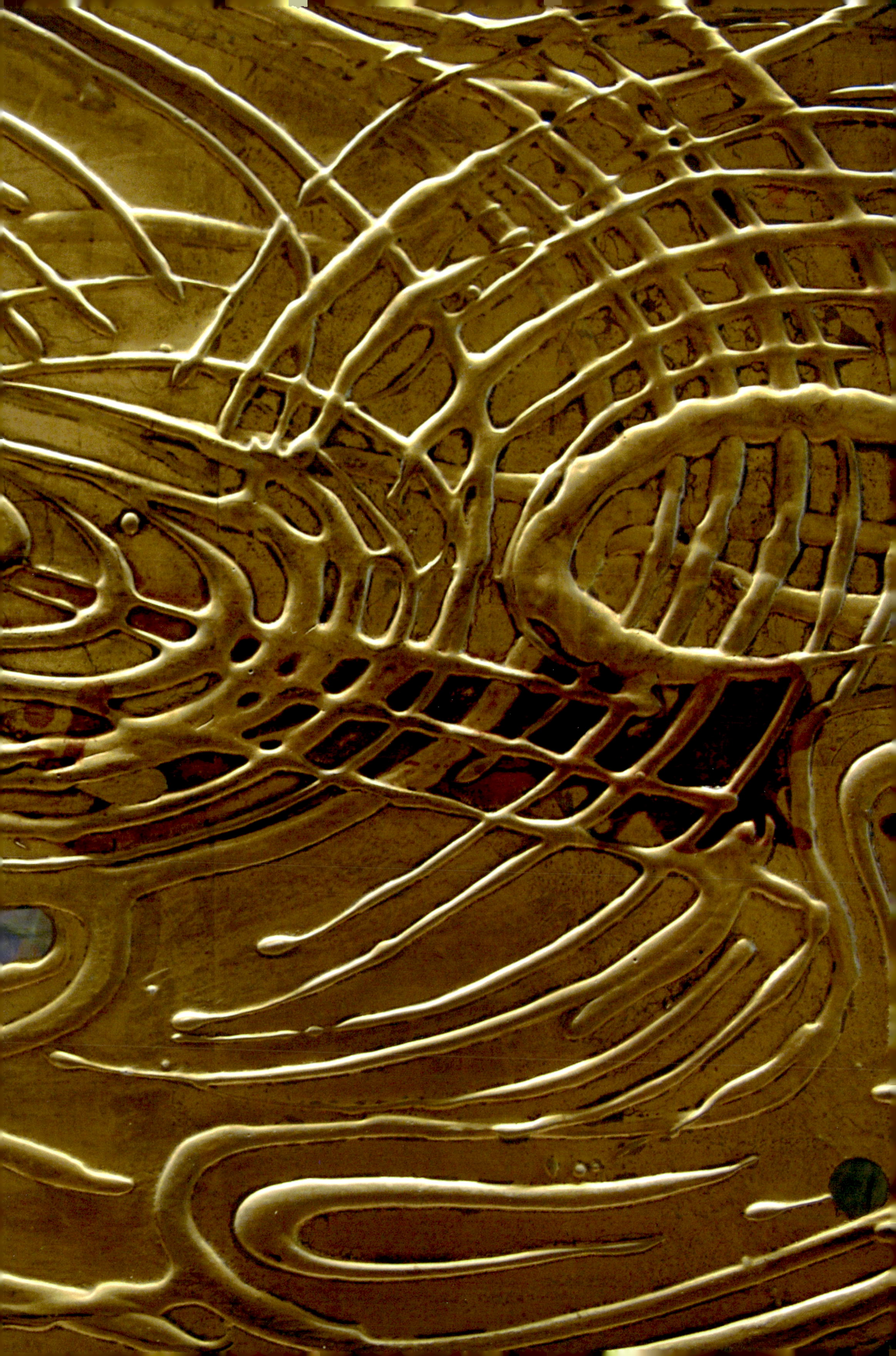

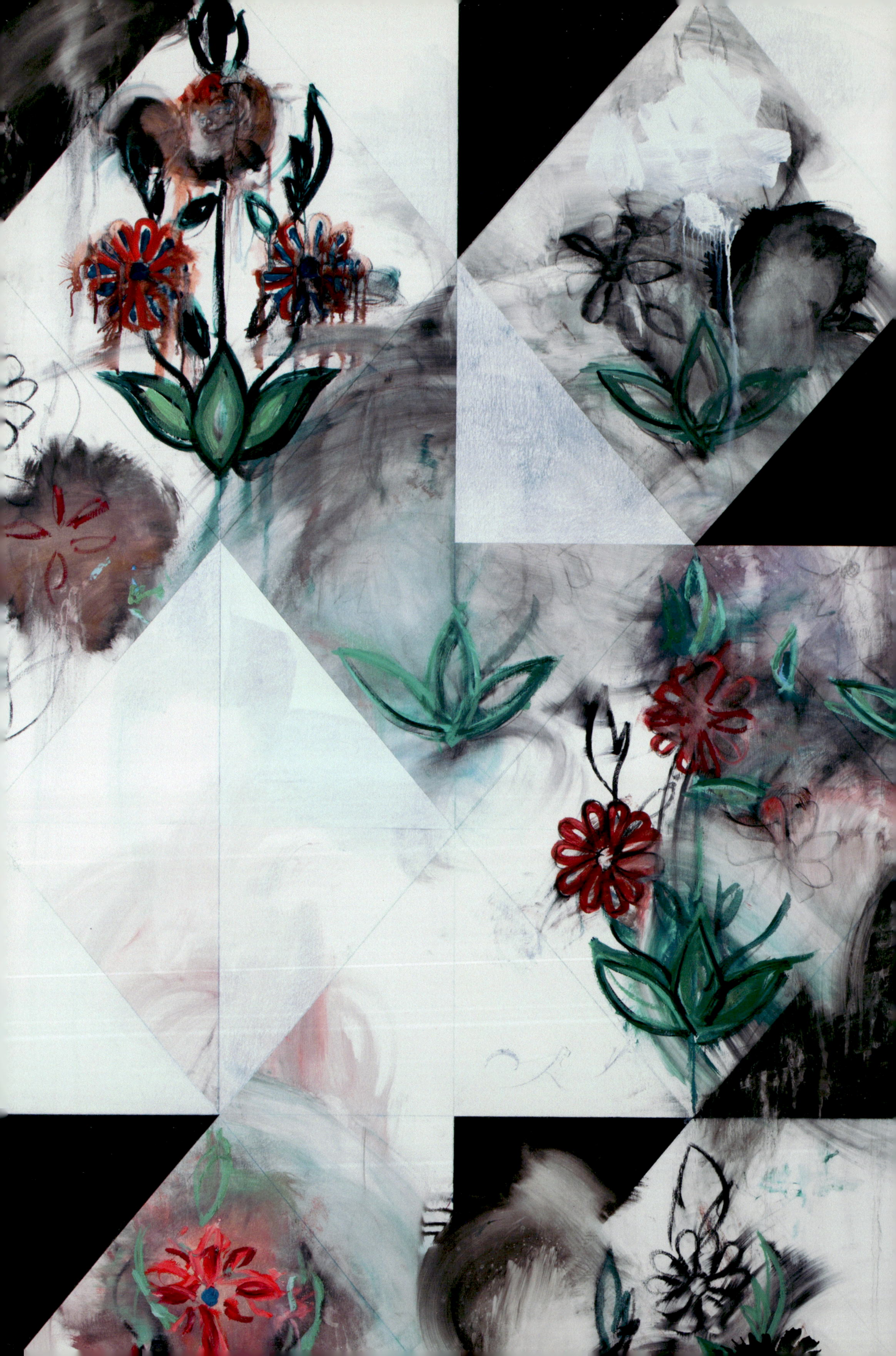

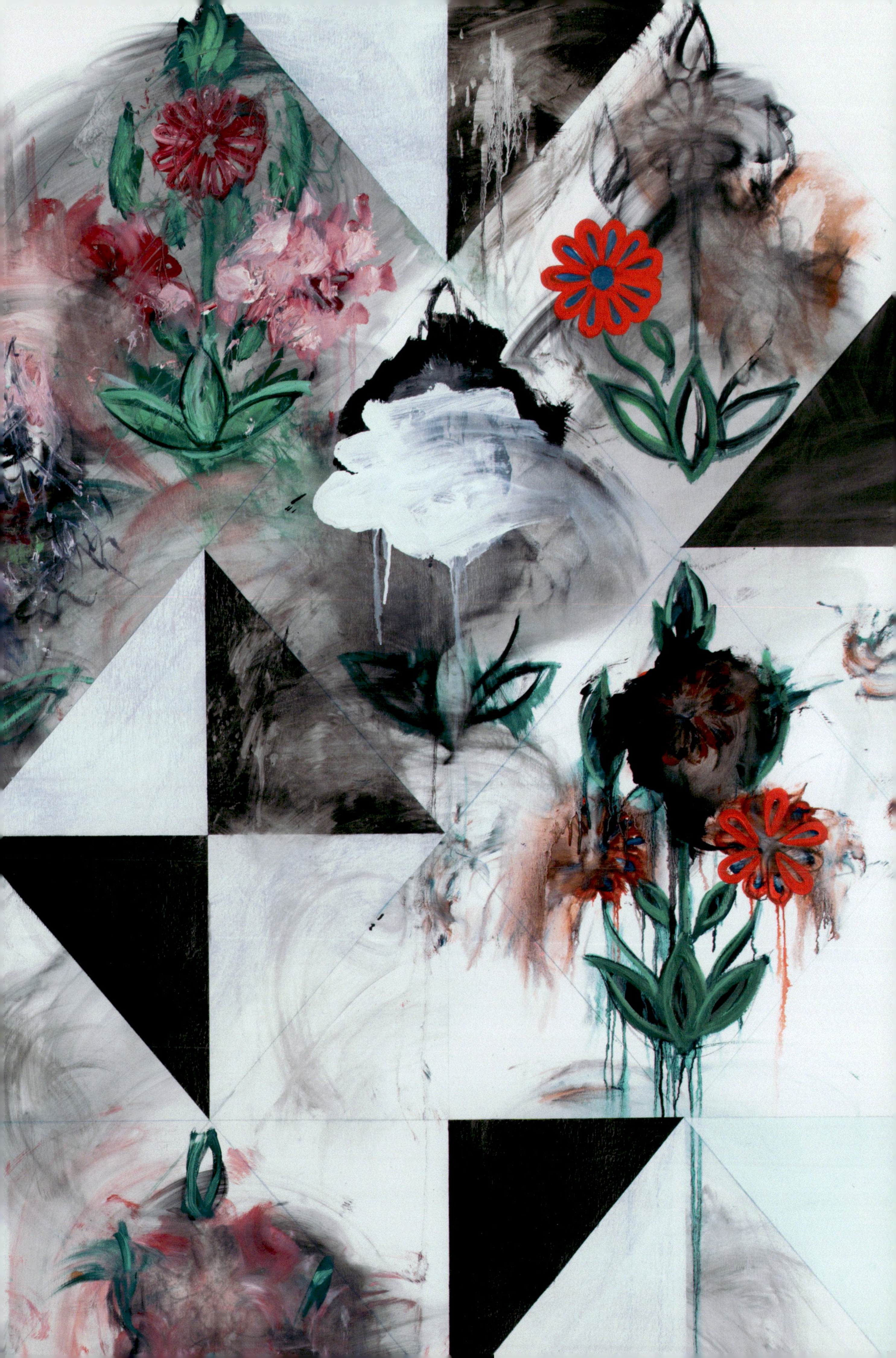

# beauty

## *A Baroque Sensibility in Recent Painting*

FUNDING FOR THIS PUBLICATION IS GENEROUSLY PROVIDED BY THE SEMMES FOUNDATION, INC.

*René Paul Barilleaux*
*Lilly Wei*
*Stephen Westfall*

# reigns

**McNAY ART MUSEUM** SAN ANTONIO, TEXAS

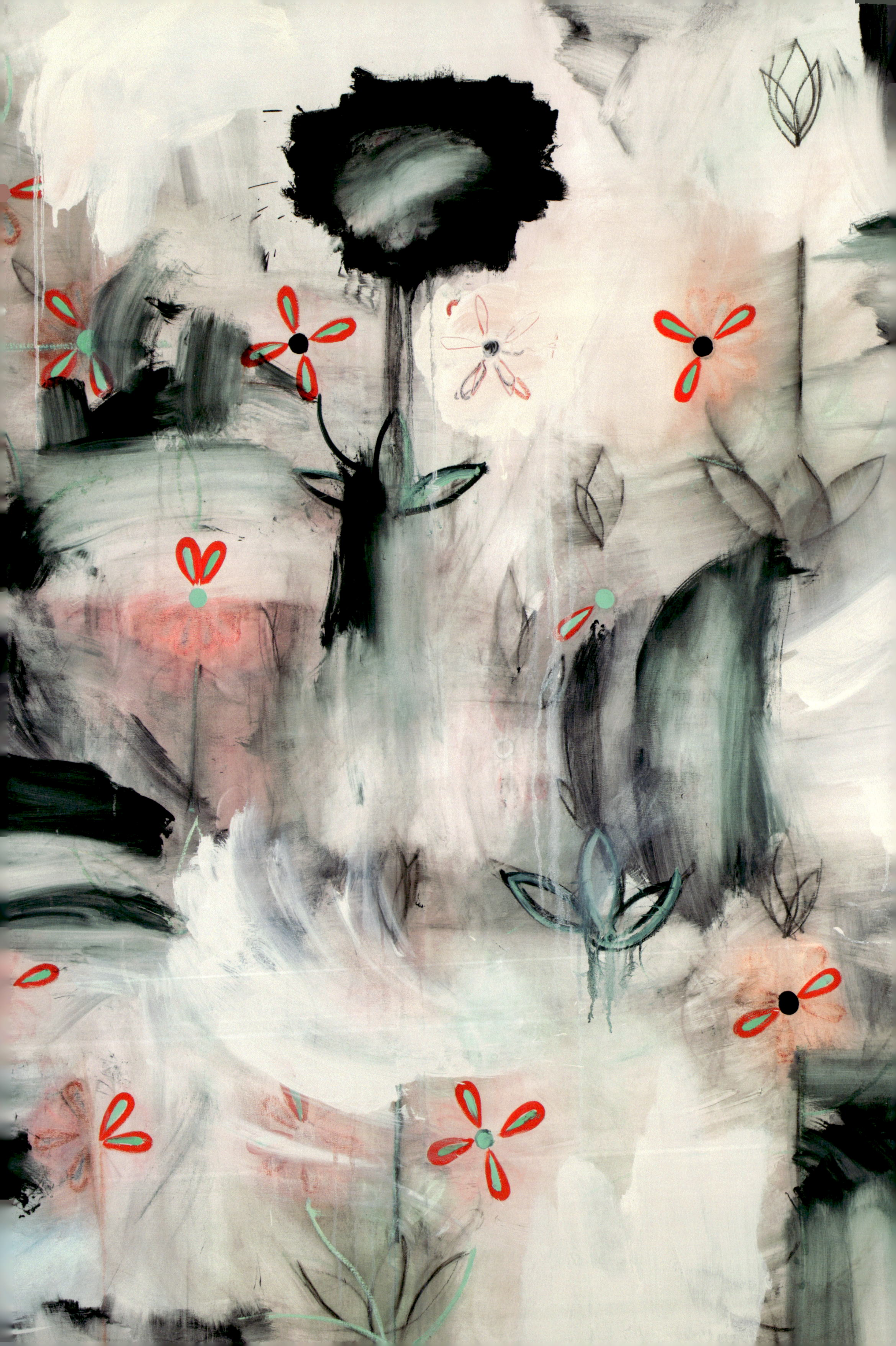

# *Foreword*

As the first museum of modern art in Texas, the McNay serves as a bridge between the art of the past and the art of the present. The museum collects retrospectively and acquires contemporary works of art. In the three exhibitions celebrating the museum's sixtieth anniversary, we reflect our collecting scope from the nineteenth century to the present.

*Beauty Reigns: A Baroque Sensibility in Recent Painting* represents the museum's commitment to the art of today. I congratulate René Paul Barilleaux, the McNay's Chief Curator and Curator of Art after 1945, for identifying an exciting direction in contemporary art, just as he did in his 2011 exhibition, *New Image Sculpture*. He organized a visually stunning survey of thirteen contemporary artists, and with his guest essayists and Marquand Books, produced a complementary, distinctive publication as a permanent document of the show. Over the last eight years of his leadership he has steadily strengthened the museum's holdings of contemporary art while simultaneously organizing a variety of exhibitions, ranging from *Andy Warhol: Fame and Misfortune*, to two new programs of wall works and video to animate public spaces in the museum.

*Beauty Reigns* is the second in the sequence of our three sixtieth-anniversary exhibitions. It was preceded by *Robert Indiana: Beyond LOVE*, a revealing retrospective of a complex, influential artist of the Pop art era whose career spans the second half of the twentieth century and continues today. Organized by the Whitney Museum of American Art, this show arrived at the McNay as a kind of homecoming, thanks to the many works by Indiana given to the McNay by the late Robert L. B. Tobin that are included in the exhibition.

*Beauty Reigns* is followed this fall by *Intimate Impressionism from the National Gallery of Art*, an exhibition of intimate-scale French Impressionist and Post-Impressionist paintings from the superb collections of Ailsa Mellon Bruce, her brother Paul Mellon, and other generous benefactors of the National Gallery of Art who collected for a domestic setting, as did Marion Koogler McNay. The strength of our founder's collection in French painting provides an ideal context for this show.

I would like to offer heartfelt thanks to the museum's Board of Trustees, led by its president, Sarah E. Harte, and all the generous exhibition sponsors and supporters of our sixtieth anniversary programs. I am grateful for their deep commitment to this museum as we celebrate this milestone in our history.

William J. Chiego
Director

# Acknowledgments

The research, organization, and production of exhibitions and publications such as *Beauty Reigns: A Baroque Sensibility in Recent Painting* go well beyond a single curator's vision. They encompass a large, diversified team. This project, and this curator, demanded the unified efforts of a wide range of individuals in order to achieve (even exceed) the intended curatorial vision. Nearly four years in the making, *Beauty Reigns* is a shared experience, and I am deeply appreciative of the dedication and focus of my many collaborators along the way.

Research for the project began with Celeste Wackenhut, the McNay's Semmes Foundation Intern in Museum Studies, 2010–2011. Three subsequent Semmes Interns built on Celeste's foundation: Katherine Kunau (2011–2012), Jacqueline Edwards (2012–2013), and most recently, Althea Ruoppo (2013–2014). Other McNay staff offered great aid, including former curatorial assistant, Edward Hayes, Jr., and current curatorial assistant (and former Semmes Intern), Jacqueline Edwards. Heather Lammers, Collections Manager & Exhibitions Coordinator, and Rebecca Dankert, Associate Registrar for Exhibitions, handled all logistical arrangements for bringing the exhibition together. Ethel Shipton, Chief Preparator, along with her dedicated team, worked to realize the beautiful installation in the McNay's galleries.

The success of this project is wholly due to the masterful creativity of the thirteen artists whose work is included in this publication and the exhibition that it accompanies: Jose Alvarez (D.O.P.A.), Kamrooz Aram, Charles Burwell, Annette Davidek, Fausto Fernandez, Nancy Lorenz, Ryan McGinness, Beatriz Milhazes, Jiha Moon, Paul Henry Ramirez, Rex Ray, Rosalyn Schwartz, and Susan Chrysler White.

Lilly Wei and Stephen Westfall contributed immensely to this publication with their insightful essays, and Marcia Goren Weser provided editorial oversight and helped shape each of the authors' words. As well, Althea Ruoppo closely assisted in every aspect; she and Craig Bunch carefully proofread layouts.

The McNay has produced a number of books in collaboration with Marquand Books of Seattle, Washington, several of which won awards. Jeff Wincapaw once again designed a dynamic volume that truly reflects the spirit and aesthetic of *Beauty Reigns*. Other Marquand staff who played key roles in this publication include Melissa Duffes, Leah Finger, Diana George, Ryan Polich, and Brynn Warriner.

In addition to the artists themselves, a number of individuals working on their behalf were instrumental in creating this book and organizing the exhibition. They are Ben Strauss-Malcolm, Quint Contemporary Art, La Jolla, California; Bridgette Mayer and Jillian Murphy, Bridgette Mayer Gallery, Philadelphia, Pennsylvania; Jacquie Littlejohn, Littlejohn Contemporary, New York; Jane Cohan and Philip Tan, James Cohan Gallery, New York; Jeffrey Lee, RYAN LEE Gallery, New York; Nancy Whitenack and Danette Dufilho, Conduit Gallery, Dallas, Texas; Sally Morgan Lehman, Morgan Lehman Gallery, New York; and Sarah Gavlak, Gavlak Gallery, Palm Beach, Florida.

Finally, my great appreciation goes to William J. Chiego, Director of the McNay, for his continued trust in me and my curatorial vision. I am grateful for the freedom to create innovative exhibitions and publications including *Beauty Reigns*.

René Paul Barilleaux

Beatriz Milhazes. **O Paraiso**, 1997. Acrylic on canvas, 70 × 74½ in. Worcester Art Museum, Worcester, Massachusetts; Charlotte E.W. Buffington Fund, 1999.2



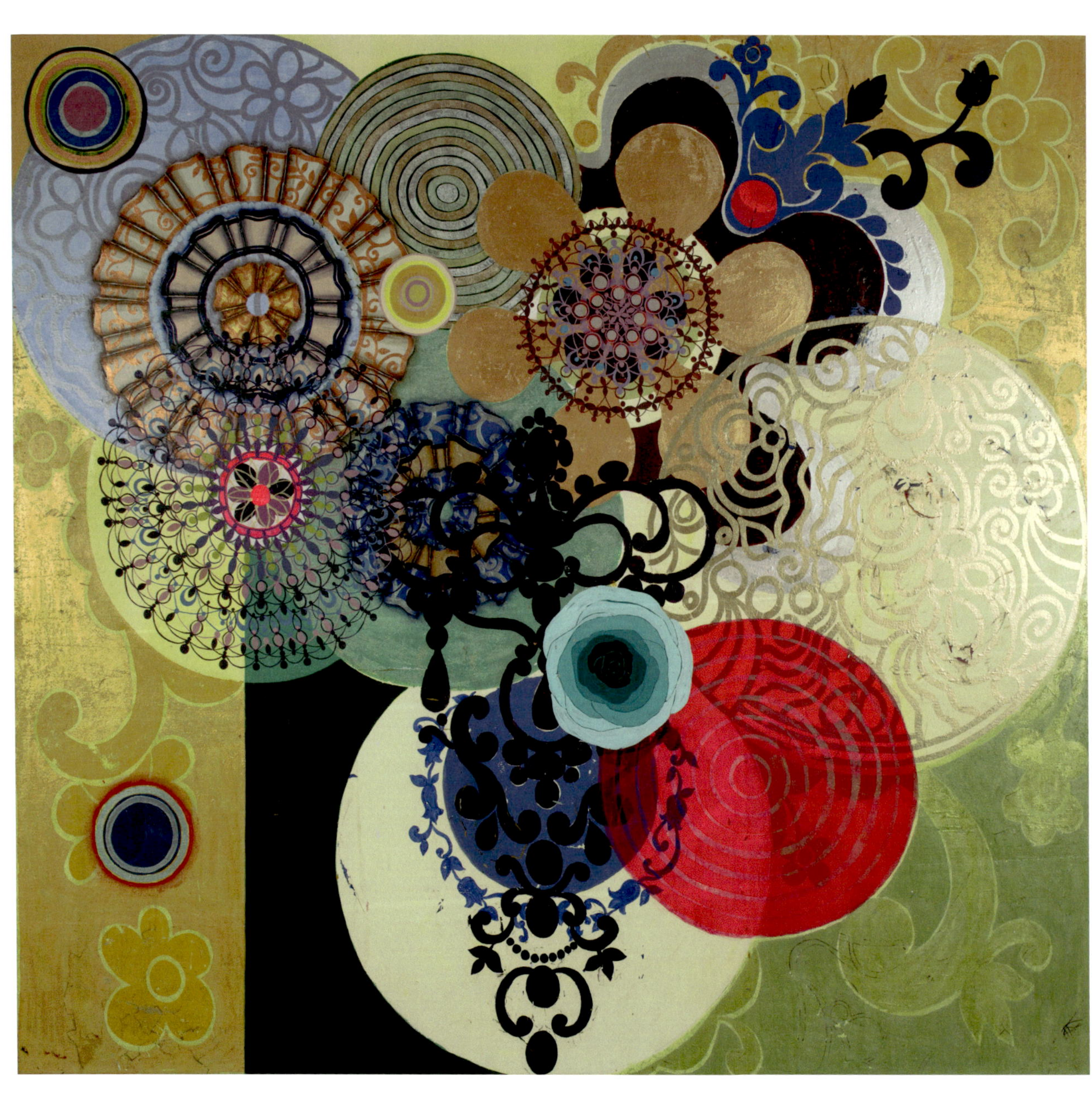

# Introduction

Abstract painting currently takes as varied and multifaceted forms as are found in the landscape of contemporary art. Expressionistic mark-making, flat and unmodulated paint application, collage, staining, stenciling, and spraying—all these techniques only hint at myriad approaches evident today. While traditional artists' materials are still employed, the wide range of components now found in abstract painting is as diverse as the imagery itself. Although it is impossible to isolate any particular direction or movement, there are shared sensibilities that unify artists separated by age, gender, location, and background.

*Beauty Reigns: A Baroque Sensibility in Recent Painting* assembles the work of thirteen intergenerational emerging and mid-career abstract painters, working in studios across the United States. Among the shared characteristics found in this highly diverse group, in whole or part, are high-key color, layering of surface imagery, use of overall and repeated patterns, stylized motifs, fragmented representation, and a tension between melancholy and the sublime. To date, little focus has been placed on works which celebrate the exoticism, exuberance, and optimism found in the work of these painters or that of the numerous others moving in similar directions.

This particular approach to abstraction evolved out of a long history of image-making. Stephen Westfall's essay on the "beautiful grotesque" traces this legacy over several centuries and sets the stage for a better understanding and appreciation of the work of these thirteen painters. Lilly Wei's contribution reflects on the nature of beauty and the sublime. She places these artists within a broader context, connecting their individual approaches not only to larger traditions but also to each other's art.

Interpretive and biographical texts offer further insight into the work of these featured individuals, while expansive portfolios give testimony to the visual feasts that their paintings have to offer. Details of artworks allow for close inspection by enlarging sections of complex surfaces. Images burst from the pages of this publication not unlike the way that the art bursts off the gallery walls.

*Beauty Reigns: A Baroque Sensibility in Recent Painting* confirms the vitality of abstract painting today. This overview requires that the viewer travel to and voyage through visual territory that seems somewhat foreign, or somewhat familiar, yet always rewarding. As art continues to evolve in unforeseen ways, the paintings surveyed here will be increasingly relevant to the overall language of abstraction: a universal language that finds its voice in a welcoming, worldwide community. In the end, beauty reigns supreme.

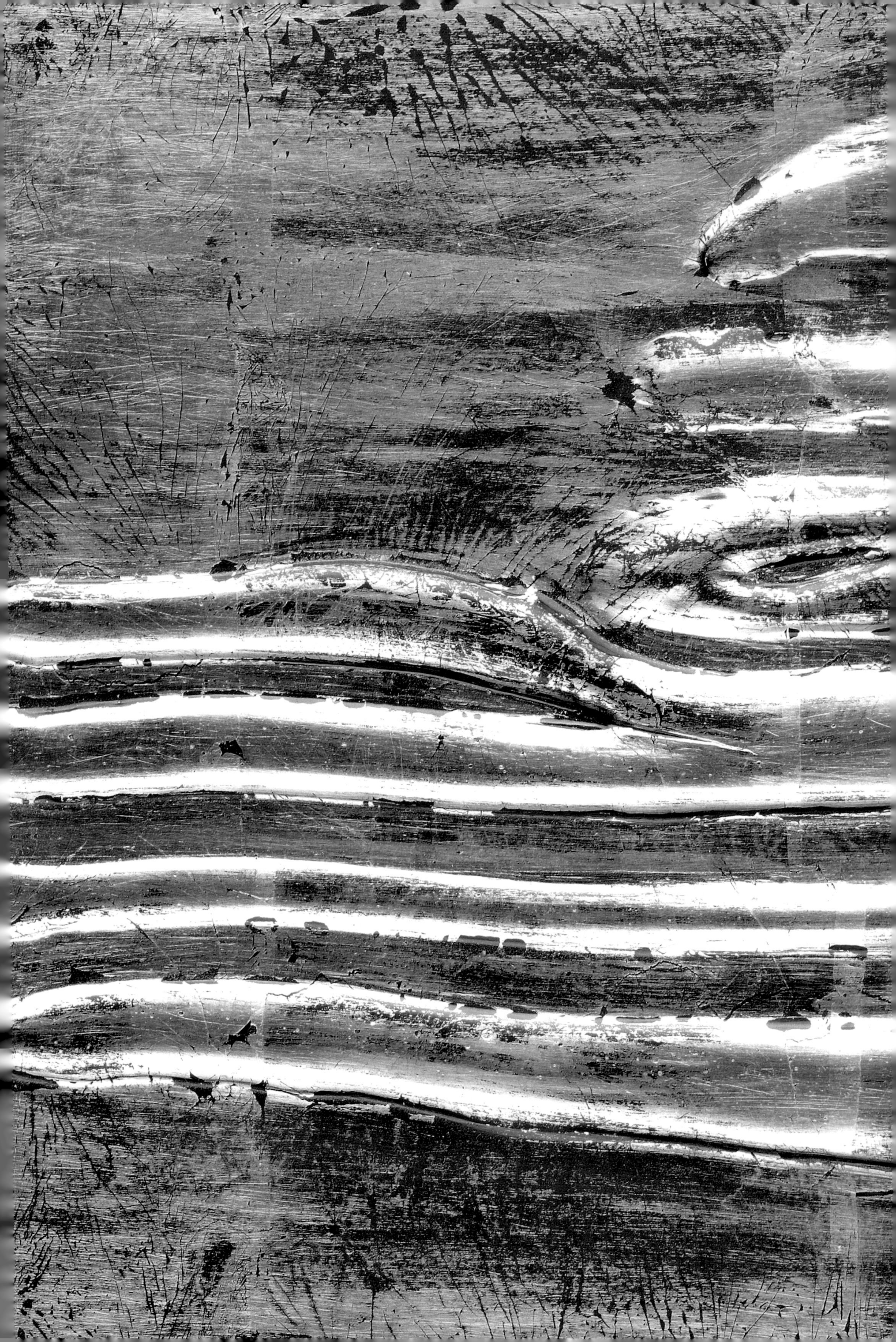

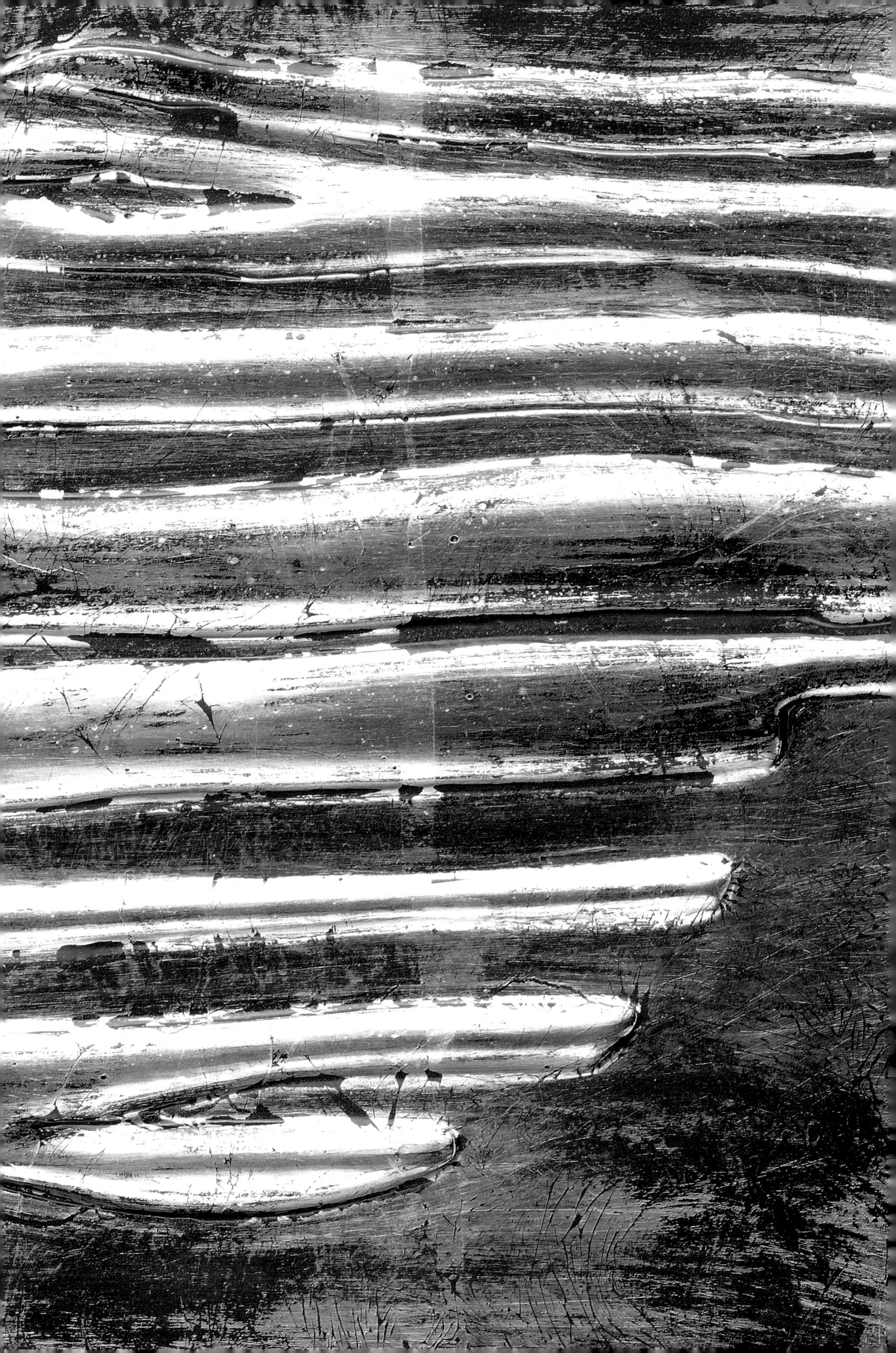

A flowering: the thirteen painters whose work is explored in this volume comprise a representative, but by no means exhaustive survey of a style of painting that opposes a reductive modernist "logic" of form. This seems overdue.

# The Beautiful

For at least several decades an artistic protest has developed against the teleology of the version of modernism advanced by the great formalist critic, Clement Greenberg (and others). In Greenberg's neo-Kantian narrative the arts progressively jettison those features of their practice that are not intrinsic to the particular medium in question. Much of the art that proceeded from this dictum has been astonishingly beautiful, yet even Shaker-like simplicity is a poor aesthetic diet.

Michael Fried correctly diagnosed Minimalism as a threat to Greenberg's paradigm in his famous essay *Art and Objecthood*,[1] because Minimalism seemed to burlesque Greenberg by taking his analysis literally. "American-type painting" was big. Minimalism went big. Should works of art be entrenched more firmly in a formal language that could be held to be exclusive to their medium? Minimalism gave us a geometrically clarified confrontation with materiality, fabrication, and scale. It was Enlightenment logic turned into an instruction sheet.

Faith in an aesthetic/perceptual revolution that would bring a unifying idea to culture was holding forth in twentieth-century art before Greenberg: And it was challenged, even if the challenge was brushed aside by dominant art discourse. One need only recall Alfred Barr's distaste for Surrealism, or the Russian post-revolutionary movement towards the utilitarian

Stephen Westfall

# Grotesque

object, to understand something of the pressure exerted on the impulse for the decorative, the fantastic, and spatial overlay in painting. That impulse may be seen here.

Between the wars the avant-garde itself was driven to choose between the apparently subjective caprices of Surrealism or a "less is more" approach, an essentializing materialism that clung both to Dada and abstract art. For the most part the avant-garde chose the latter, perhaps because it seemed less decadent in the face of the apparent failures of capitalism and the tragic backdrop of The Great War.

There were other voices and contrary impulses. There always are. Max Ernst's *frottage* landscapes from the early 1940s, such as *Europe after the Rain* (1940–42), are perhaps the most open evocation of the grotesque in twentieth-century painting. Their frothy, hallucinatory geology directly recalls the walls of the grottos that name the style. But the original "grotto" was a palace, Nero's Domus Aurea. The curling foliage-into-animal imagery decorating its walls gave birth to a late Renaissance and early Baroque style of decoration.

This style played with all the pagan metamorphoses that Classical harmonies and the rationality of High Renaissance realism and proportionality were supposed to dispel like light casting back shadow. The tension between these polarities of fantasy and rationality, caprice and order, runs back a long way. Vitruvius loathed grotesque ornament at least as much as Barr and Greenberg detested Surrealism.

As John Elderfield points out in his great catalogue essay for the Museum of Modern Art's Morris Louis retrospective in 1986–87, Horace gave us the phrase *Ut pictura poesis*, in asserting that painting "should appeal to the intellect rather than to the senses."[2] Renaissance theorists such as Alberti used Horatian criteria to contrast different types of pictures:

Leon Battista Alberti, for example, contrasted ennobling pictures—those fulfilling the intellectual, didactic implications of Horace's idea—with pictures of an opposite kind, whose justification was that if painting is a kind of poetry, then it might be a specifically poetic kind of painting—a relaxing, harmonious kind of painting similar in its effects on the human mind to that of music—which would "help to restore the tired spirits of the man of affairs."[3] This is to justify a hedonistic, lyrical art devoted to pastoral subjects rather than (and besides) a moralistic, epic art devoted to ennobling subjects (also, in effect, to justify Venetian painting next to Florentine). Whereas the intellectual interpretation of the Horatian idea was fulfilled in an emphatically urban, civic art, expressive of the

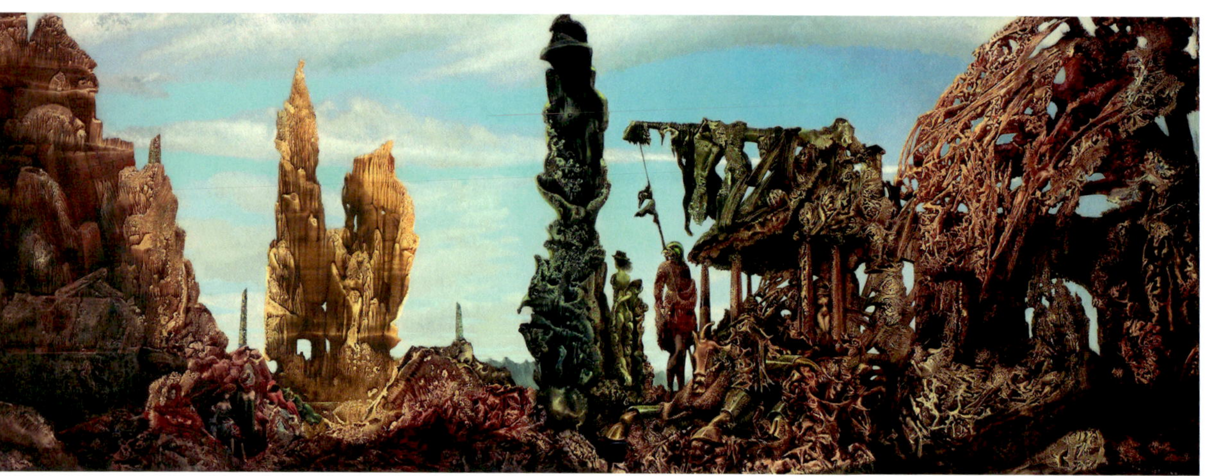

Max Ernst (German, 1891–1976). ***Europe after the Rain***, 1940–42. Oil on canvas, 21 9/16 × 58 3/16 in. Wadsworth Atheneum Museum of Art, Hartford, Connecticut; The Ella Gallup Sumner and Mary Catlin Sumner Collection Fund, 1942.281.


> ordering of affairs in a rational, organized society (whose biblical archetype was the city of Jerusalem), the instinctive interpretation was fulfilled in a rural, pastoral art, which imagined an existence prior to and apart from society itself (its archetype being the paradisal garden). *The two interpretations (and the polarities I am using to describe them), as manifested in the practice of painting, were never totally distinct, but in practice the intellectual interpretation produced a more heroic and proclamatory art of regularized accent and meter, and the instinctive, a more introverted and private art of increasingly asymmetrical and irregular rhythms.*[4] [emphasis added]

The preceding is an effective outline of the break between "decorative" *grotesquerie* and the tradition of "ennobling" painting with which it has had to contend. I envision the image of Yosemite Sam as a pirate stomping desperately on the bilge-hold of his ship as the arms and teeth of snarling crocodiles try to break out. Maybe crocodiles aren't in your image of the relaxing, hedonistic pastoral, but I tend to think of them as Freud's "return of the repressed."

The garlanded metamorphoses of the grotesque are evocations of the pastoral, the opposition of Orphic lyricism to dispassionate reason. They are also *eros* to Horace's poetic *logos*. The pastoral and *eros* are not synonymous, but their alliance is a necessary complement to what Elderfield describes as "an emphatically urban, civic art, expressive of the ordering of affairs in a rational, organized society." Without their presence, *logos* atrophies into Law, and if banished they return as monsters, as Goya so brilliantly showed us.

I perceive that the thirteen artists in *Beauty Reigns* are inheritors of the *grotesquerie* style of ornament that flourished in the Baroque era and which also winds a thread or a vine tendril back to the Domus Aurea. This is the metamorphosis of ornamentation that decorates and comprises the painted pilasters framing both interior and exterior landscape views in the wall paintings of Pompeii and Herculaneum.

It is a thread that winds through the *drolleries* in the margins of Middle Ages manuscripts. It reaches across the Mediterranean to Islamic "arabesques." It comes into our present ornamental culture that has little to do with the progressive nullifications of Western thought: tin foil, plastic gel, and plastic flower altars in barrio culture. It is in Persian and Navajo weavings, voodoo hex designs, and more. *Grotesquerie* has existed on the margins of art and has withstood official disapproval for millennia. Now it seems poised to return to a place of acceptance and even prominence in the creative psyche.

The Domus Aurea was rediscovered by accident in the late fifteenth century when a Roman on the Palatine Hill fell through a hole in the earth into a chamber festooned with decorative frescoes of vegetal vines turning into creatures and then back again. The effect was electric among Italian artists and probably

**Corner of a room with two frescoed walls.**
Domus Aurea, Palatine Hill, Rome, Italy.
Nimatallah/Art Resource, NY.

**Wall decoration with grotesques.**
Roman wallpainting. Casa dei Vettii, Pompei, Italy.
Scala/Art Resource, NY.

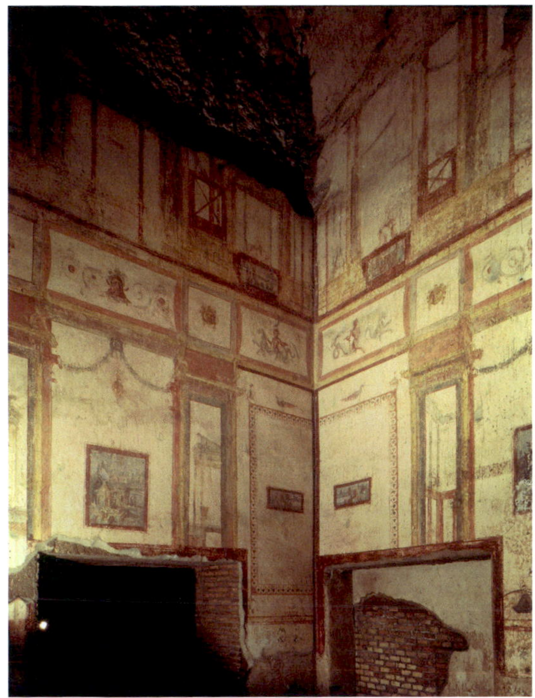

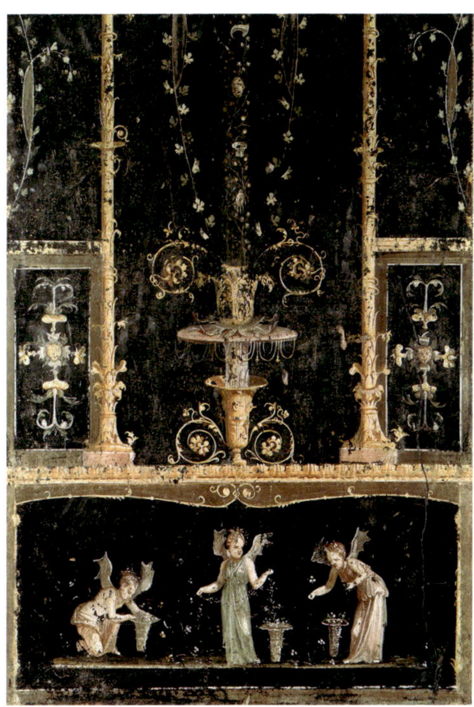

helped catalyze the painting of vegetation in Italian oil painting.

Raphael and Michelangelo adopted the grotesque style for their own decorative passages, perhaps most famously in the frescoes of the four Stanze di Raffaello, the public rooms of the papal apartments in the Vatican. Raphael's Stanze are best known for large frescoes such as *The School of Athens* and *Disputation of the Holy Sacrament*, but the interstitial spaces framing the larger scenes, especially on the ceilings, are sites of riotously inventive *grotesquerie.*

The clearly pantheistic origin of this imagery not only relegated it to the margins in ecclesiastical imagery, but also rendered its very existence problematic. In the Stanze di Raffaello, the symbolism of color and scale helped keep things under control. The scenes from triumphant Christendom were dominant in scale and vivid color. Raphael's *grotesquerie* was confined to the interstitial spaces and rendered in a stone-imitating *grisaille*, which had the effect of making it seem like decoration from a bygone era. It both was and wasn't, obviously. Raphael's decorations were conceived and executed in his and the church's present, even as they drew their inspiration from the freshly uncovered past.

The conceit of the pagan past framing the spatial and chromatic glory of the church and providing a pedestal for historical succession was a cloak that allowed the church to assume it was in control, even as the artist's riotous invention in pagan motifs was set free to charm, beguile, and inflame other imaginations. After the opening of the Domus Aurea, the *djinn* could not be put back in the bottle.

I don't think I am mixing cultural metaphors: the *djinn* are the demigods predating (then incorporated by) monotheistic Islam. More than a thousand years after Nero built his palace, the looping and extended linear traceries of the Domus Aurea *grotesquerie* would come to be known as *arabesques* as successive tides of Islamic empire-building would sweep across the Mediterranean.

Make no mistake, the grotesque is partly a *djinn*: elemental (fire), protean, predating the "progressive" history of monotheism, a tempter and occasionally a deliverer. Its animistic core could be petrified in *grisaille* for a while, but sooner or later it was going to bloom into color, sprout wings, and take to the air.

Raphael's pupil, Giulio Romano, constructed a pleasure palace, the Palazzo del Te, for Federico II Gonzaga, Marquess of Mantua, beginning in 1524. It was completed in just 18 months. Yet a team of painters and plasterers under Romano's direction took the next ten years to complete an astounding array of murals and architectural ornament in the salons. Their very titles reveal the rampant play let loose from the Domus Aurea: *Camera di Amore e Psiche*, with paintings of the Olympian gods banqueting and wooing; *Sala dei Cavalli*, with paintings of elegantly stylized horses; and the *Camera dei Giganti.*

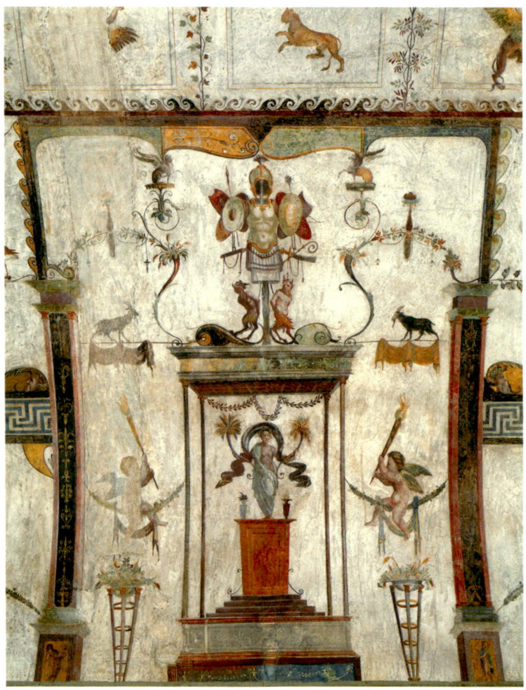

Raphael (Raffaello Sanzio) (Italian, 1483–1520) (School of).
**Vault decoration with "grotteschi."** Logge, Vatican Palace, Vatican City, Italy.
Scala/Art Resource, NY.

In the latter, Romano's Mannerist masterpiece, the *Battle of the Giants,* includes a deep spatial illusionistic dome above the clouds and smoke, with writhing bodies and caricatured expressions of the anguished giants. By 1630 war had overtaken Mantua; the palace was abandoned, and Romano's riot of beasts and gods stood as empty as the rooms of the Domus Aurea.

To commission the pantheistic subject matter of *grotesquerie* was partly to declare a separation between one's power and that of the Church of Rome. It was one of the growing indicators of the rise of secular power within the city-states and even within the offices of the Church.

After the Council of Trent, the Church struck back against the licentiousness of pagan subject matter in painting. It was led by Cardinal Gabriel Paleotti, a dogged critic of Mannerist pagan symbolism. The Counter-Reformation's attempt to slam the lid not only on the Protestant Reformation, but also on the gods and demigods of the reopened Classical world, was one of the great schisms and struggles of the Baroque era.

The sobriety and tangibility of the (relatively) mature Caravaggio and the Spanish *Caravaggisti* (Ribera, Zurbarán, Velázquez, and Murillo), contrast with the exuberant inventiveness of Rubens and, later, Tiepolo. Both of the latter are invigorated by the energy of the grotesque, even as they seek commissions from the endlessly reconstituting and still powerful Catholic church (which continued to believe in the power of images).

In the Italian states at this time we have the spectacle of immensely powerful families, who harbor hopes of seeing one of their own elevated to Cardinal or even Pope, commissioning glorious paintings of warm-blooded Greco-Roman deities. Divine beings are shown frolicking, fighting, and shooting hot glances at each other while civilization crumbles outside the walls of the palace.

Rome had already been sacked by the rebellious troops of Holy Roman Emperor Charles V in 1527. Plague was unleashed a few years later. By the late sixteenth century the population of Rome had dwindled to less than 10,000 inhabitants.

The Farnese family commissioned Annibale Caracci to paint *Loves of the Gods,* the second-largest ceiling painting in Rome next to the Sistine Chapel, for their Palazzo in 1597 (it was completed in 1608). Pietro da Cortona painted another great ceiling painting, *Allegory of Divine Providence and Barberini Power* (1633–39) at the Palazzo Barberini, and also the story of Aeneas at the Palazzo Pamphilj (1651–54). These paintings teem with beautiful naked and near-naked bodies sporting on the ground and hovering in mid-air among plants and animals, the elevated pastoral garden of the gods. Even if Divine Providence is a Christian "personification," her happy, natural worldliness is borrowed from the pagan pastoral.

Giulio Romano (Italian, 1499–1546). ***The Battle of the Giants***. Ceiling fresco. Palazzo del Te, Mantua, Italy.
Erich Lessing/Art Resource, NY.

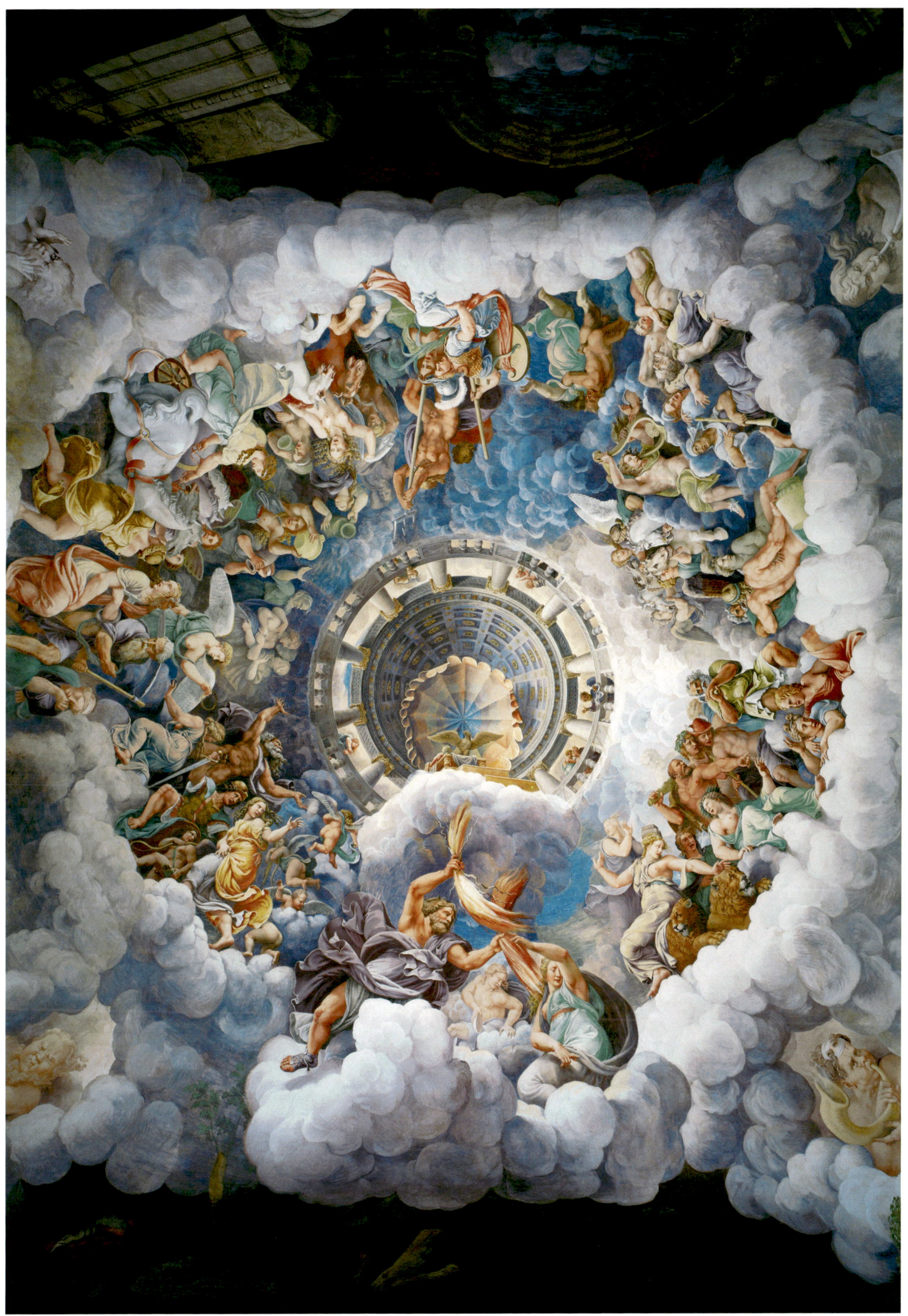

Carracci Gallery, Palazzo Farnese, Rome, Italy.


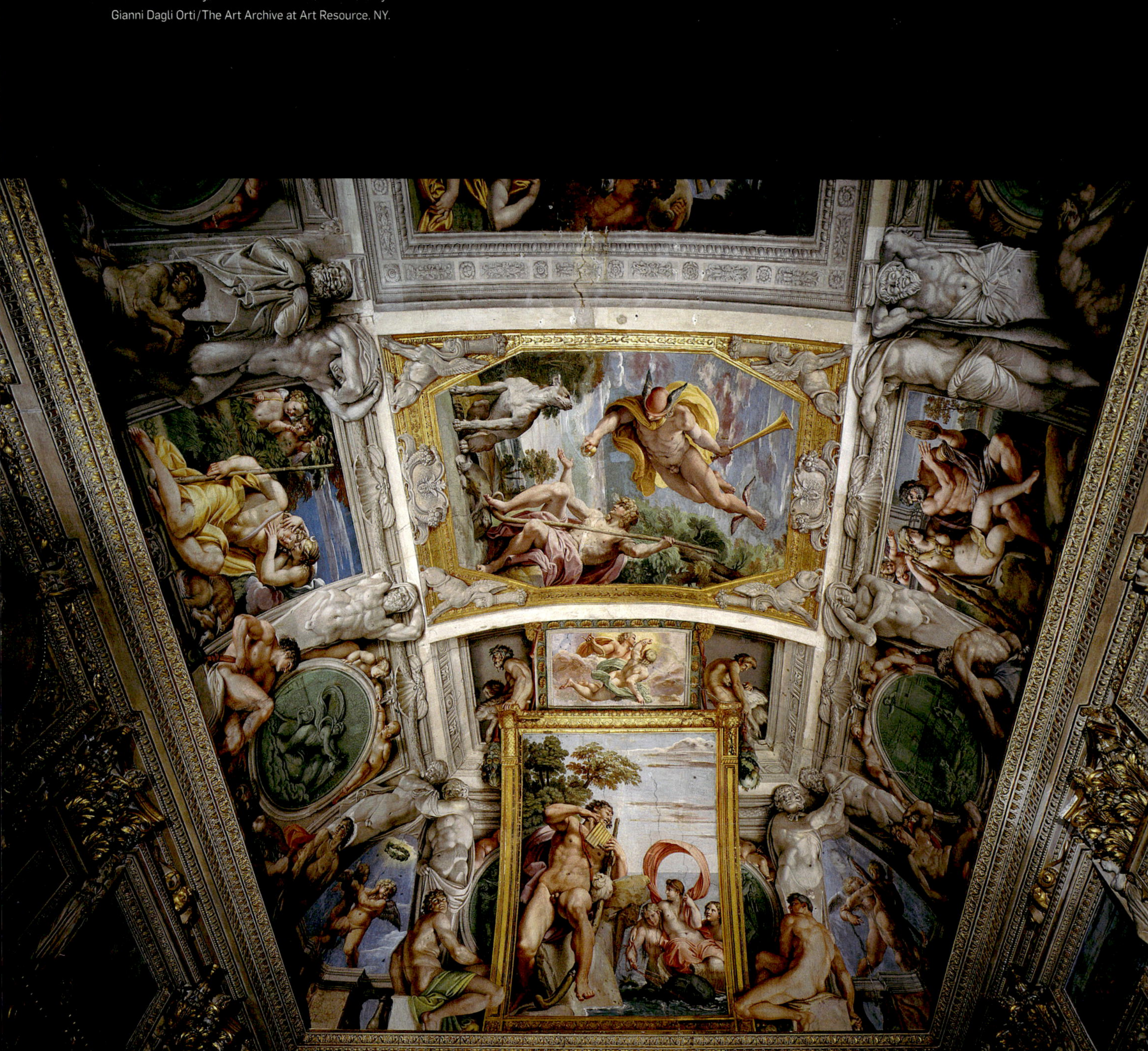

Nicolas Poussin (French, 1594–1665). ***Landscape with Man Killed by a Snake***, probably 1648. Oil on canvas, 46½ × 77⅞ in. National Gallery, London, Great Britain; Bought, 1947 (NG5763).


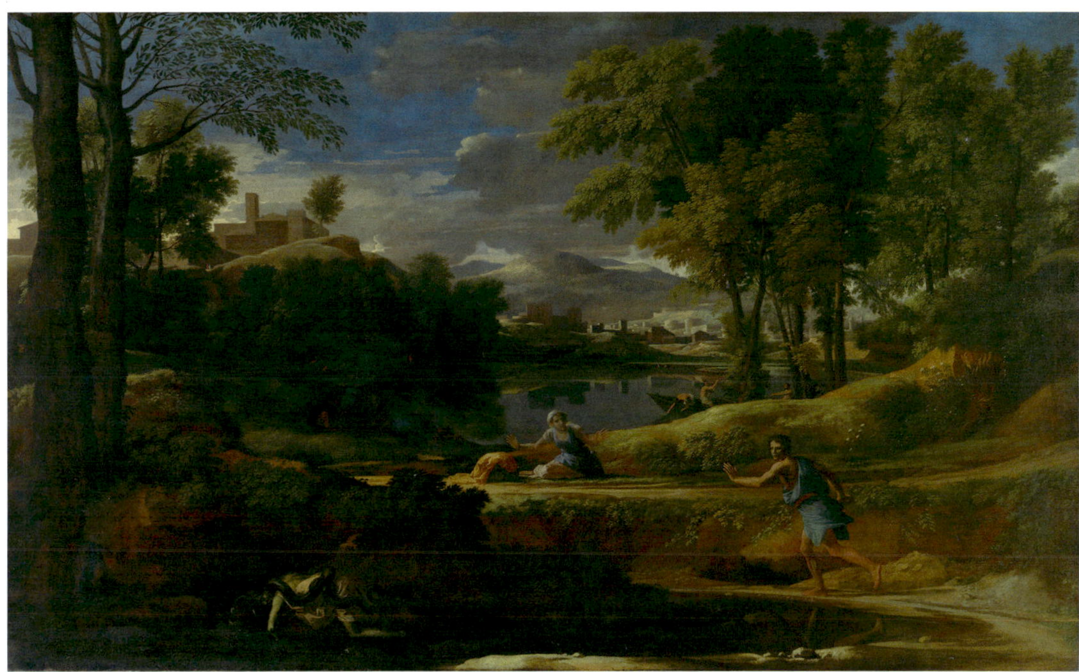

These paintings are crowded with figures even as Rome itself had been depopulated by strife and corruption. Against this backdrop the debate between High Baroque humanism and the advocates for Counter Reformation takes on a particular urgency and poignancy. Pietro da Cortona famously debated his rival, Andreas Sacchi, about the appropriate number of figures in a painting.

Sacchi argued that having fewer figures enabled concentration on conveying the thoughts and emotions of the chief protagonists and a clearer narrative space. Cortona argued that a greater number of figures could introduce meaningful subplots to the grander narrative, and that there was a greater decorative or design potential with more figures.

The Counter Reformation view represented by Sacchi was to gain the upper hand, due in large part to the undeniable talents of the *Caravaggisti*: the Gentileschis, Guercino, and the Spanish mentioned above (Ribera was from Naples, which was controlled by Spain). It is also commonly held that Poussin was to carry on the Sacchi point of view, but elements of grotesque invention attend several of his paintings, such as the writhing serpent in *Landscape with Man Killed by a Snake* (probably 1648), a descendant of Altdorfer's dragon and parent to Turner's sea monsters.

One might notice that in the celebratory humanism of the High Baroque painting that was not restrained by the Counter Reformation, bodies are also linked as garlands. In their multiplicity they become pattern, as Cortona anticipated. The linked patterns of both vegetal and human garlands were described as "arabesques" ("rabeschi") by Italian Renaissance writers, under the mistaken belief that they were derived from Islamic decorative motifs.

In fact the original "S" and "U" volutes of classic decorative arabesque derive from Imperial Roman decoration such as that found in the Domus Aurea. Nevertheless, the term "arabesque" is extremely useful in describing the transformation of the ordinary into the exotic. Thus *grotesquerie* is a form of marginalization in the discourse of European Art even as linear invention is one of the persistent geniuses (derived from "djinn") of Islamic art.

An example of the migration of Islamic style is the intricately outlined central diamond pattern known as the "Saltillo," from the town of Saltillo in central Mexico. The town is the chief producer of the *serape*, a colorful Mexican blanket typically worn over the shoulder until it is unfurled for warmth or shade.

The diamond has its origins in Islamic design, possibly going back even further to ancient India and China. It was brought to Spain during the Moorish occupations, and eventually found its way to Rome and Sicily. Michelangelo and Antonio da Sangallo, the Younger used it in the decorative brickwork on the façade of the Palazzo Farnese.

The Spanish brought the diamond that was to become the Saltillo to Mexico, where it became a central organizing image in both textiles and tile work.

Antonio da Sangallo, the Younger (Italian, 1483–1546) and Michelangelo (Italian, 1475–1564). **Façade of the Palazzo Farnese** (detail), 1514–49. Palazzo Farnese, Rome, Italy.
Andrea Jemolo/Scala/Art Resource, NY.

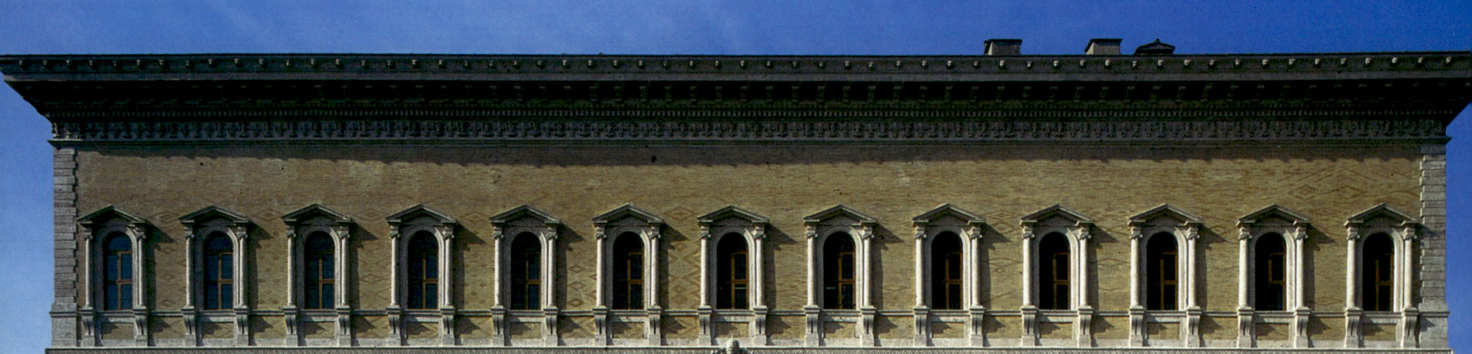

By the late nineteenth century Navajo weavers started incorporating it into their own textiles in patterns that occasionally rivaled the complexities of carpets from the Caucasus. In its simpler iterations, the shape anticipated the boldest geometric painting of the twentieth century.

The Counter Reformation really settles in Spain, where despite the genius of its painters little of the exuberant intermingling of reason and caprice takes place until the advent of Goya. His *caprichos* are executed with a lightness of touch that rivals and usually surpasses the greatest decorative painters of Imperial and Renaissance Rome. They also strike a note of mordancy, reaching its nocturnal apogee in the Black Paintings that forever changed the alignment of the artist's relationship to patronage by creating a persistent uncertainty as to whether or not the commissioning power is being mocked.

Michelangelo, Veronese, and Peter Brueghel the Elder, among other artists, had their run-ins with authority and took their vengeance in their pictures through moral narratives and caricature. But none applied such consistent pressure to the normative narratives of his patrons as Goya. Virtually all of his portraits of Spanish royalty fall into the realm of *grotesquerie* as surely as Daumier's later caricatures.

After Goya, the sleep of Reason was to remain a calling to artists willing to stare into the abyss of psychic discontent. That this subject betrayed a profound anxiety over accepted socio-political / economic power relations was self-evident. Subsequent artistic movements such as Symbolism, the Jugendstil, Nabis, Fauvism, Expressionism, and Surrealism were all seen not only as challenges to accepted norms of "realism," but also as purveyors of an intermittently frightening decadence (which may strike some without historical empathy today as campy).

Greenberg understood that even painting that more closely followed the "ennobling" path of reason, or *logos*, could not protect itself from its own marginalization by an increasingly distrustful middle class. But art has only ever been able to transform itself, not the rest of culture (except, perhaps incrementally, through the transformative education of the artist).

The artists in *Beauty Reigns* have immersed themselves in the lexicon of *grotesquerie* and *arabesque* because their own temperaments and backgrounds find fuller expression in its attributes. The linear patterning, multiple forms, decorative motifs, pastoral *eros*, global cultural motifs, and often explosive color are qualities that have come to mean more, especially through Beat esotericism, Buddhist imagery, psychedelia, and digital technology. To revisit John Elderfield's quote, the art here is a "hedonistic, lyrical" art that finds the pleasures of painting and fresh invention in this complex, multi-sourced field of reference.

Is it Baroque? Not if we are thinking of the Baroque style that set new standards for a theatrical "realism" through mastery of the illusionistic movement of curving volumes. The imagery in nearly all of these

Francisco de Goya y Lucientes (Spanish, 1746–1828). ***The Family of Carlos IV***, ca. 1800. Oil on canvas. 110¼ × 132¼ in. Museo Nacional del Prado, Madrid, Spain.


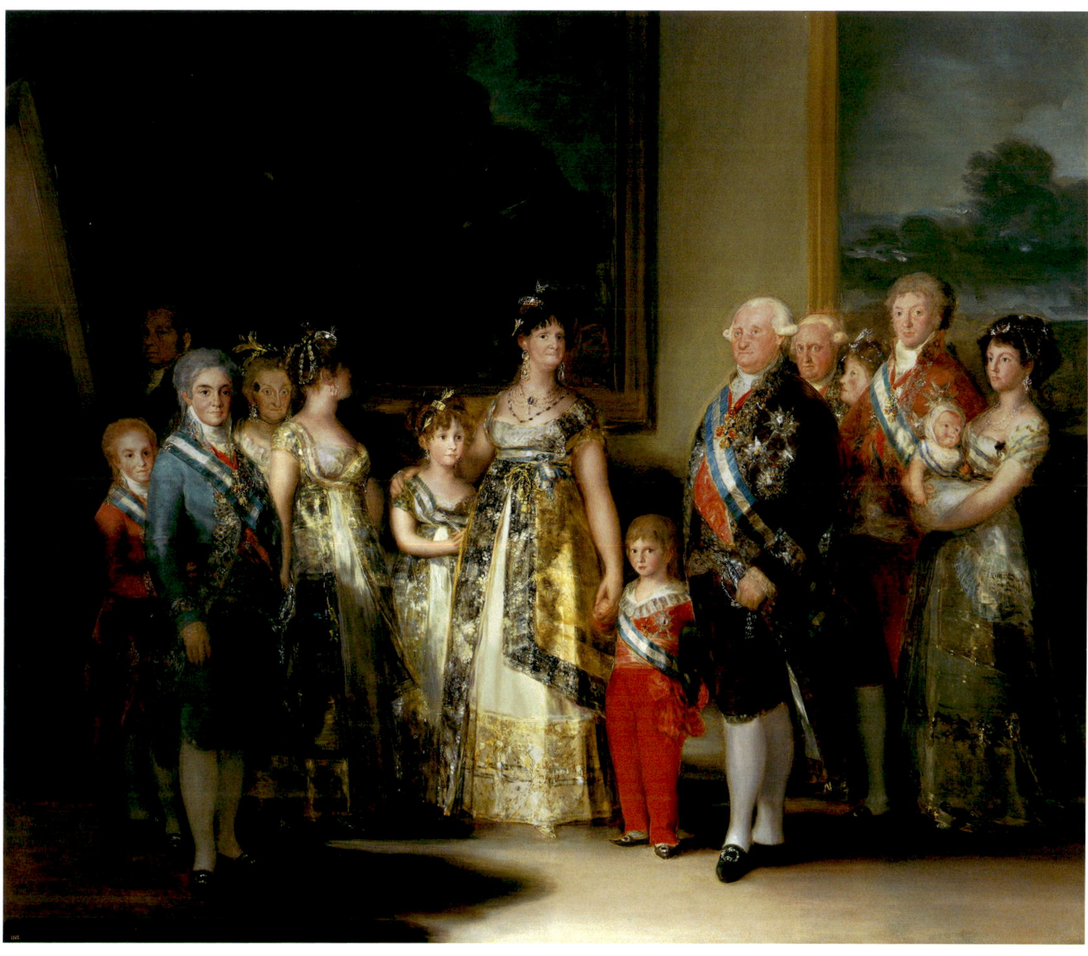

paintings is ligatured, even hieratic. Its presentation is as frontal and emblematic as the standard grid, if with more overlay. But it was in the Baroque era that painting found its contested modernity in an open tension between high and low, Christian and pagan, the Classical Orders and foreign motifs, narration and decoration (which is always producing another narrative).

Geographical distances have closed and cultural diversity is altering the mainstream at a more rapid pace than ever. Yet the anxieties and exhilarations of the Baroque feel familiar to our present because it was the threshold of a widespread understanding that culture had a past that could inform a burgeoning, unpredictable future.

The artists surveyed here find themselves poised with their paintings on an analogous threshold. The complexities they are negotiating won't be simplified or resolved by a unifying historical idea. What their imagery represents is the coexistence of multiple subjectivities, of simultaneous and diverse effects: a multi-level spatiality for the mind that may be as revolutionary as the spaces for the embodied imagination opened up by the release of the household gods that began with falling through a hole.

NOTES

1. Michael Fried, "Art and Objecthood," *Artforum* 5 (June 1967): 12-23.
2. John Elderfield, *Morris Louis* (New York: The Museum of Modern Art, 1986), 45.
3. E.H. Gombrich, *Norm and Form: Studies in the Art of the Renaissance* (London and New York: Phaidon, 1971), 114, cited in Elderfield, *Morris Louis*, 188, 191.
4. Elderfield, *Morris Louis*, 45.

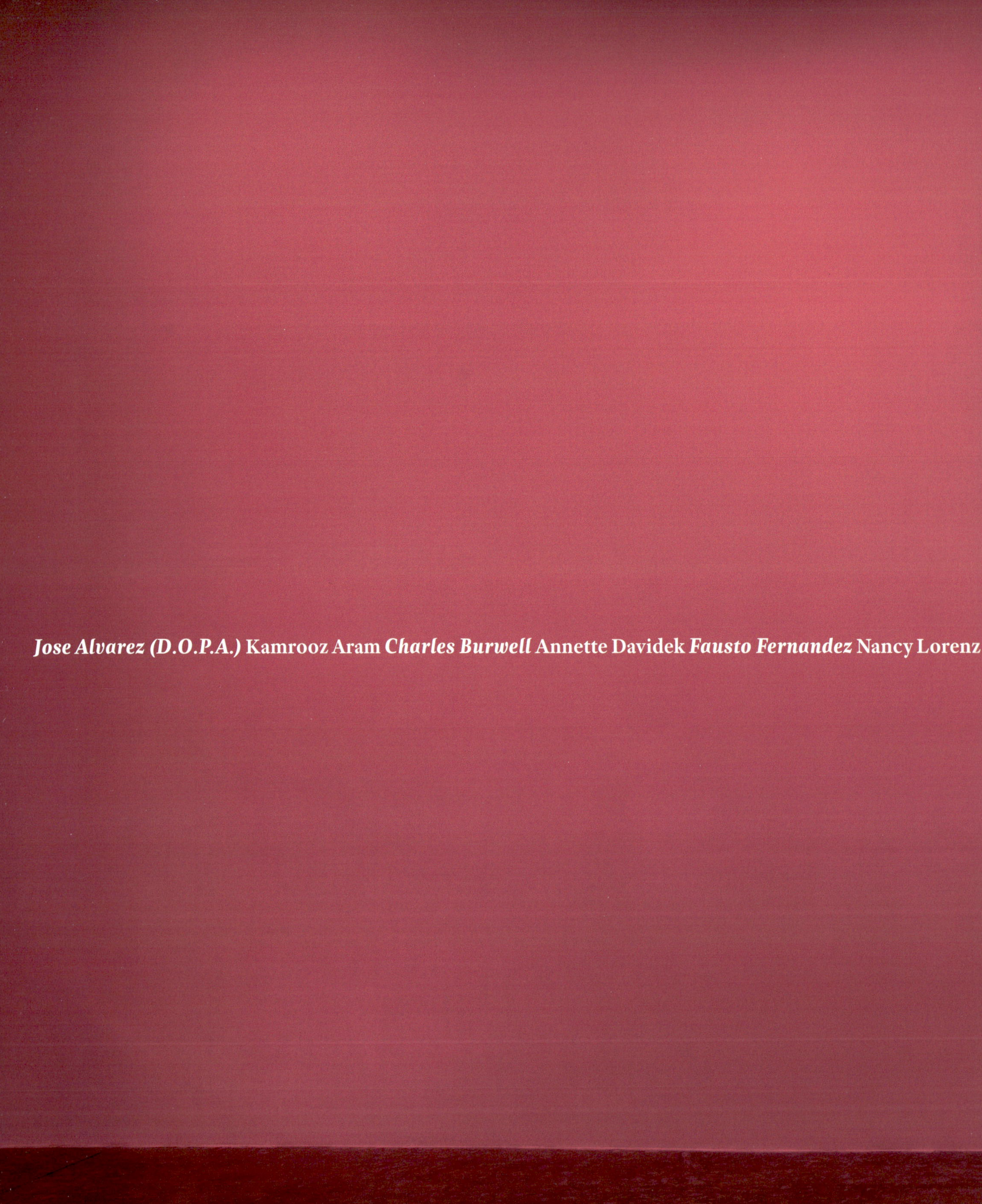
*Jose Alvarez (D.O.P.A.)* Kamrooz Aram ***Charles Burwell*** Annette Davidek ***Fausto Fernandez*** Nancy Lorenz

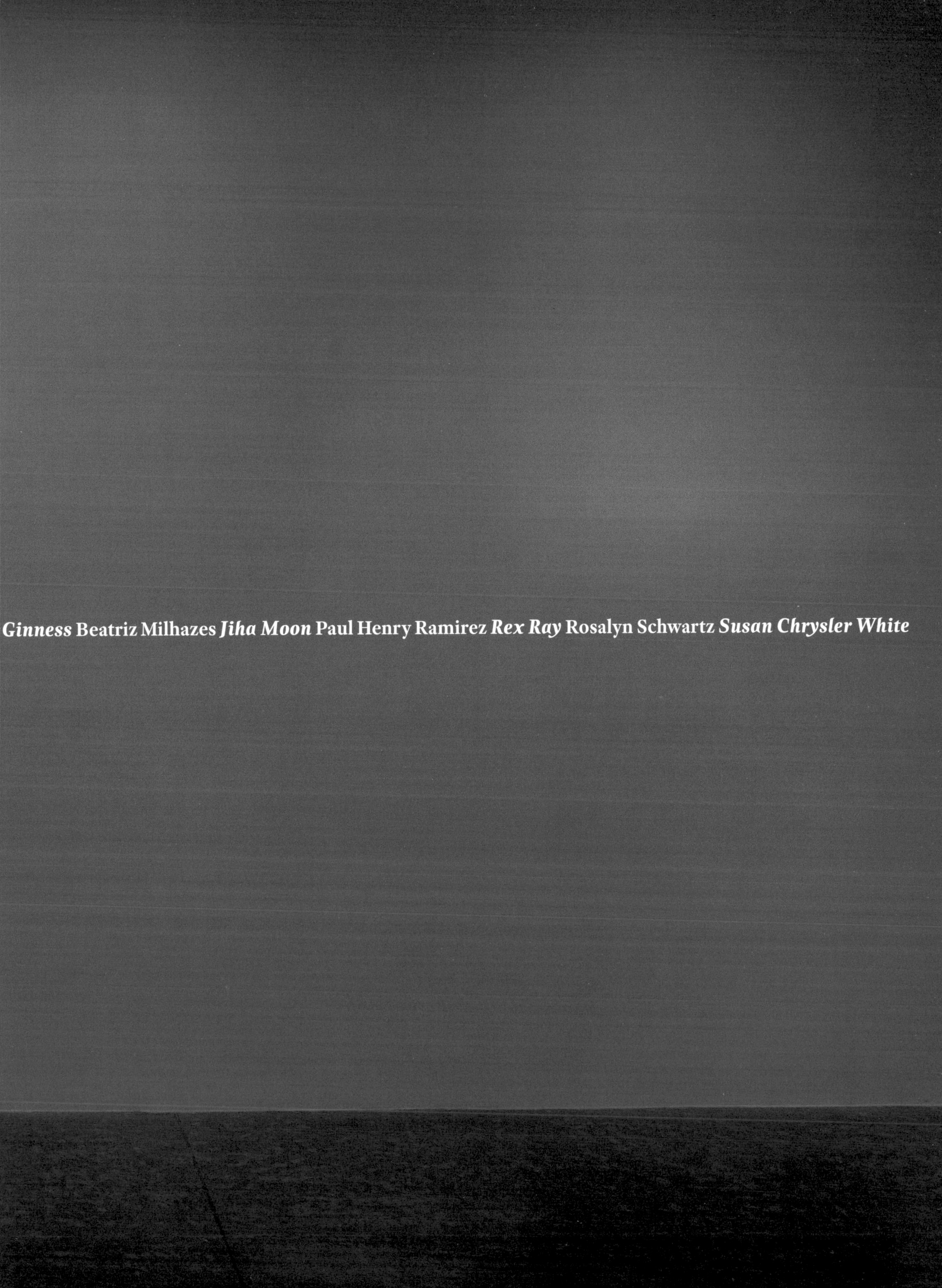
*Ginness* Beatriz Milhazes *Jiha Moon* Paul Henry Ramirez *Rex Ray* Rosalyn Schwartz *Susan Chrysler White*

# Jose Alvarez (D.O.P.A.)

Born 1961

The hallucinogenic collages of Jose Alvarez (D.O.P.A.) incorporate a wide range of exotic materials including porcupine quills, feathers, mica, sequins, and mineral crystals. Alvarez juxtaposes these slightly dimensional elements with images that he fashions from traditional art-making supplies to produce lush, often psychedelic works. Stylized motifs recalling flowers, plant forms, and tiny creatures float across glistening planes which oscillate among vivid colors that bounce back and forth. The works' overall compositions force the viewer's eyes to move at a fast pace, absorbing the sheer visual beauty while dissecting the many intricate details.

Other works take a more minimal approach in the form of circular assemblages, incorporating materials such as mineral crystals. While reductive in appearance, their reflective surfaces shimmer from light striking the surface, and echo the glimmering imagery found in Alvarez's illusionistic paintings and collages.

In addition to these discrete, one-of-a-kind, two- and three-dimensional objects, Alvarez also makes sumptuous videos that animate the static wall works and push his imagery into new yet closely aligned directions. The artist overcomes the limitations imposed by working on paper, canvas, or panel, and further pushes his art's physical boundaries by covering entire wall surfaces with digitally printed wallpaper. Individual works often hang over the papered walls to further exploit the optical effects.

The sources from which Alvarez draws his inspiration are as wide ranging as the materials he uses to create his works, including scientific, cosmological, and mathematical theories, anthropological research, and visionary ritual practice. He transforms these abstract and elusive points of origin into real shapes, giving tangible form to intangible ideas, concepts, and beliefs.

A Venezuelan native, Jose Alvarez (D.O.P.A.) studied at the School of Visual Arts, New York, during the 1990s. For the past decade he has shown paintings, collages, and videos, in addition to creating installations. In 2002 his art was included in the Whitney Museum of American Art's *Biennial* exhibition; in 2007 in a solo exhibition at the Kitchen, New York; and in 2012 he covered the lobby walls of the Norton Museum of Art in Palm Beach, Florida, with his digital wallpaper. Alvarez is based in Fort Lauderdale, Florida.

JOSE ALVAREZ (D.O.P.A.)
DEYVI ORANGEL PEÑA ARTEAGA

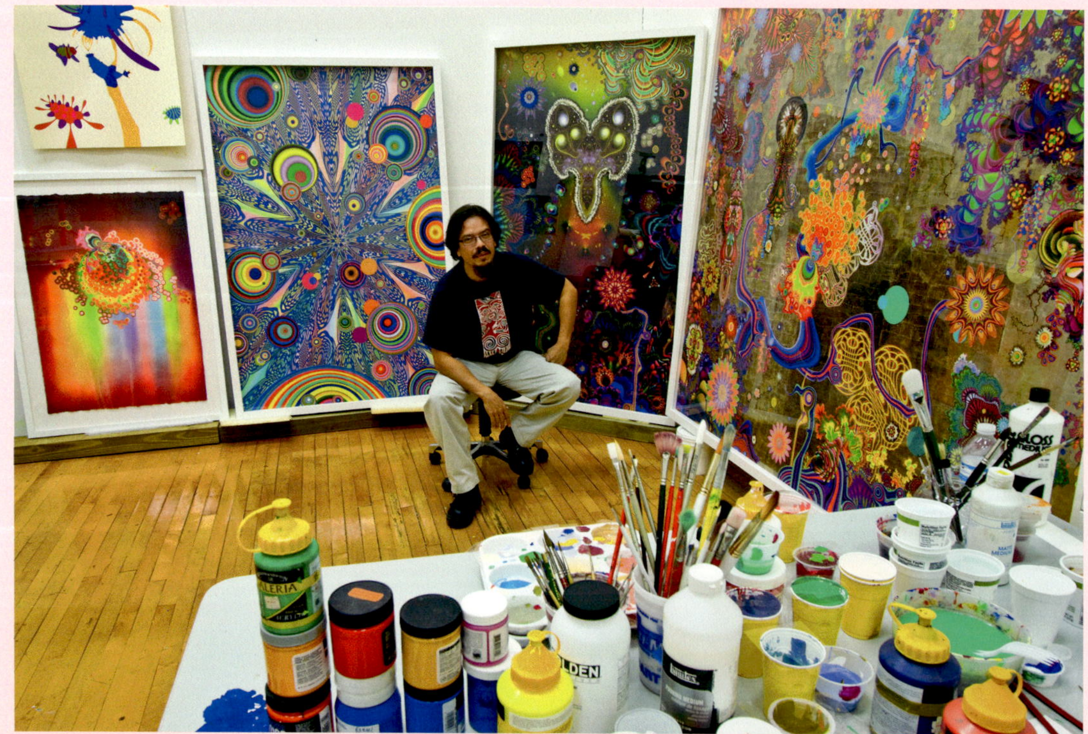

Courtesy of the artist and Gavlak Gallery, Palm Beach, Florida.

# *Kamrooz Aram*

Born 1978

Ornamentation and decoration play key roles in the art of Kamrooz Aram, as do symbols, patterning, and geometric forms. Drawing on his Iranian origins, Aram investigates the confluence of the exotic, the decorative, and the abstract in his paintings, collages, and assemblages of wall works and objects. History and ethnicity serve as sources of inspiration for the artist, who mines the decorative traditions and fine art heritage of both the Middle East and the cultures of Western Europe and America. Aram works from one series to another series, which are perhaps disparate in look and feel but united in their tension between tradition and modernism.

Aram employs a range of techniques in creating his work, including enhancing and reducing the painted surfaces by processes of wiping and sanding, as in a recent group of works. These paintings are created using an additive and reductive process, through which there emerges a physical temporality—as past, present, and future unite in a single moment. Ghostly pictures underlie boldly painted ones, anticipating new, evolving images.

In another series, paint is applied in a direct manner, rendering an image head-on and fully in the present. Still other, more recent endeavors extend the two-dimensional into three dimensions by including objects on shelves or pedestals placed in dialogue with paintings and collages.

Color plays a unique role in this body of work: Aram uses color with careful thought and precision. While some works lean towards monochrome, others, equally challenging, run riot in their explosion of a bold palette. The artist deftly shifts between the two approaches, employing color to satisfy both conceptual and visual functions.

Kamrooz Aram was born in Shiraz, Iran, and now resides in Brooklyn, New York. After completing a Bachelor of Arts at the Maryland Institute College of Art in Baltimore in 2001, Aram earned a Master of Fine Arts from Columbia University, New York, in 2003. He began exhibiting his work soon after graduate school, including a solo exhibition at the Massachusetts Museum of Contemporary Art, North Adams, in 2006. Work by Aram is found in the collections of the Cincinnati Art Museum, Ohio; Honart Museum, Tehran, Iran; and the Herbert F. Johnson Museum of Art, Cornell University, Ithaca, New York.

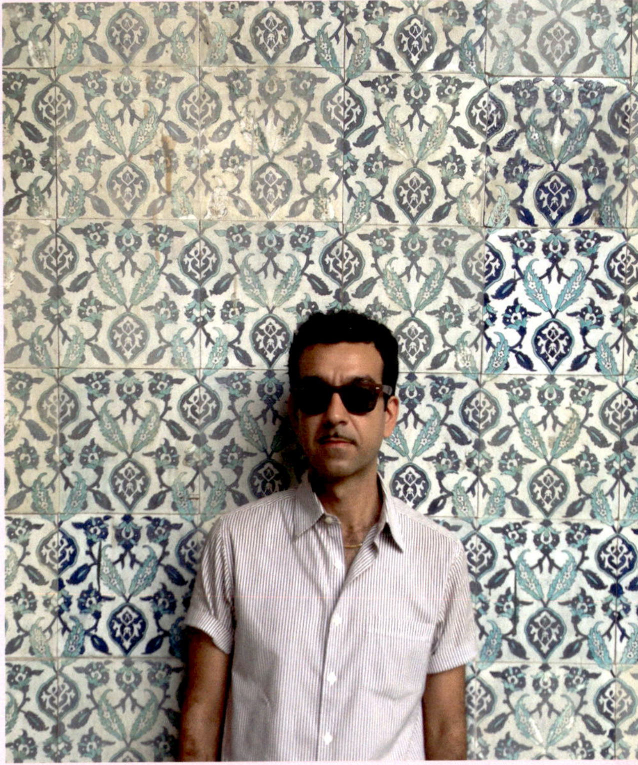

Courtesy of the artist and Green Art Gallery, Dubai, United Arab Emirates.

# Charles Burwell

Born 1955

Courtesy of Bridgette Mayer Gallery, Philadelphia, Pennsylvania.

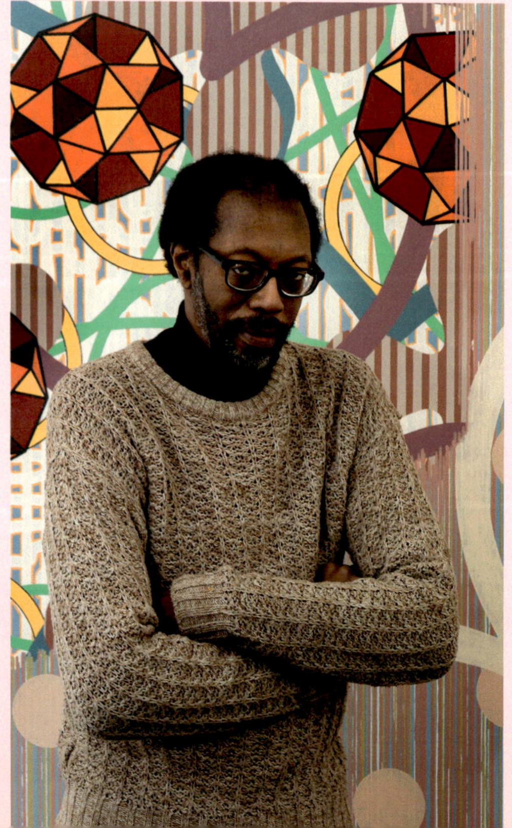

Charles Burwell builds the compositions of his oil and acrylic paintings through two primary elements: linear marks and layered imagery. Tightly structured and boldly painted, the works allude to textile design, wallpaper, and Pattern and Decoration art from the 1970s. Familiar shapes and repeated geometric motifs are woven together with strong circuitous lines, creating an illusion of deep space within the picture plane while simultaneously reveling in the physical layering of the paint itself. Burwell's harmonious palettes further enhance the works' strong graphic qualities, adding an aura of playfulness and increasing their visual satisfaction.

Burwell studied painting during the 1970s, at a time when American art (and painting in particular) was at a crossroads. He specifically points to Mark Tobey, Jack Tworkov, Cy Twombly, and Agnes Martin as early influences, twentieth-century artists whose work represents a wide range of approaches—from juicy, gestural expressionism to cool, contemplative abstraction. However, as different and distinct as is the work of each of these individuals, their art is united in a dependence on line, from which Burwell draws ongoing inspiration.

In addition to line, Burwell's complex compositions are further galvanized by the lack of a central subject or form, causing the eye to roam across the surface of the canvas. In the process of looking, the viewer discovers image bits that slowly connect many fragmented forms. Altering the scale of the paintings does not result in shifts in their compositional components either. Whether working small or large, Burwell employs the same strategy for organizing the lines, shapes, and colors within the rectangular perimeter.

Finally, like many artists who emerged before the digital era, Burwell began to use the computer to assist in developing his imagery and palette. Digital imaging can quicken the entire creative process while allowing for greater experimentation with composition and color. He has also incorporated digital imaging to produce mixed-media works.

A Philadelphia, Pennsylvania, native, Charles Burwell received a Bachelor of Fine Arts from Tyler School of Art, Temple University, Philadelphia, in 1977, and a Master of Fine Arts from Yale University School of Art, New Haven, Connecticut, in 1979. He has exhibited his paintings for nearly forty years, and his work is found in museum collections including the Cleveland Museum of Art, Ohio; Delaware Art Museum, Wilmington; Philadelphia Museum of Art; Pennsylvania Academy of the Fine Arts, Philadelphia; and the Studio Museum in Harlem, New York. The artist continues to live and work in his hometown.

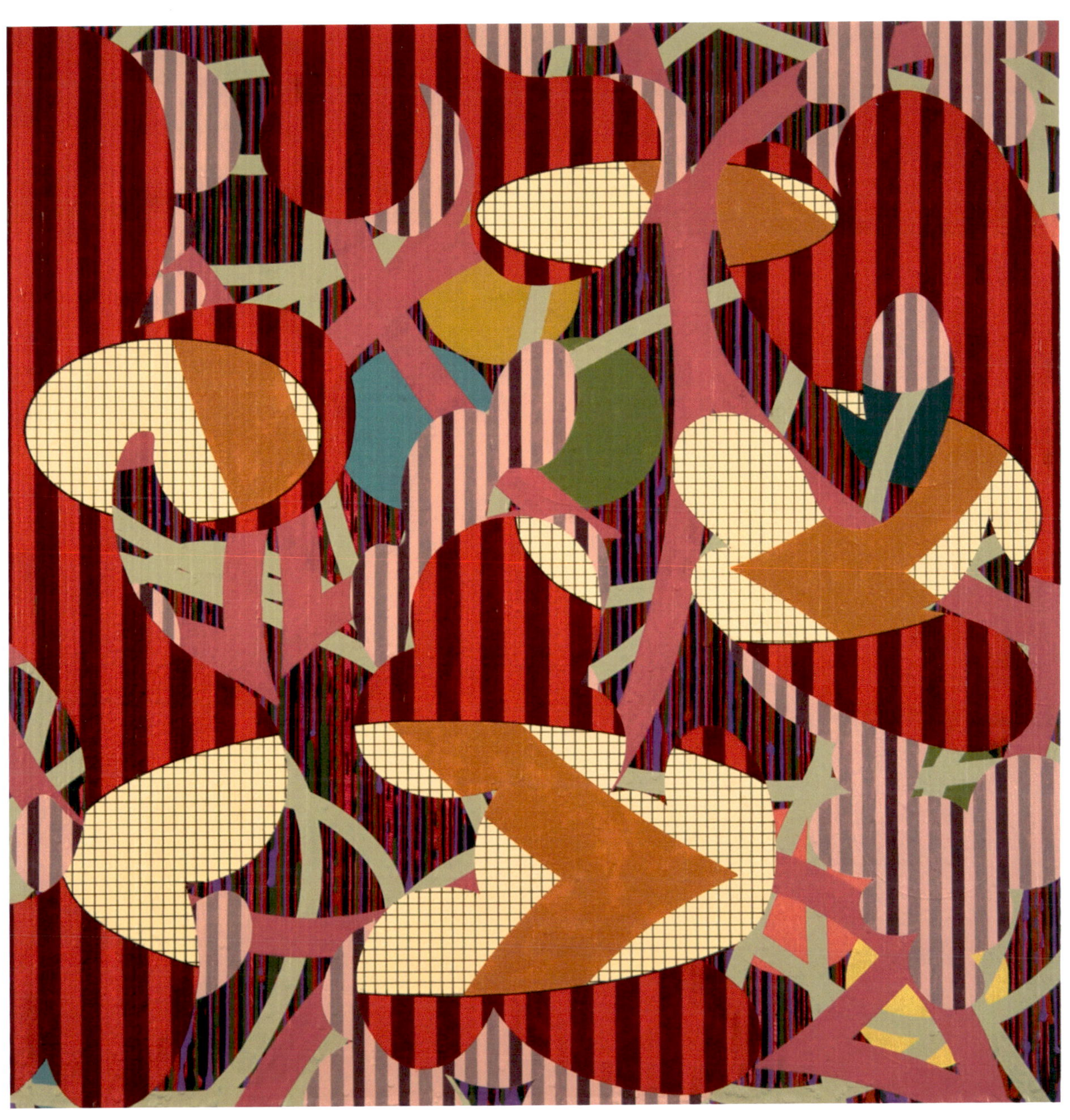

Charles Burwell, **Compression Grid No. 1**, 2012. Acrylic on panel, 24 × 24 in. Courtesy of Bridgette Mayer Gallery, Philadelphia, Pennsylvania

Jose Alvarez (D.O.P.A.), **Untitled #3**, 2009. Collage, flocking, and crystals on paper, 20 × 13 in. Collection of Bill Mercur
Courtesy of the artist and Gavlak Gallery, Palm Beach, Florida

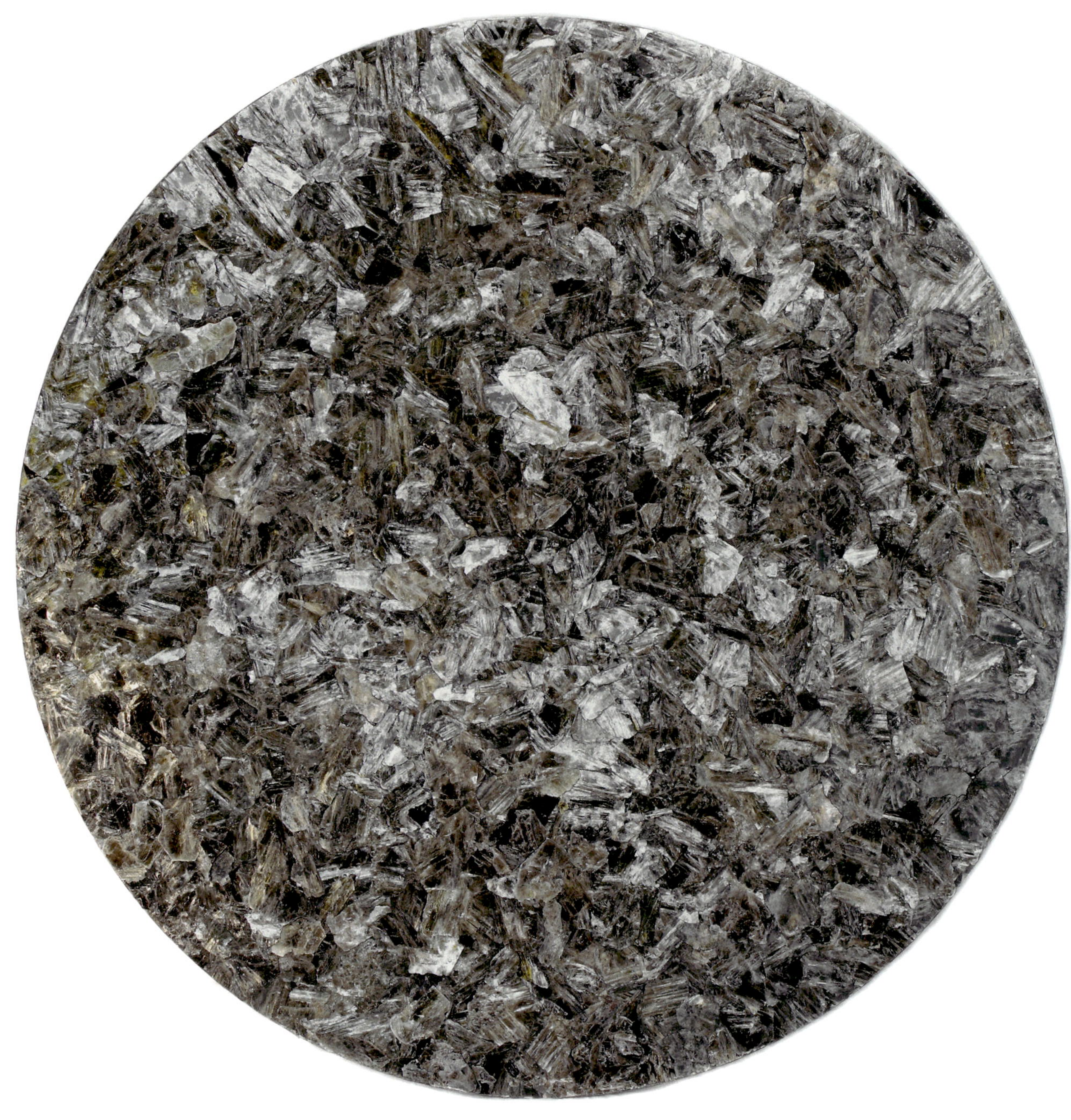

Jose Alvarez (D.O.P.A.), **Regolith (In the Darkness the Silver Disc was the Only Light)**, 2011. Mineral crystals with resin on wood, 72 × 72 × 4 in.
Collection of Jane Holzer. Courtesy of the artist and Gavlak Gallery, Palm Beach, Florida

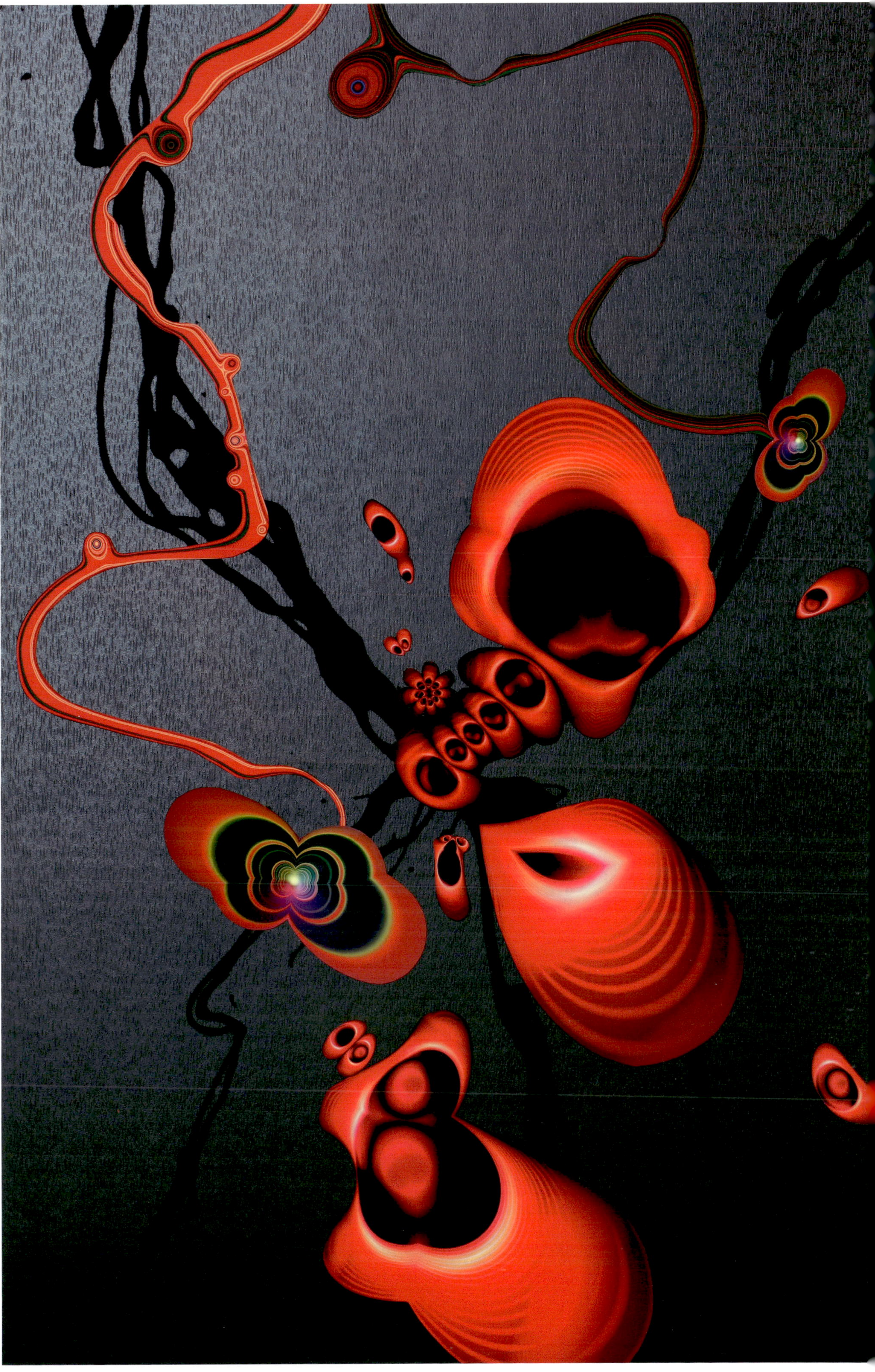

Kamrooz Aram, **Ornament for Anxious Interiors (1–4)**, 2012. Oil and acrylic on linen, 48 × 40 in. each
Courtesy of the artist and Green Art Gallery, Dubai, United Arab Emirates

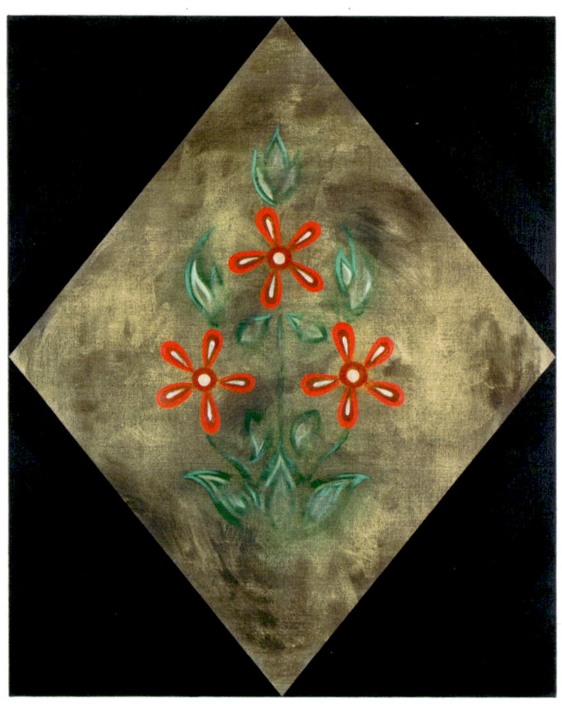

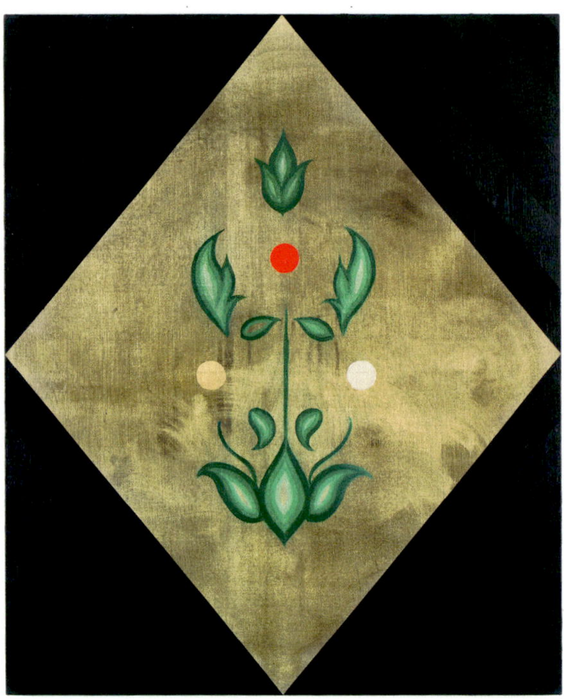

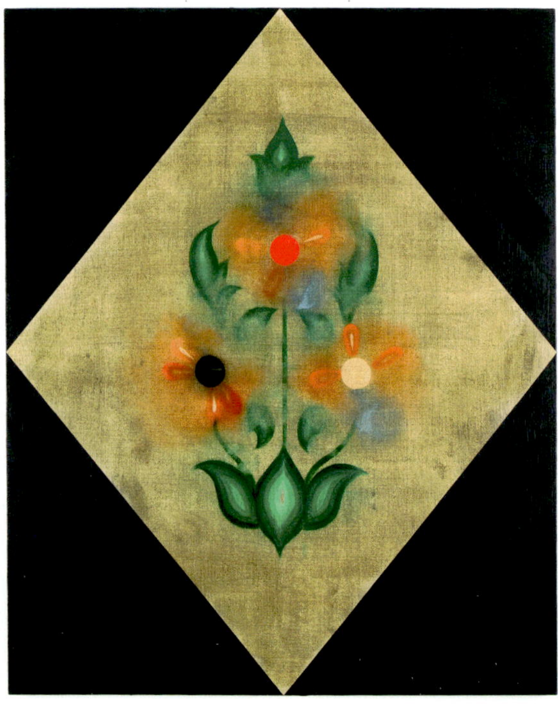

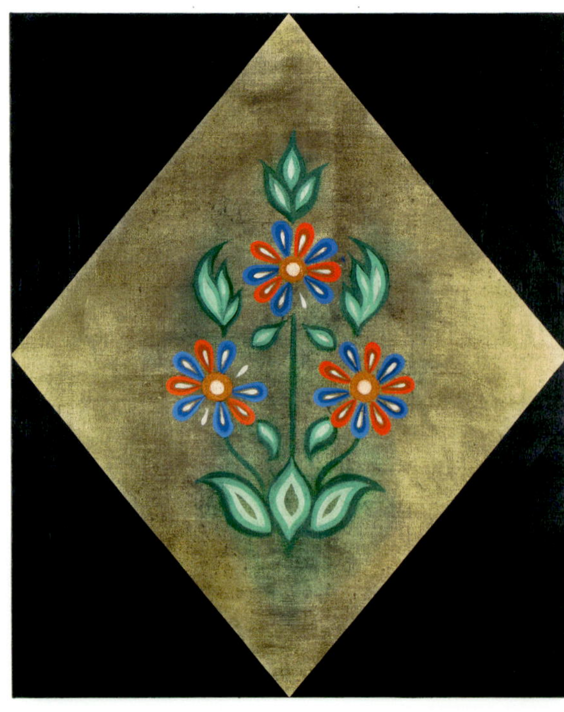

Charles Burwell, **Imposition**, 2012. Acrylic on panel, 24 × 24 in. Courtesy of Bridgette Mayer Gallery, Philadelphia, Pennsylvania

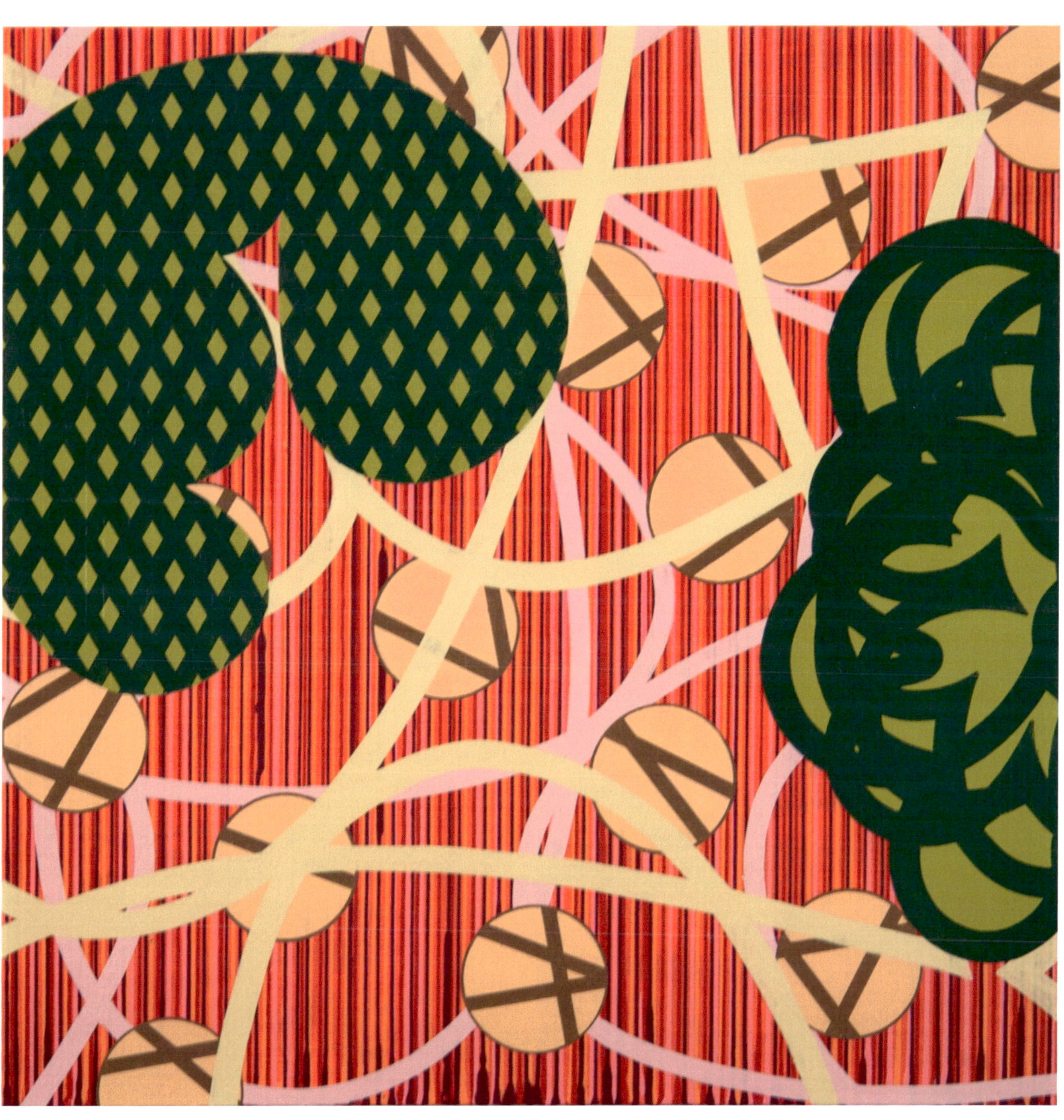

Kamrooz Aram, Studio view: Brooklyn, New York, 2013. Courtesy of the artist and Green Art Gallery, Dubai, United Arab Emirates

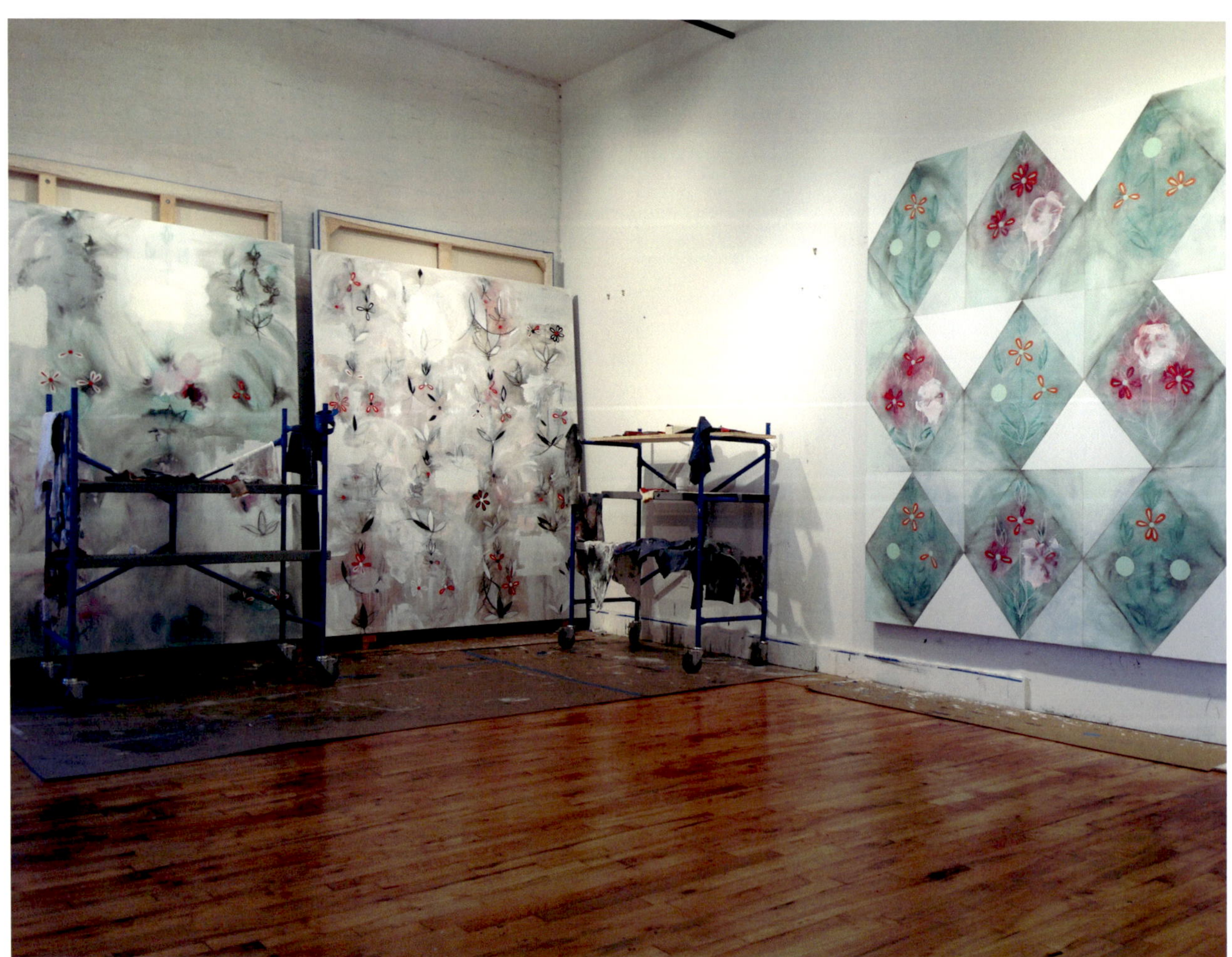

Kamrooz Aram, Studio view: Brooklyn, New York, 2013. Courtesy of the artist and Green Art Gallery, Dubai, United Arab Emirates

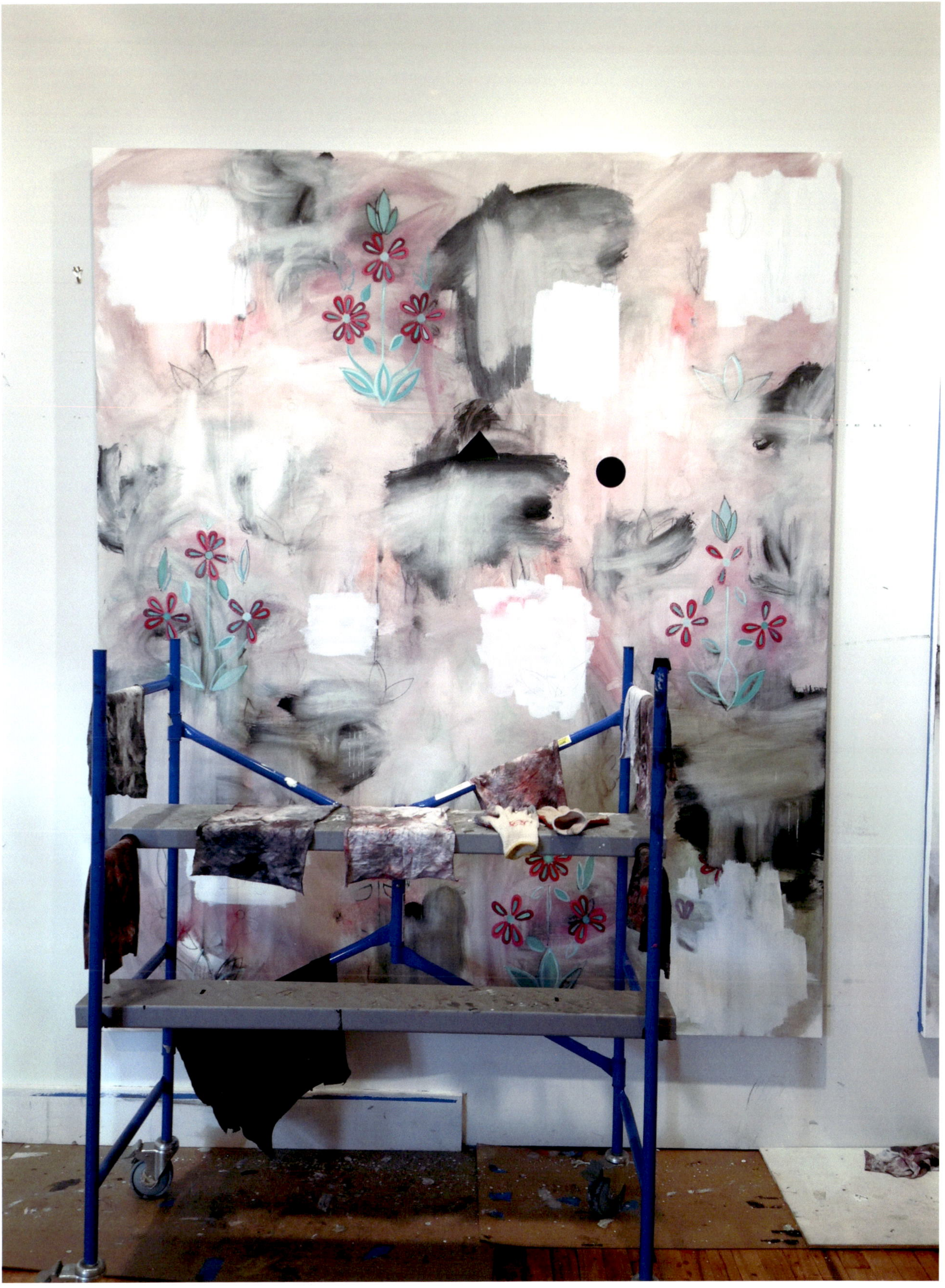

Kamrooz Aram, **Untitled (Fana' #5)**, 2010. Oil on canvas, 44 × 36 in. Courtesy of the artist and Green Art Gallery, Dubai, United Arab Emirates

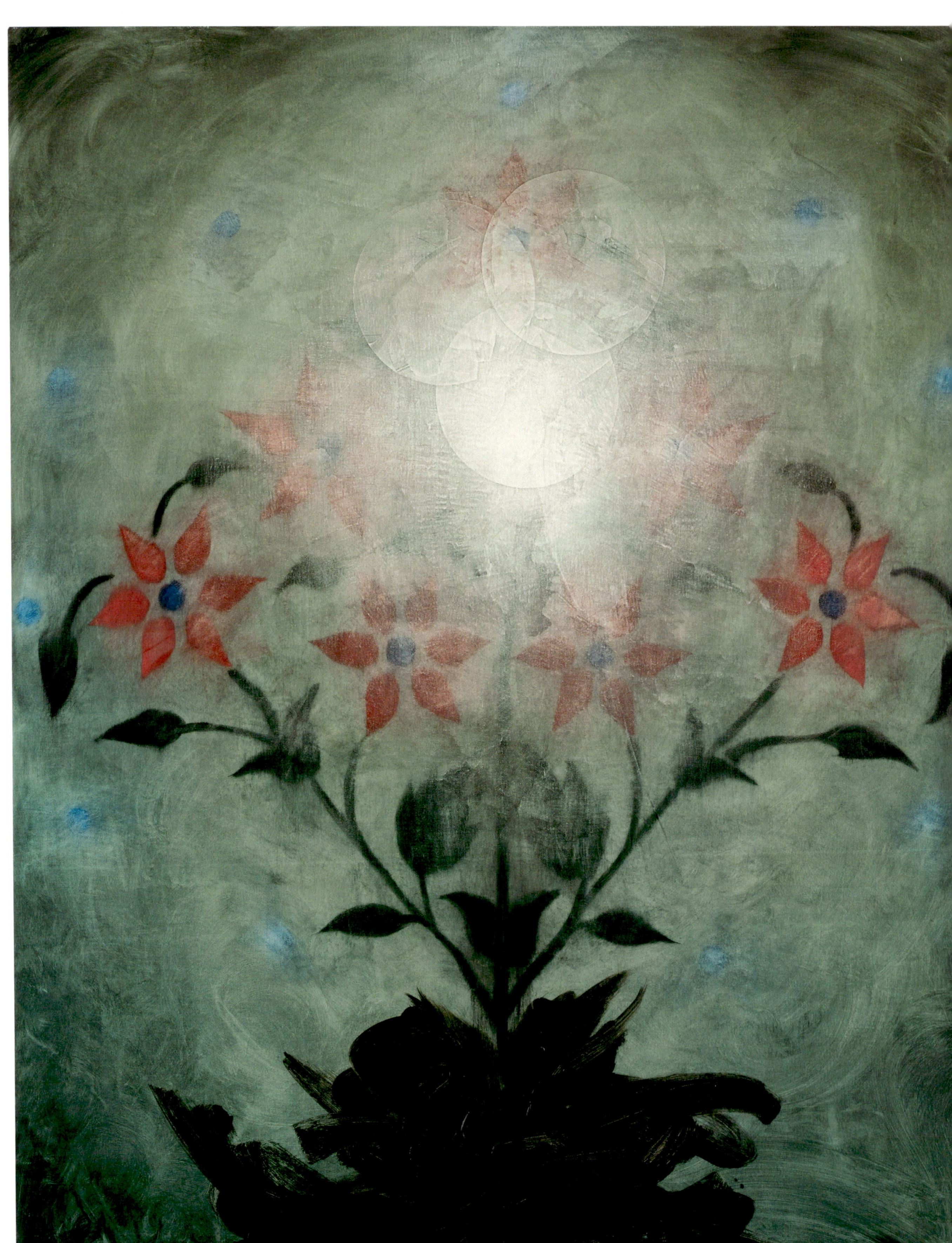

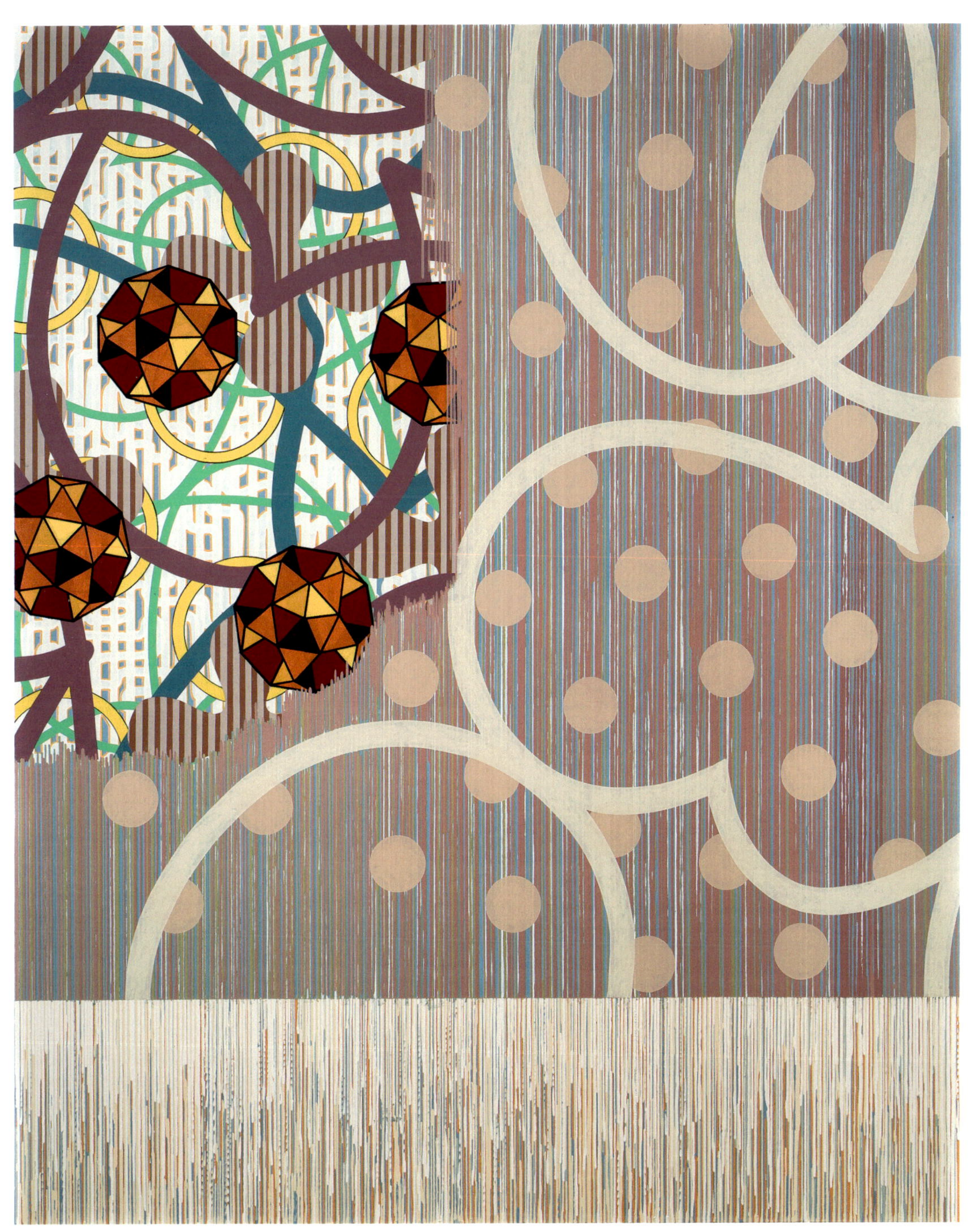

Charles Burwell, **On Becoming**, 2012. Oil on canvas, 96 × 78 in. Courtesy of Bridgette Mayer Gallery, Philadelphia, Pennsylvania

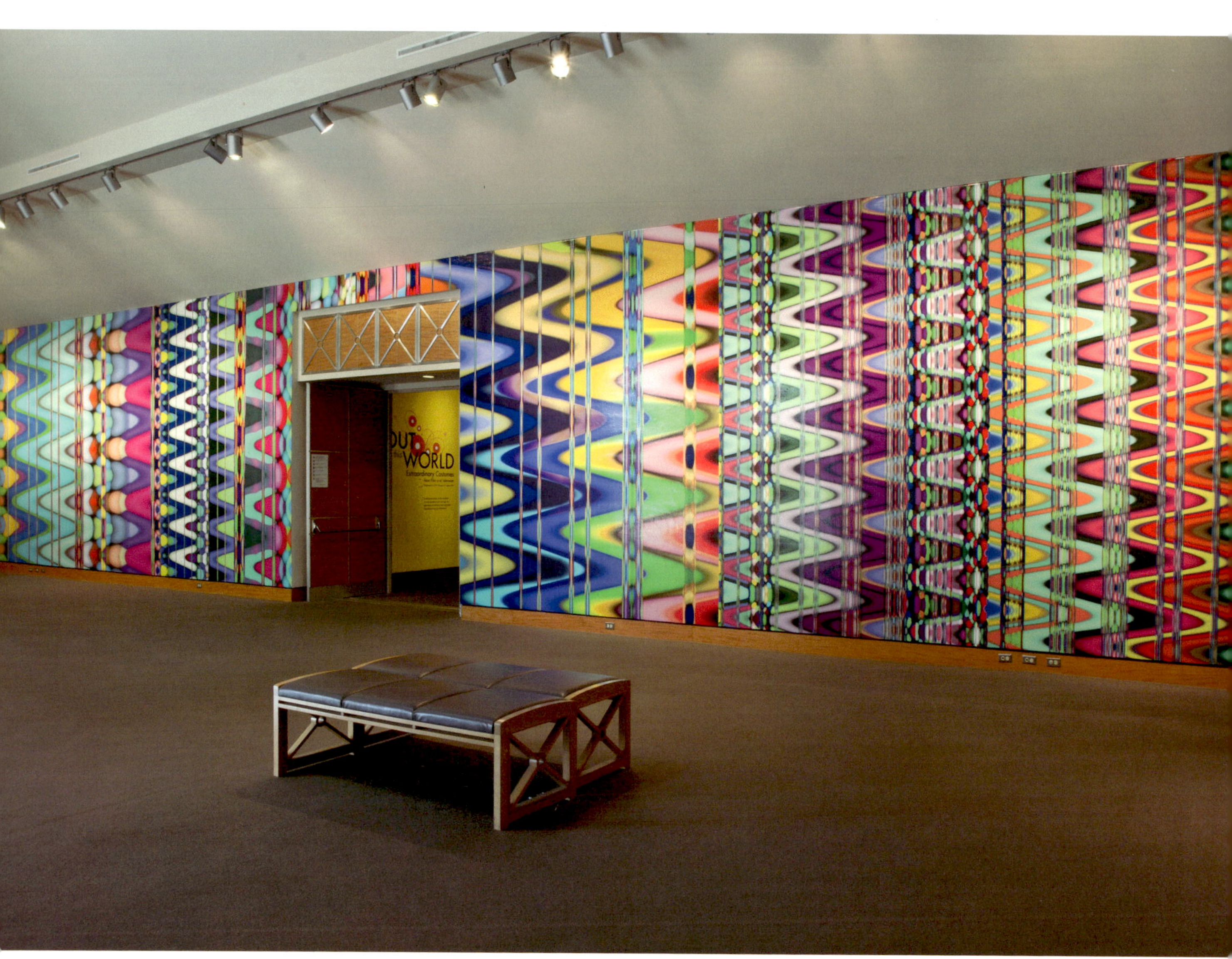
this WORLD
Extraordinary Costumes

Jose Alvarez (D.O.P.A.), **Vibrating Strands of Energy**, 2011. Vinyl, 156 × 672 in. Installation views: Norton Museum of Art, West Palm Beach, Florida
Courtesy of the artist and Gavlak Gallery, Palm Beach, Florida

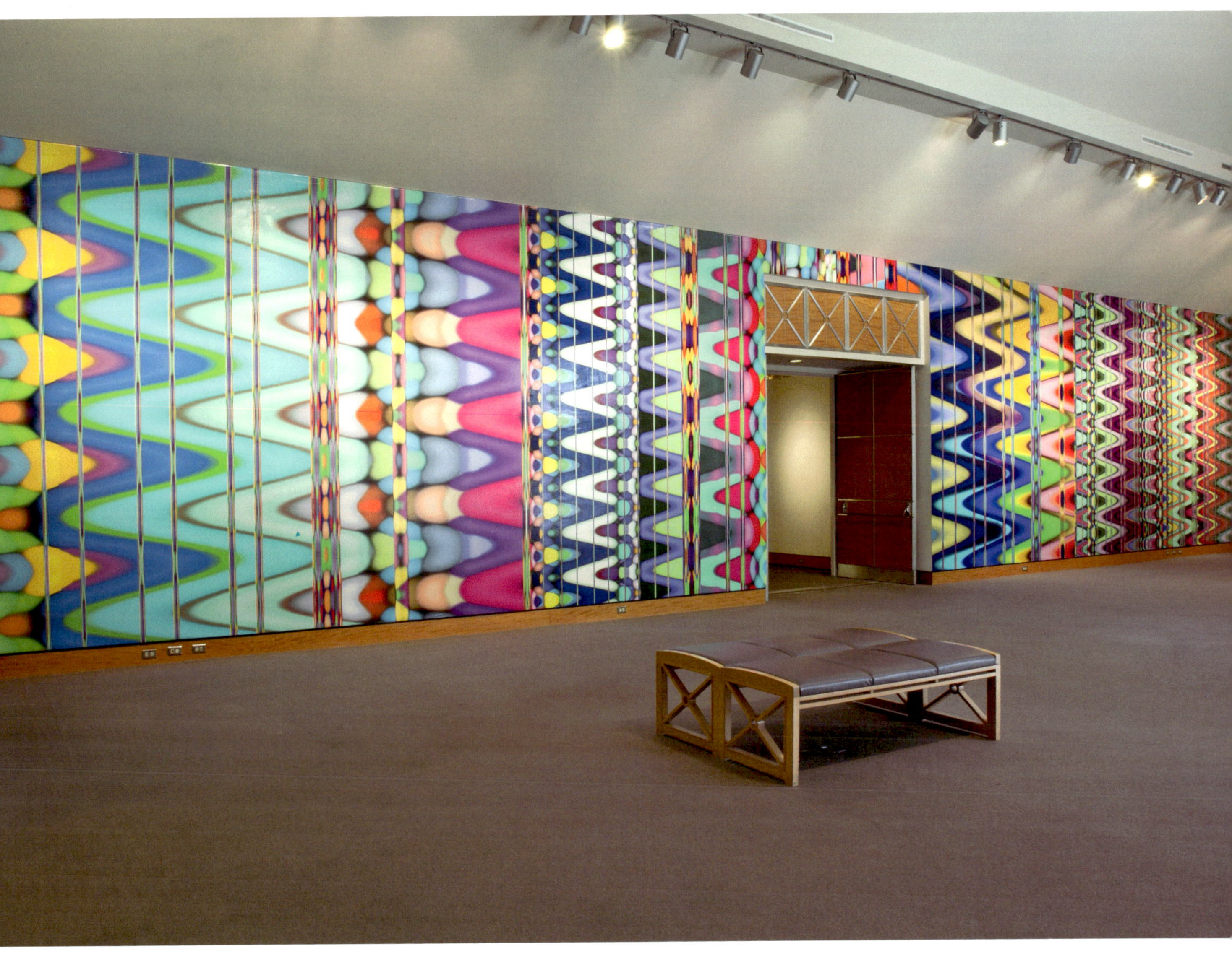

Jose Alvarez (D.O.P.A.), **The Myth** (detail), 2008. Crystals, mica, feathers, porcupine quills, enamel, acrylic, and colored pencil on paper, 72 × 44 in. Collection of Carlos and Rosa de la Cruz. Courtesy of the artist and Gavlak Gallery, Palm Beach, Florida

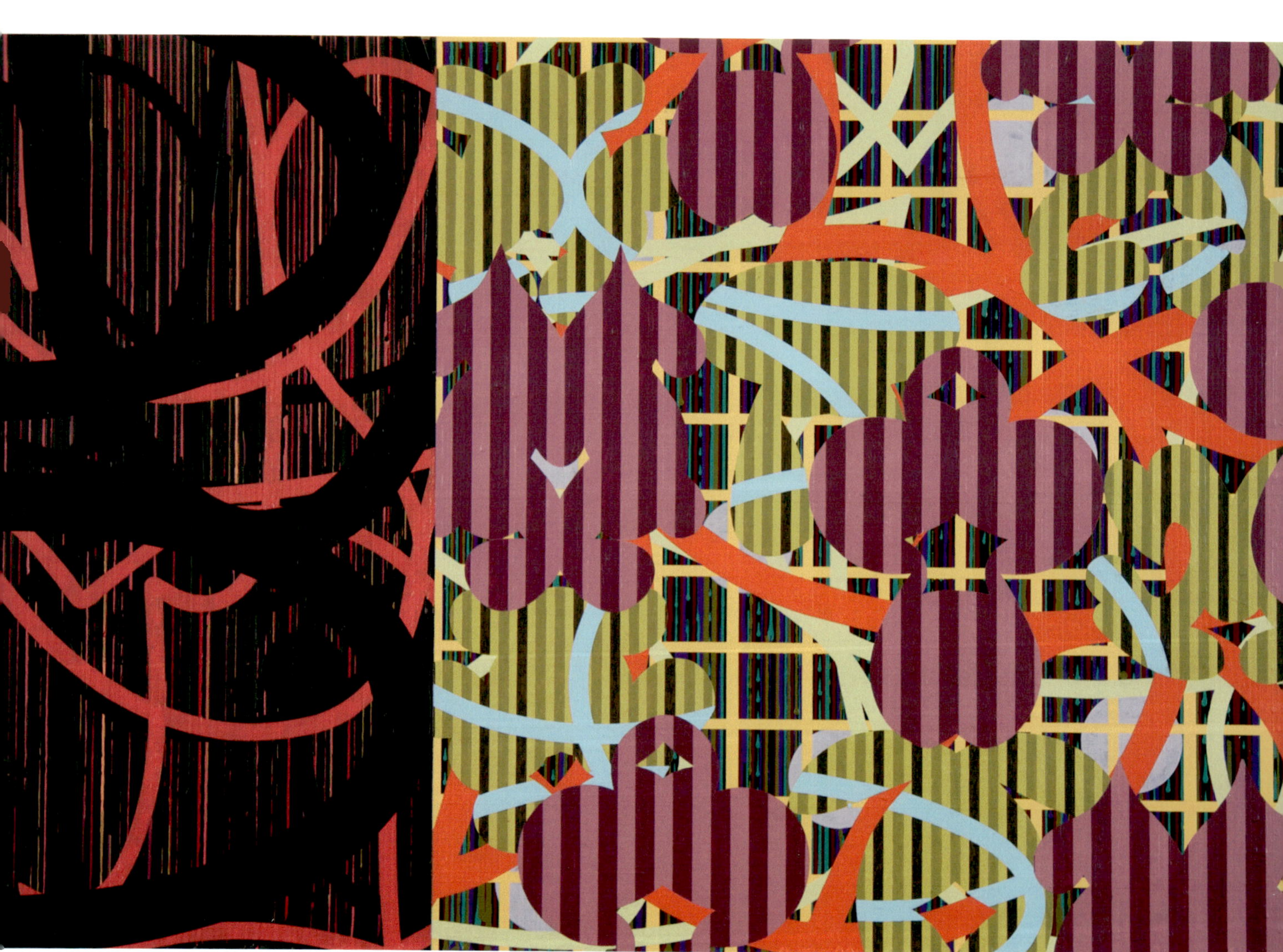

 Charles Burwell, **Around, In and Out**, 2012. Acrylic on panel, 24 × 36 in. Courtesy of Bridgette Mayer Gallery, Philadelphia, Pennsylvania

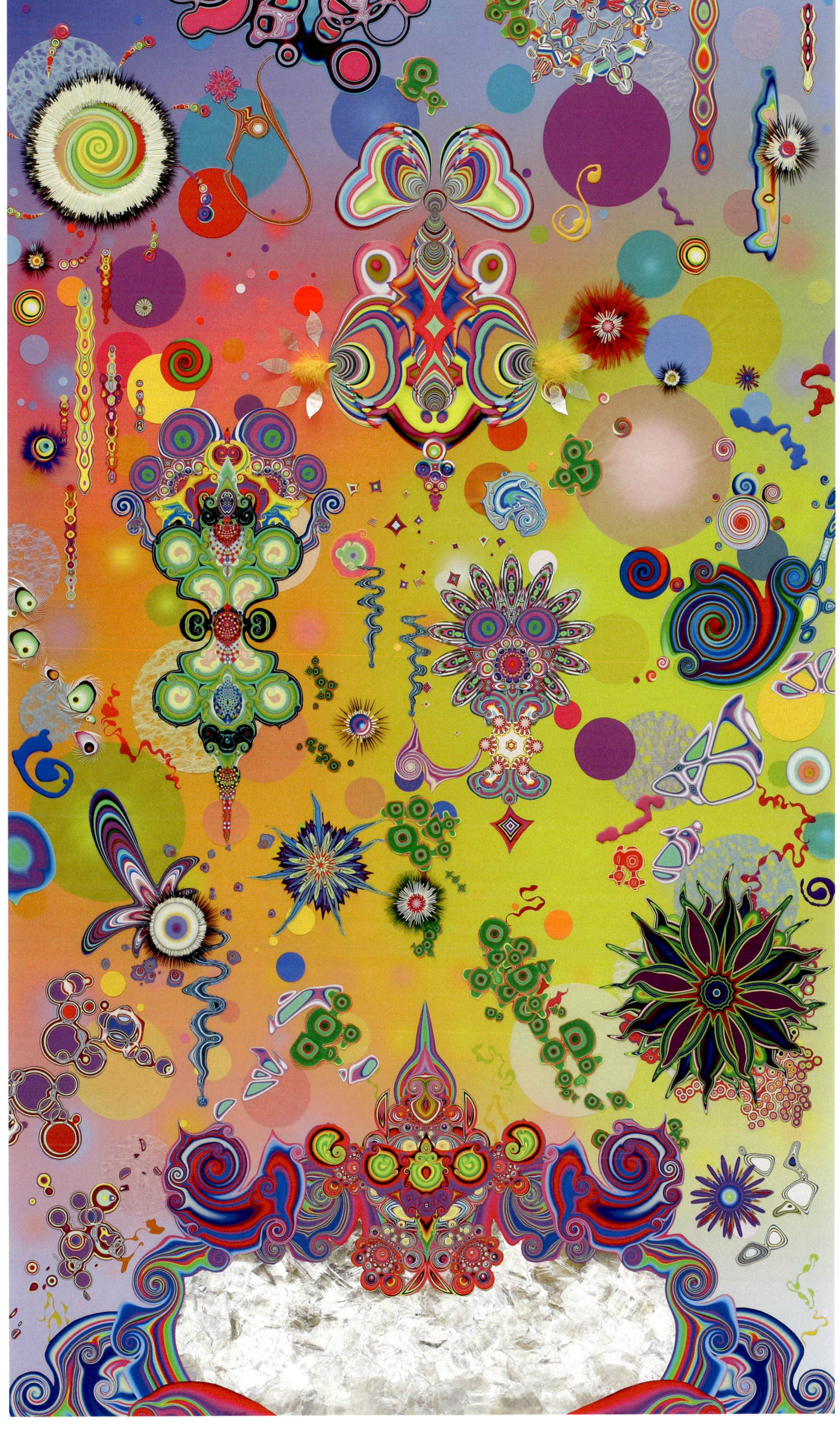

Kamrooz Aram, Installation views: **Negotiations**, Perry Rubenstein Gallery, New York, 2011

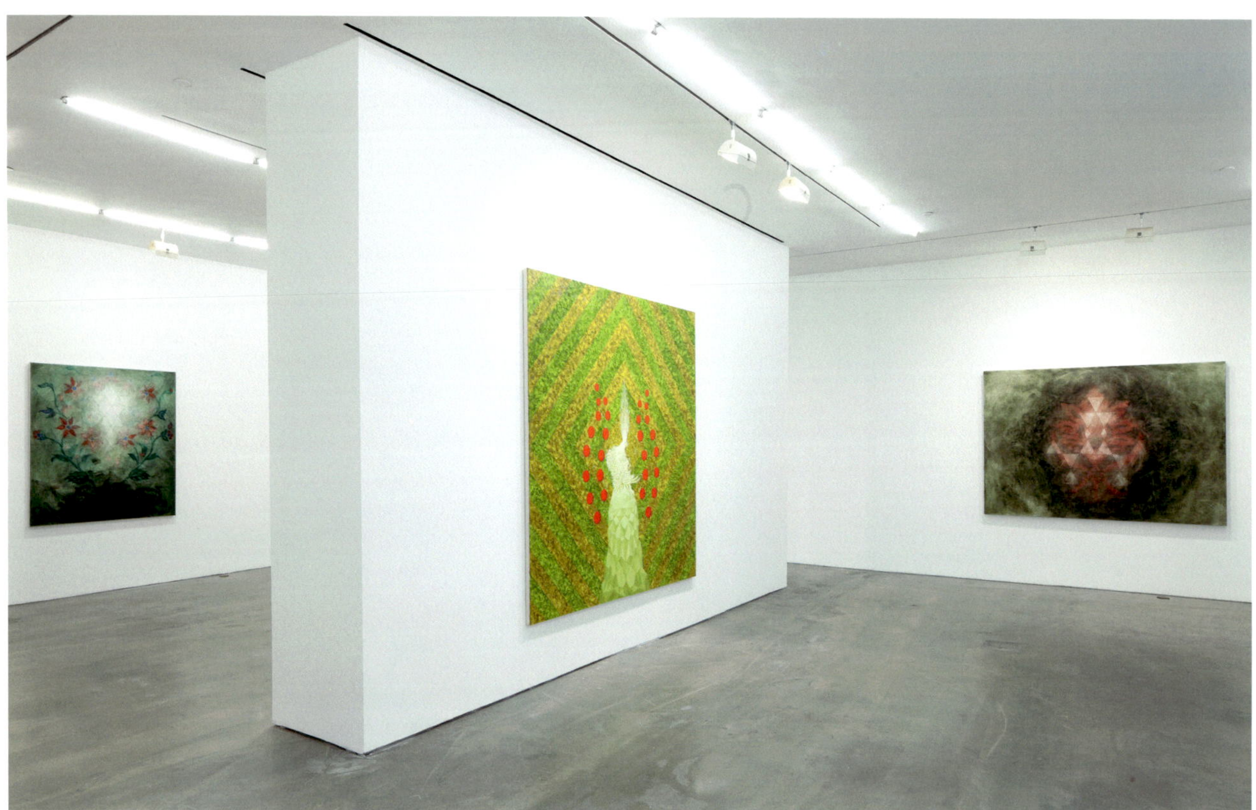

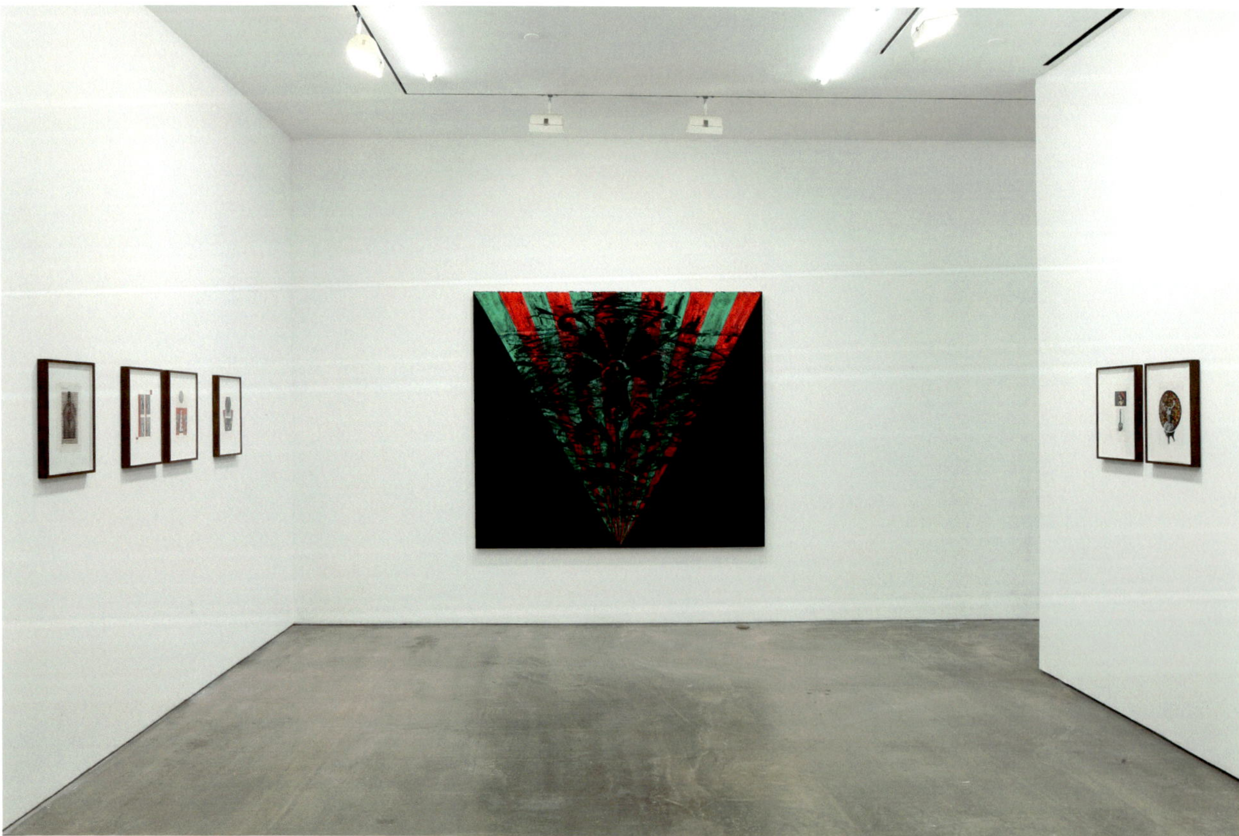

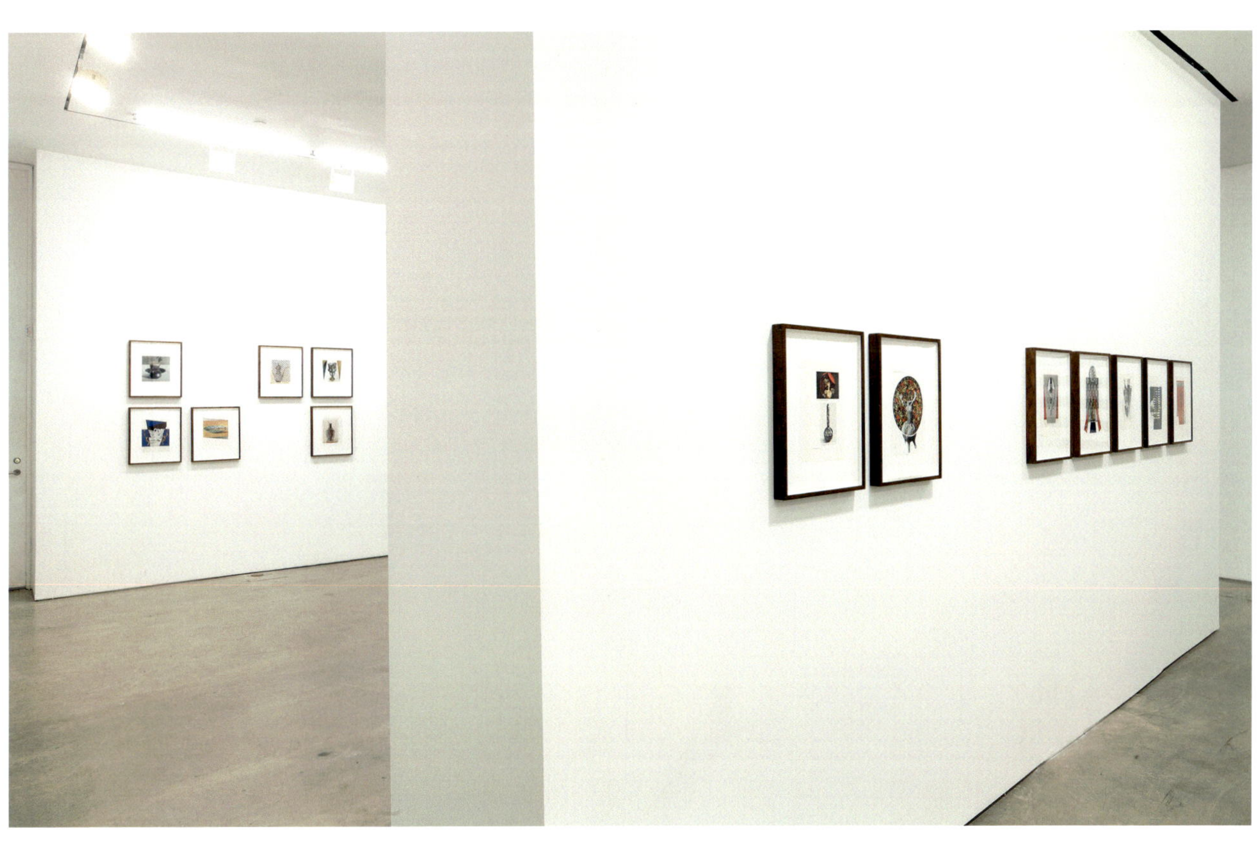

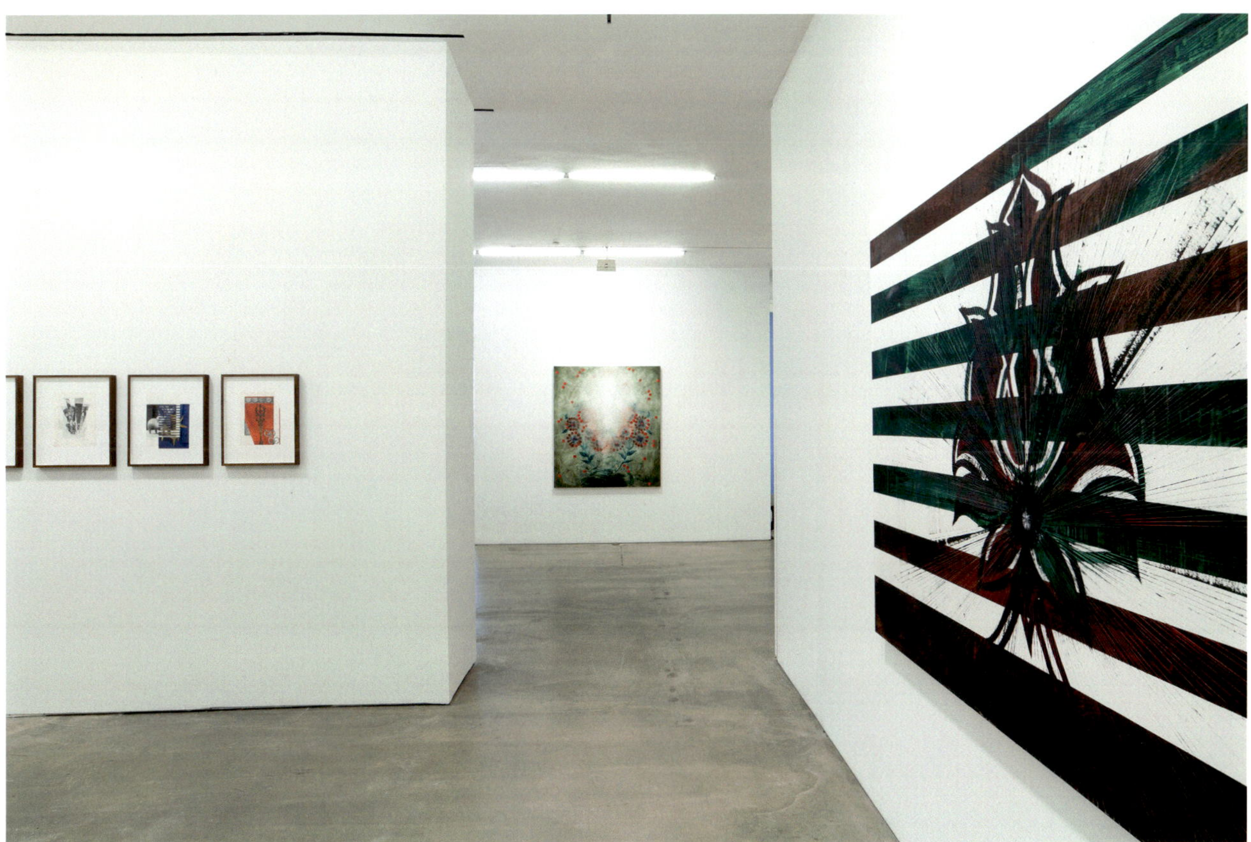

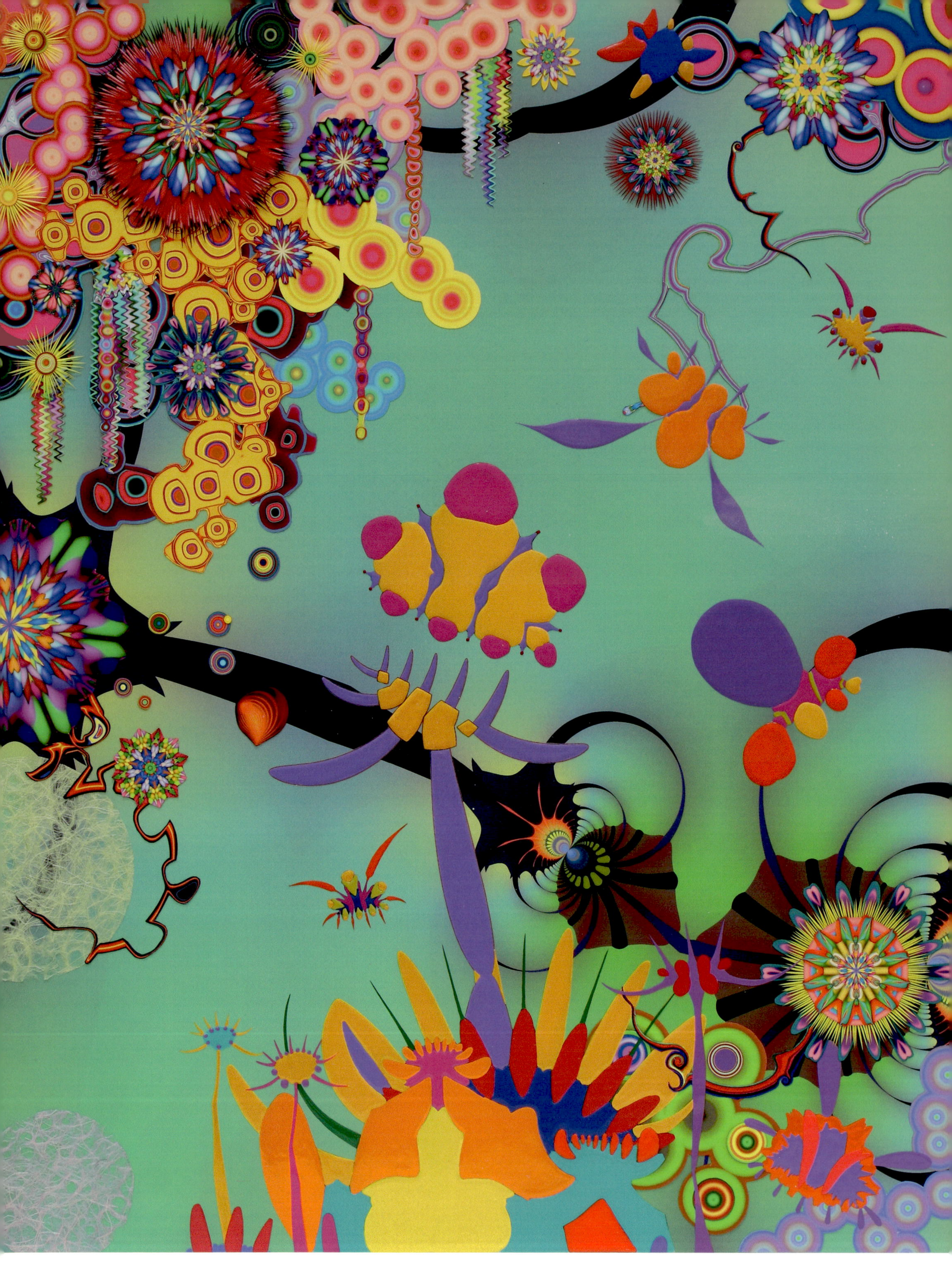

Jose Alvarez (D.O.P.A.), **Hydra** (detail), 2011. Acrylic, quills, feathers, ink, and mixed media on paper, 35⅞ × 30 in. Collection of Tom Lee and Ann Tenenbaum
Courtesy of the artist and Gavlak Gallery, Palm Beach, Florida

Charles Burwell, **Interior, Interior**, 2010. Oil on canvas, 52 × 40 in. Courtesy of Bridgette Mayer Gallery, Philadelphia, Pennsylvania

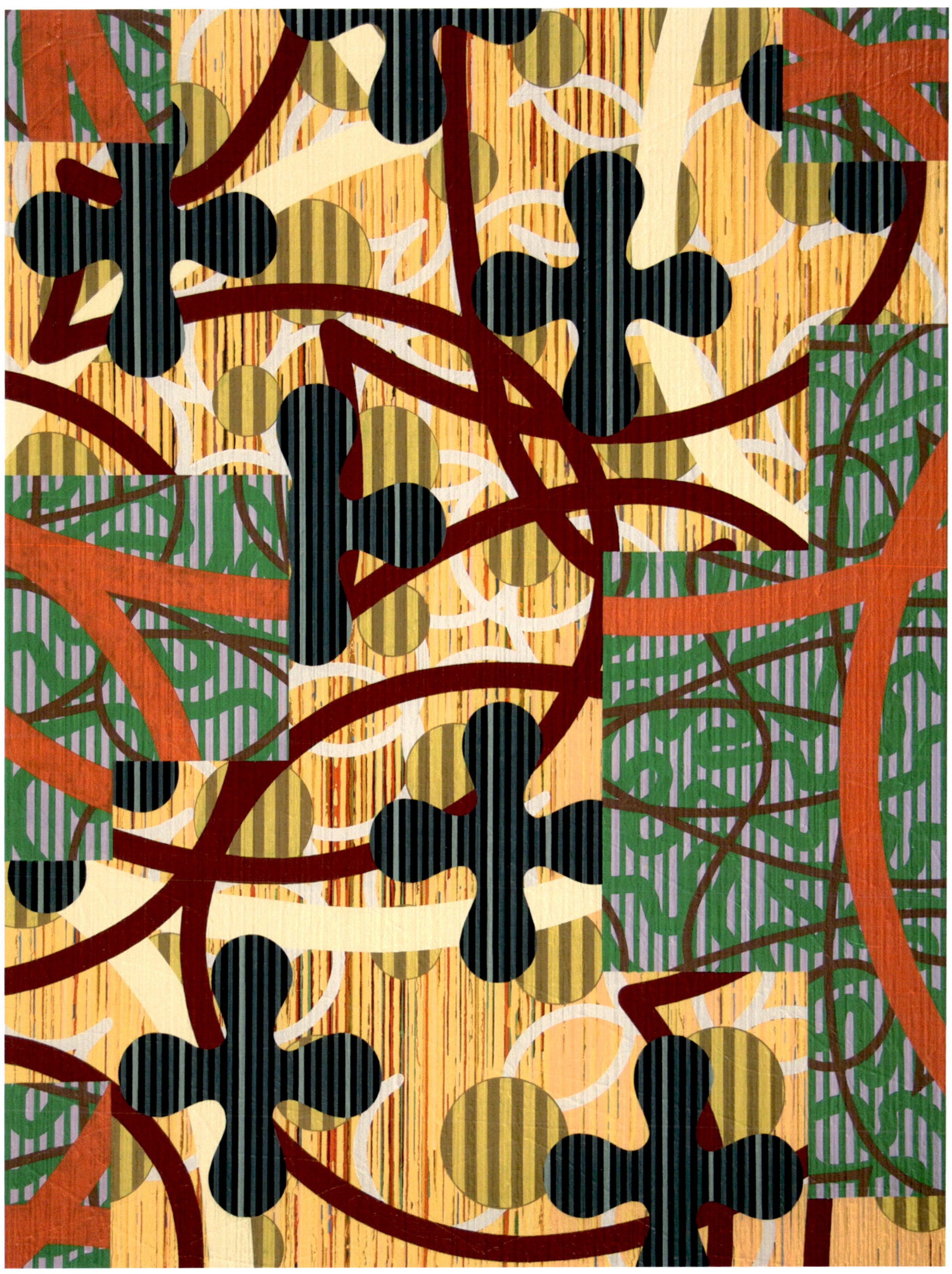

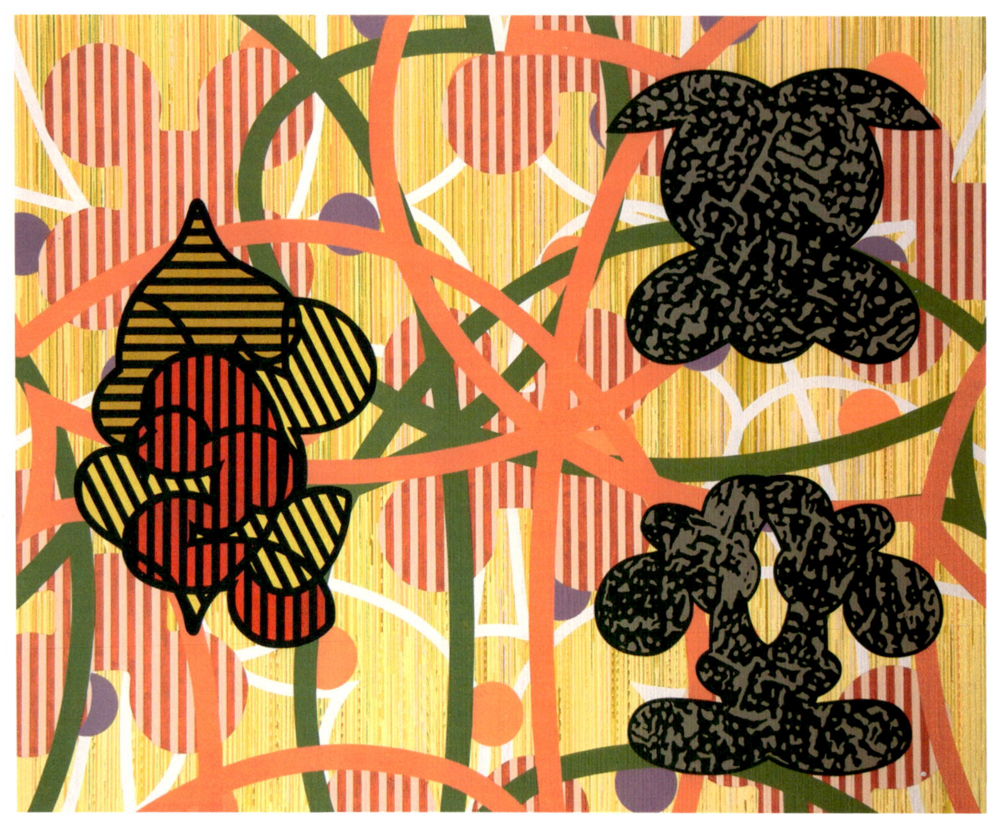

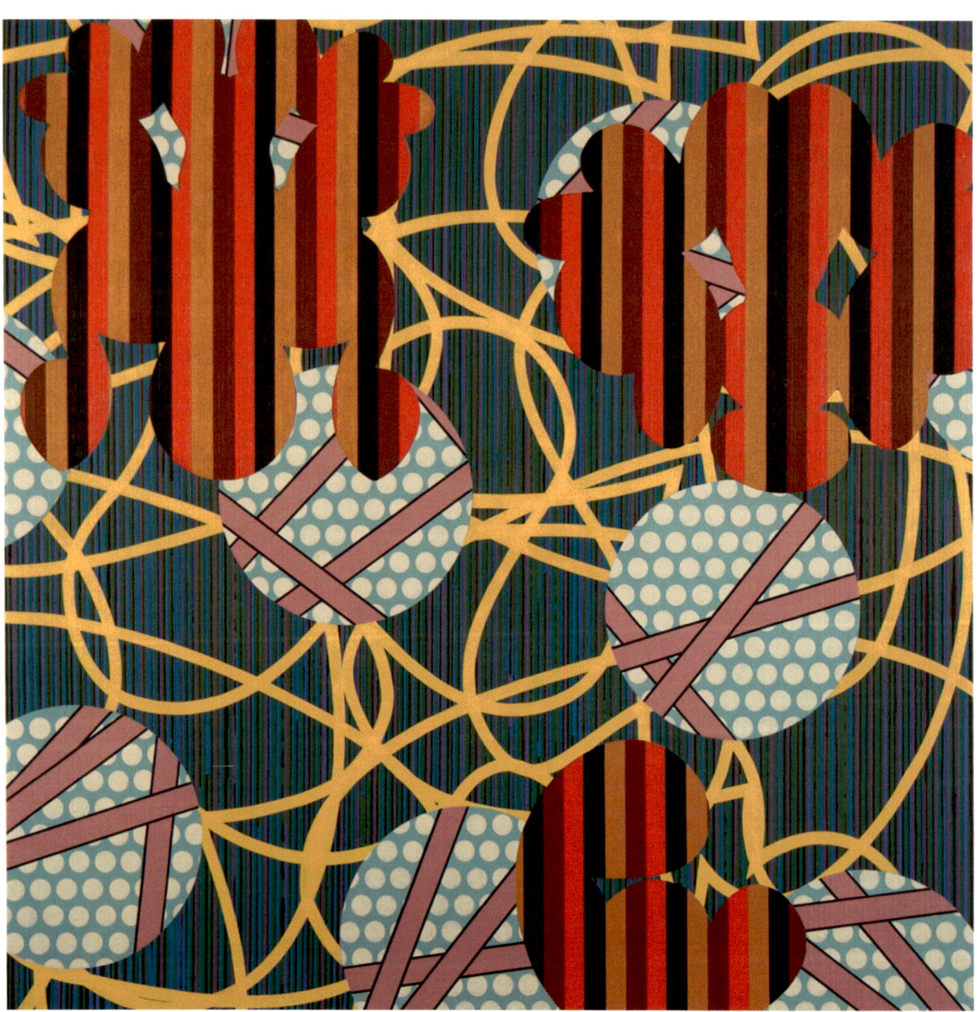

Charles Burwell, **Map Overlay No. 1**, 2012. Acrylic on canvas, 48 × 60 in. Courtesy of Bridgette Mayer Gallery, Philadelphia, Pennsylvania

 Charles Burwell, **Warm Wave**, 2012. Acrylic on canvas, 47 × 47 in. Courtesy of Bridgette Mayer Gallery, Philadelphia, Pennsylvania

Jose Alvarez (D.O.P.A.), **Vitraya Ramunang**, 2011. Acrylic, watercolor, ink, colored pencil, feathers, and collage on paper, 36⅛ × 28⅛ in.
Collection of Joan Genser. Courtesy of the artist and Gavlak Gallery, Palm Beach, Florida

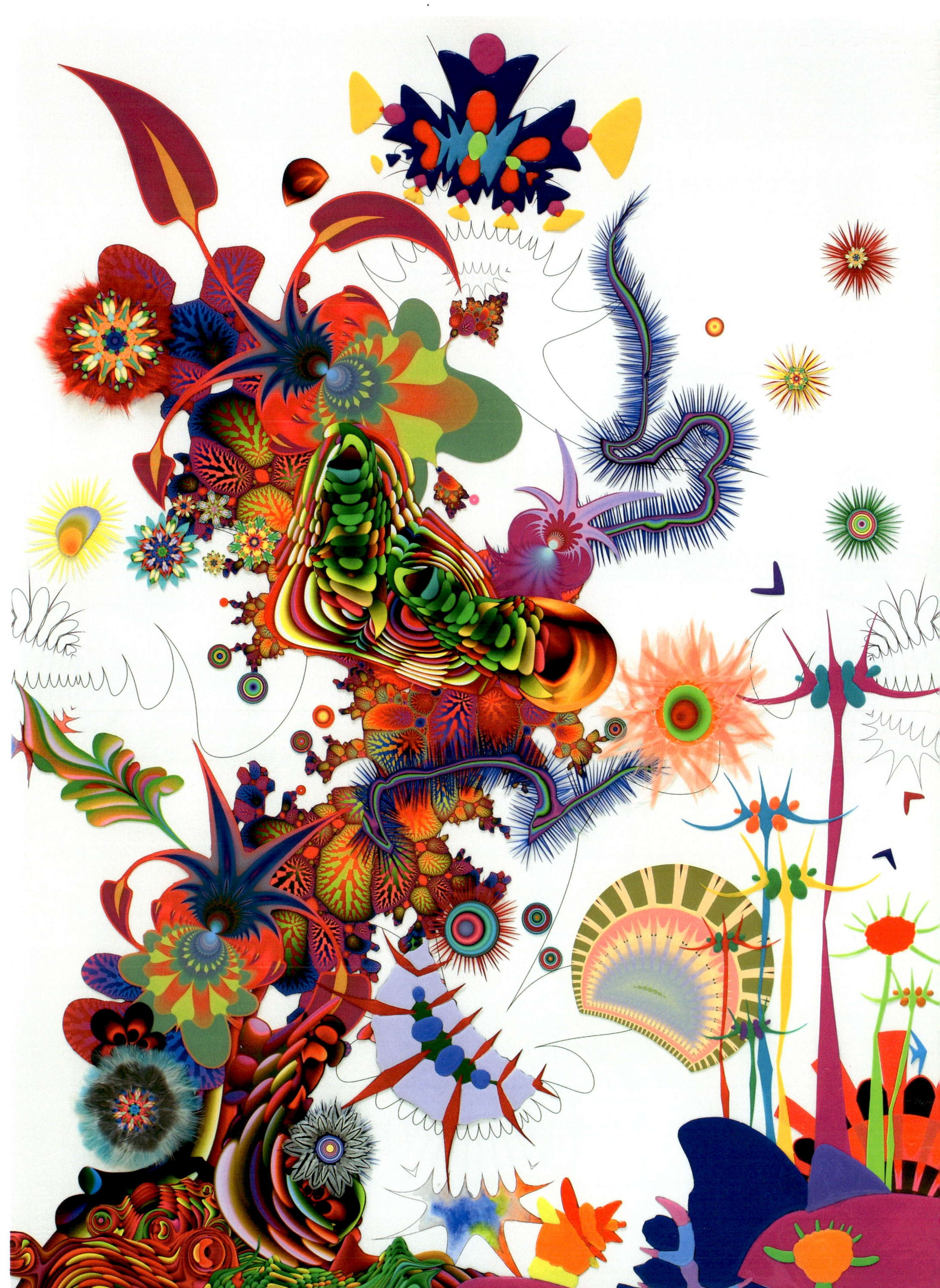

# Annette Davidek

Born 1957

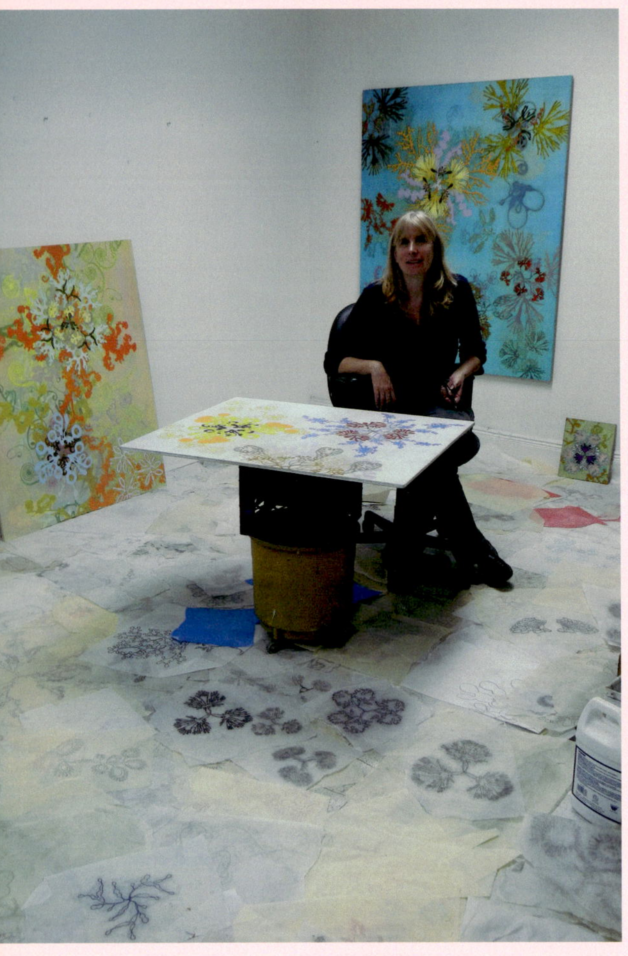

Courtesy of the artist and Littlejohn Contemporary, New York.

The surfaces of Annette Davidek's luminous panel paintings are populated by details from nature, including flowers, branches, coral, microscopic organisms, and "found" diagrammatical sources. However, the manner in which the imagery is enlarged, reduced, stylized, and then recombined pushes these often familiar forms into the realm of abstraction. Davidek builds her compositions with layers of thin paint on wood surfaces, creating a push-pull of scale and depth that is both flat and volumetric.

A characteristic that binds much of her work is the way the artist juxtaposes crisp, boldly colored images over a background of ghosted forms. This layering creates a dynamic foreground / background relationship and emphasizes the imagery's flatness while at the same time referring to real space. Sometimes, the formal qualities of Japanese prints come to mind: for example, in the way that space is organized within the picture plane. Other times, the imagery recalls decorative embellishments found on fine porcelains or wallpapers, as details float freely in space.

Davidek's keen sense of color pushes the palette in directions and combinations outside of nature, enhancing the paintings' seductive qualities as well as their visual reward. Vibrant hues sit alongside soft pastels, and nearly fluorescent pigments cause particular elements to pop out. On casual encounter, the viewer may perceive these works as representational. On closer inspection—taking into account everything from composition to color—they emerge unmistakably as abstract.

Annette Davidek was born in Flint, Michigan, in 1957. She received a Bachelor of Fine Arts from the University of Michigan, Ann Arbor, in 1979, and in 1990, she earned a Master of Fine Arts from Hunter College of The City University of New York. Davidek has exhibited her paintings since the early 1990s and is based in Brooklyn, New York.

# *Fausto Fernandez*

Born 1975

Fausto Fernandez makes art that both mirrors and explores relationships in life. Everyday objects, such as tools or flowers, or diagrammatic sources, including sewing patterns, are used to investigate how individuals relate to one another or develop complex routines and rituals for daily living.

Fernandez layers these identifiable subjects with abstract elements in dense arrangements, resulting in large compositions that serve as metaphors for human interaction. Fernandez's messages are not always readily apparent to the viewer, but his underlying concepts serve as the roadmap to drive the art in a number of different, yet related, directions.

The surfaces of Fernandez's works are built up in layers of paint, collage, and drawing materials. In this process, he melds gestural brushwork and intuitive mark-making with fragments of realism, including the human face and form. Strong lines and geometric shapes anchor the free-floating elements, which Fernandez masterfully weaves together.

Occasionally, a photographic portrait surfaces; recently, a series of faceless portraits obscures the identities of the subjects. Like many artists of his generation, Fernandez borrows freely from the art of the past, in both his approach and his imagery. As a result, his work takes a multiplicity of forms.

In college Fernandez studied graphic design along with painting, and his skills as a designer make a strong imprint on his paintings and collages. Again, like his contemporaries, he moves comfortably between the worlds of fine and applied arts, rejecting traditional hierarchies that influenced many artists of previous generations. In recent years, Fernandez has pushed his work even further in creating large public projects.

A native of El Paso, Texas, born in 1975, Fausto Fernandez spent his first twenty-five years in Ciudad Juárez, Chihuahua, Mexico. In 2001 he received two Bachelors of Fine Arts from the University of Texas at El Paso: one in painting and one in graphic design. After several years in Phoenix, Arizona, Fernandez relocated to Los Angeles, California, where he currently lives. He regularly exhibits his paintings and in 2013 completed a public work for the Phoenix Sky Harbor International Airport.

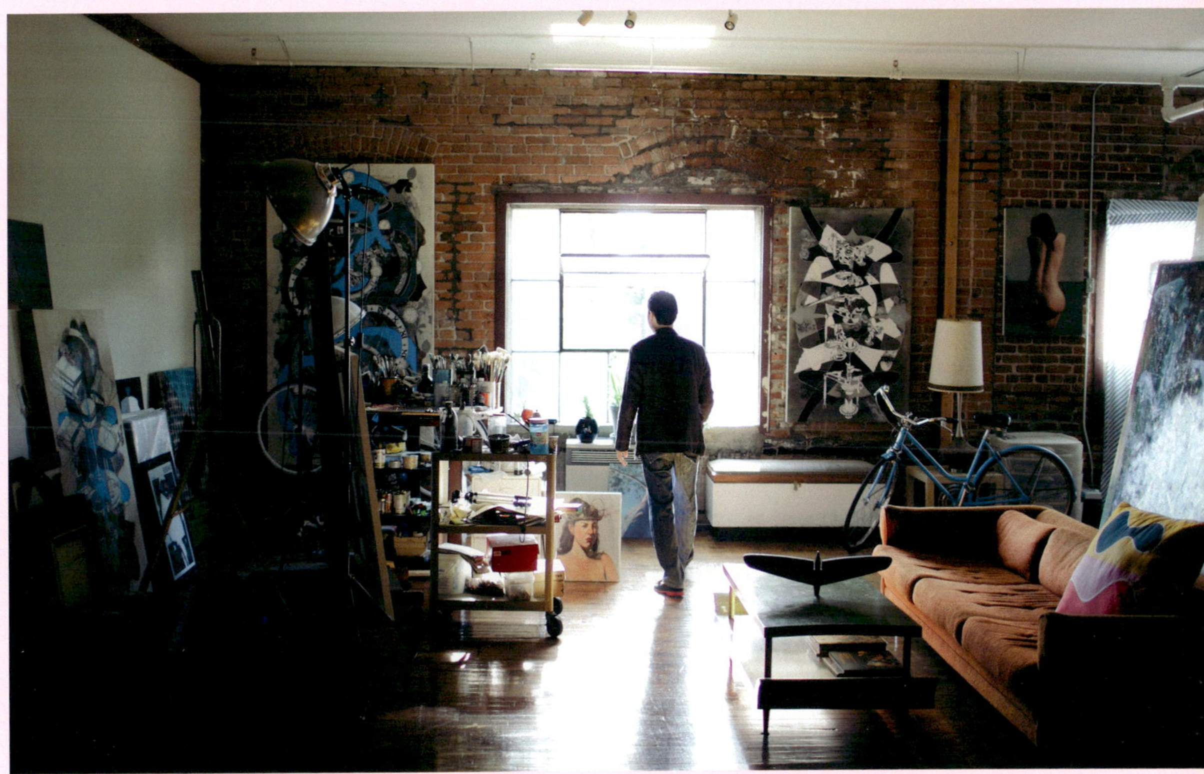

Courtesy of the artist.

# *Nancy Lorenz*

Born 1962

Extended stays in Japan have had a significant impact on Nancy Lorenz's luminous paintings and objects. She sensitively melds elements of Eastern decorative traditions with intuitive, gestural mark-making to create shimmering abstractions. Lorenz's works fuse these opposing approaches in her imagery. Moreover, her use of exotic materials—including mother-of-pearl, lacquer, and metallic leaf—adds a unique dimension that is quite unlike that seen in the work of other contemporary abstract painters.

Elements of the landscape and references to nature pervade Lorenz's paintings on panel, often reinforced by a work's title. The reflective surface of water, vaporous cloud forms, or falling rain showers inspire the artist and translate into her iridescent abstractions. Their imagery extends beyond the pictures' perimeters and floats off into the surrounding space, further emphasizing connections to landscape vistas, vast bodies of water, and the expanse of sky. The panels' surfaces are often covered in gold or silver leaf, then incised and inlaid with mother-of-pearl. These materials, while rarely found in current painting, have histories in both Western and Eastern traditions, and they cause Lorenz's art to waver between high concept and fine craft.

Lorenz also makes traditionally designed folding screens that bear the same imagery as her paintings and are created from the same luxurious materials. Another significant aspect of her production includes creating permanent site commissions. She collaborates with interior, fashion, and product designers. She embellishes the surfaces of furniture and decorative boxes. Whichever format her works take, however, they are all unified by a shared sense of visual restraint, surface tactility, and inherent elegance.

Nancy Lorenz was born in North Plainfield, New Jersey, in 1962. In 1985 she received a Bachelor of Fine Arts from the University of Michigan, Ann Arbor, and in 1988, a Master of Fine Arts from the Tyler School of Art, Temple University, in Philadelphia, Pennsylvania, and Rome, Italy. For nearly two decades, her work has been included in solo and group exhibitions, and is found in public and private collections worldwide. She lives and works in New York.

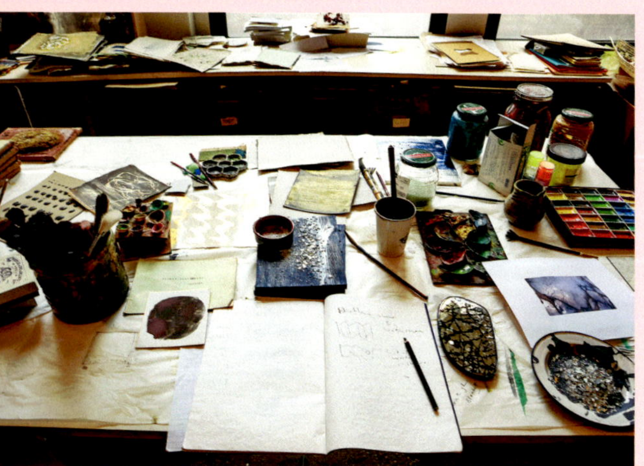

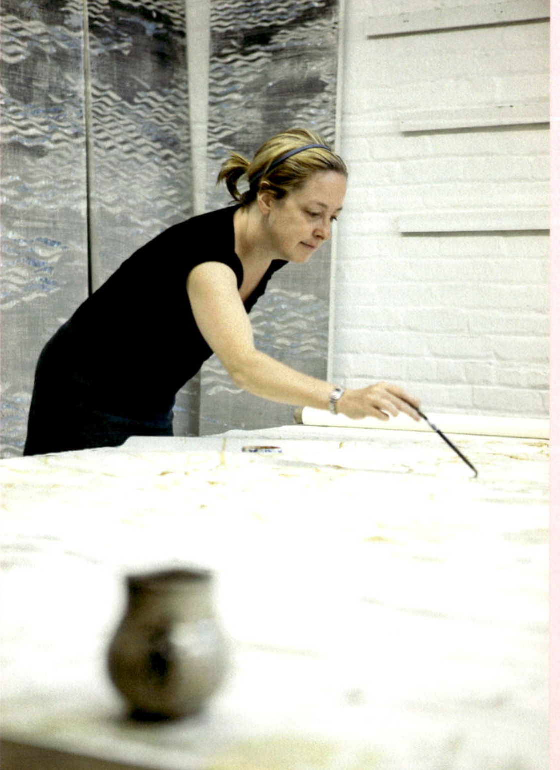

above: Studio view: New York, 2013. Courtesy of the artist.
right: Courtesy of the artist.

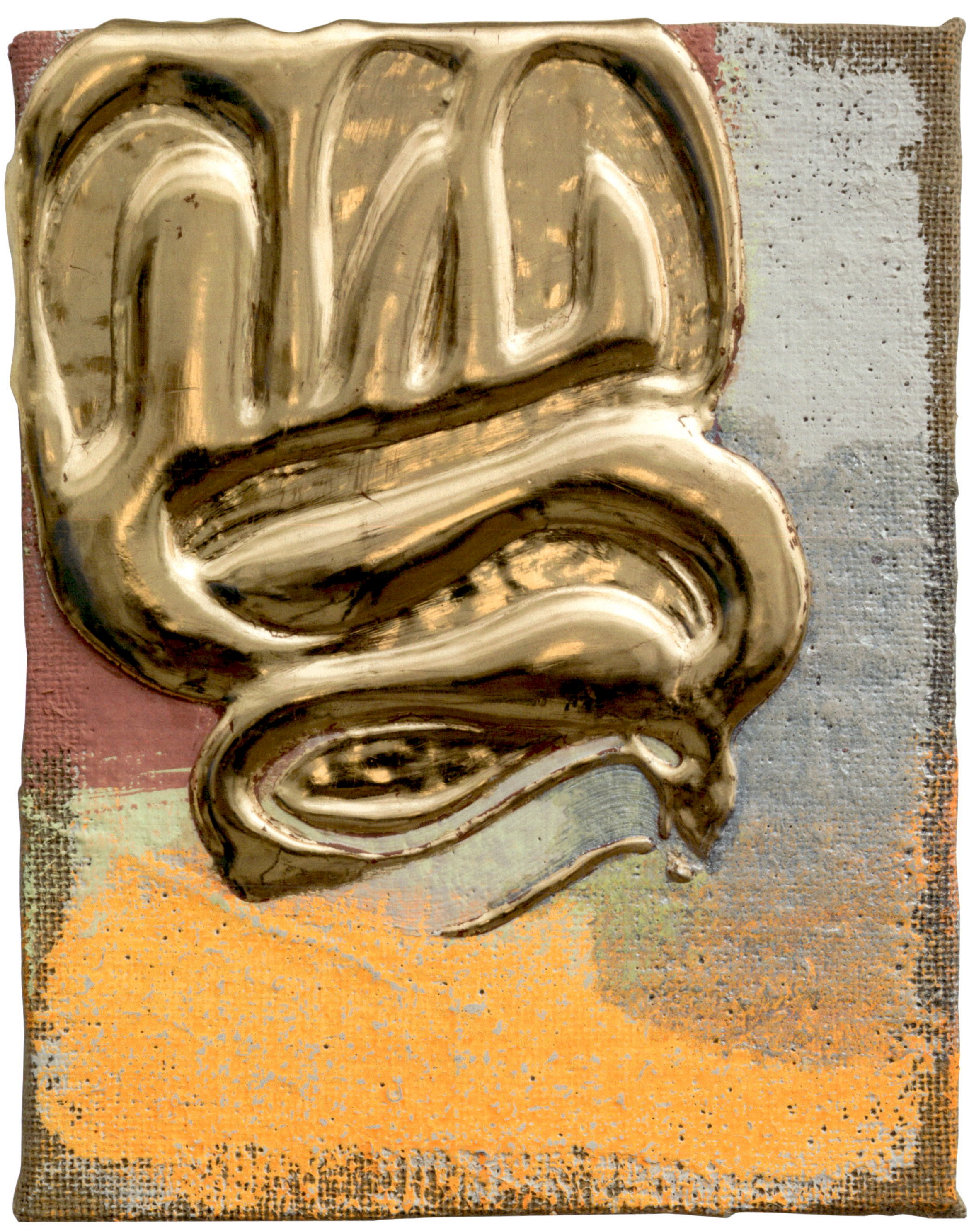

Nancy Lorenz, **Red Gold Pour**, 2013. Gesso, gilder's clay, red gold leaf, and pigment on burlap, 10 × 8 in. Collection of Lucy Schwalbe. Courtesy of the artist

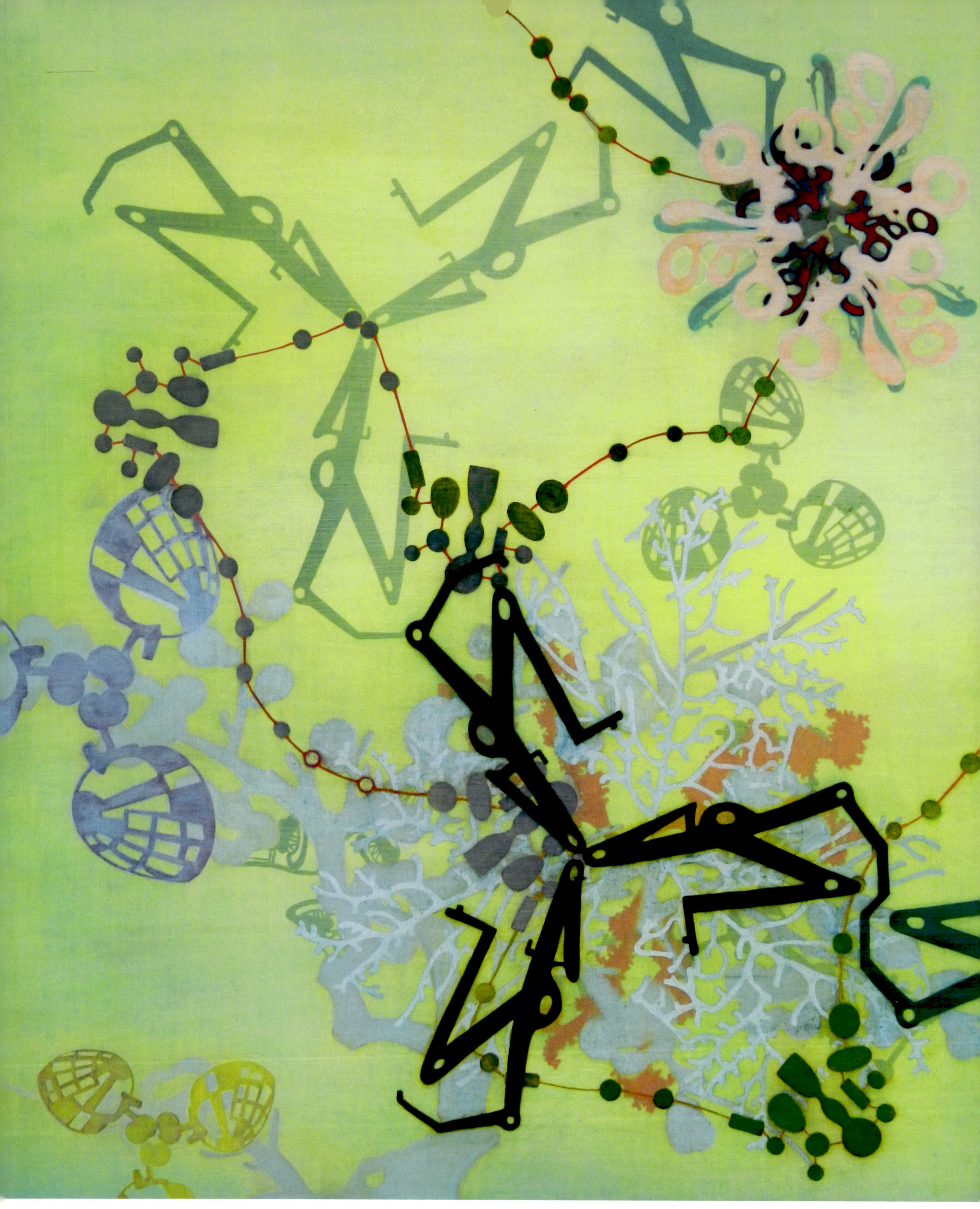

 Annette Davidek, **Untitled**, 2011. Oil on birch panel, 48 × 42 in. Courtesy of the artist and Littlejohn Contemporary, New York

Fausto Fernandez, **Main Rotor Assembly #2**, 2010. Collage, acrylic, and spray paint on canvas, 60 × 36 in. Courtesy of the artist

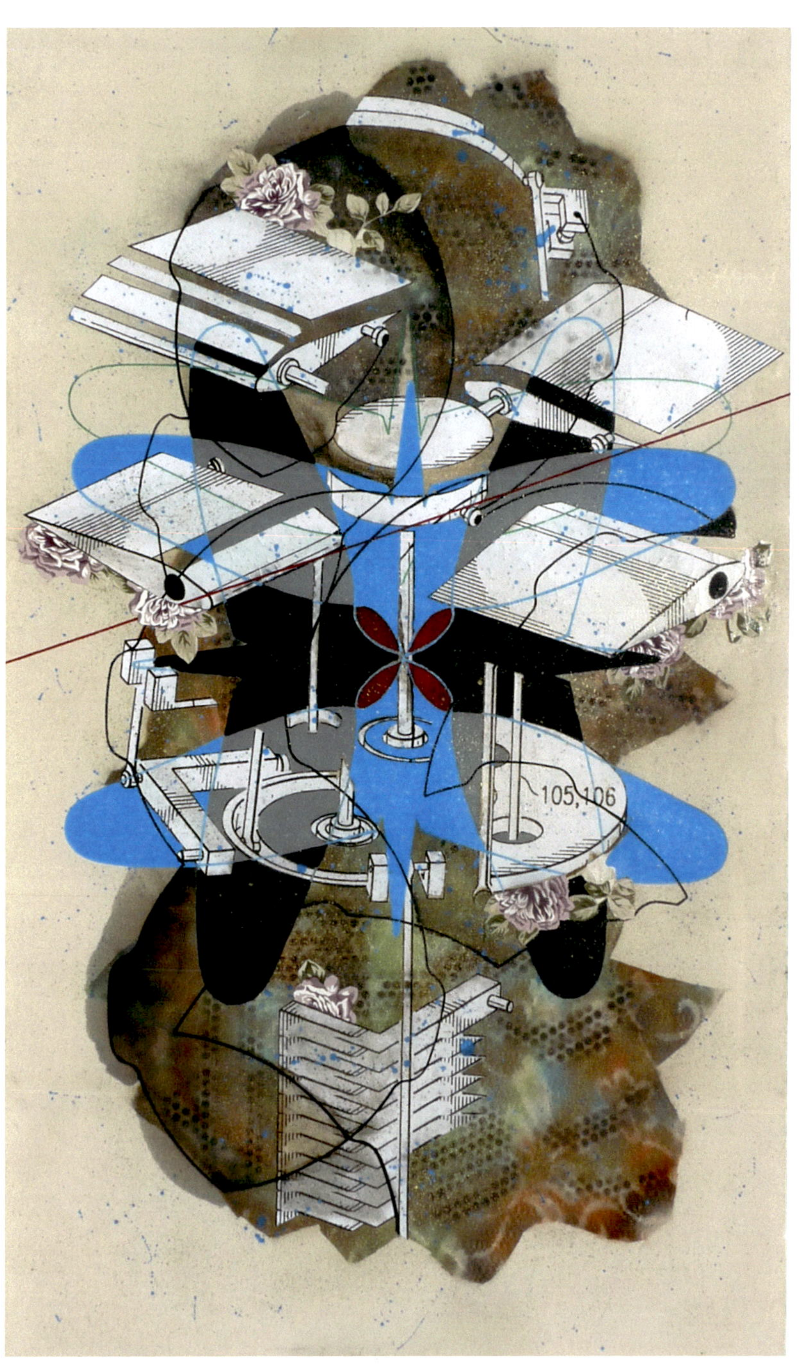

Nancy Lorenz, **Reclining Buddha**, 2007. Gold leaf and mother-of-pearl on panel, 36 × 72 in. Private collection
Courtesy of the artist and Chahan Gallery, Paris, France

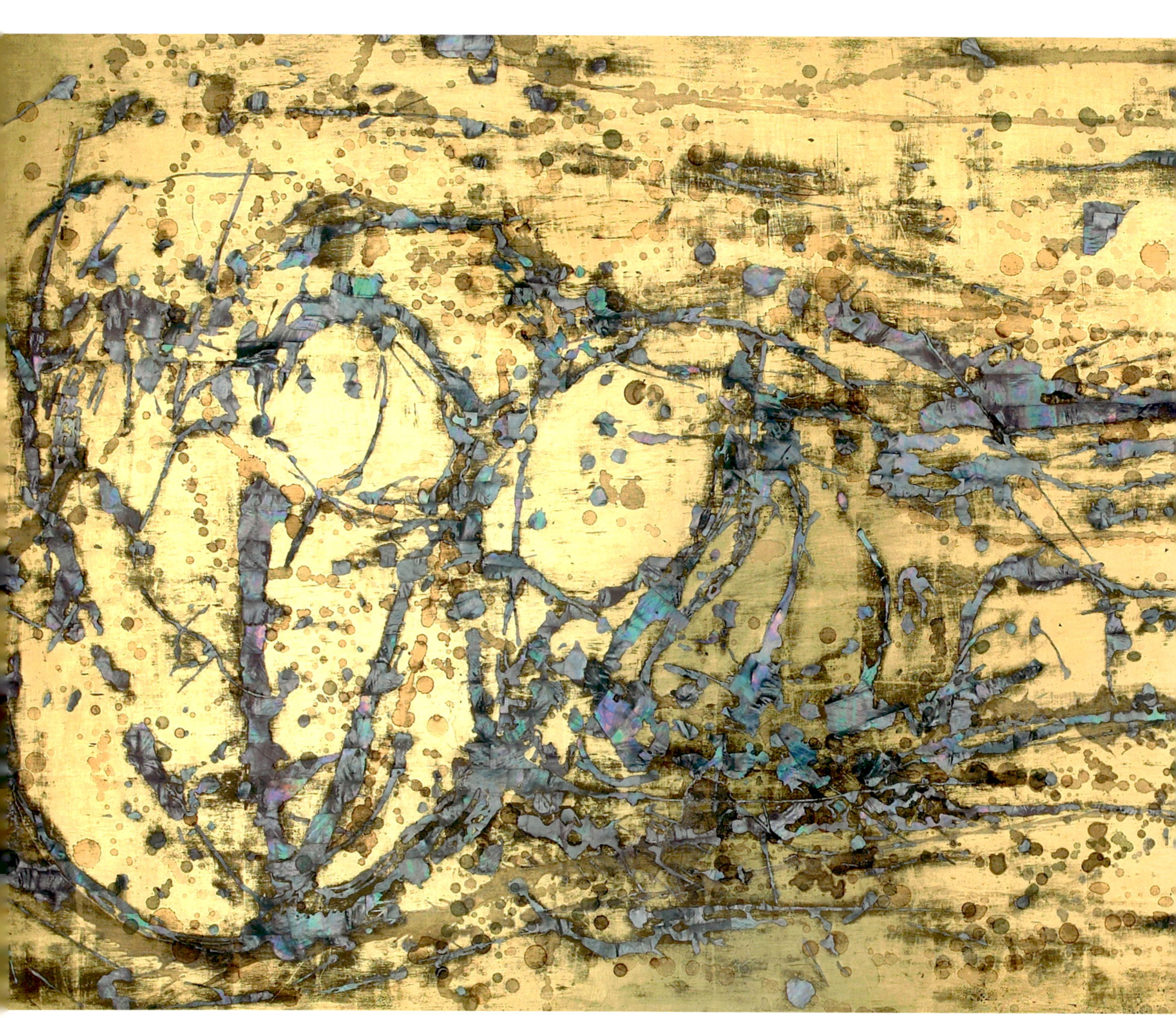

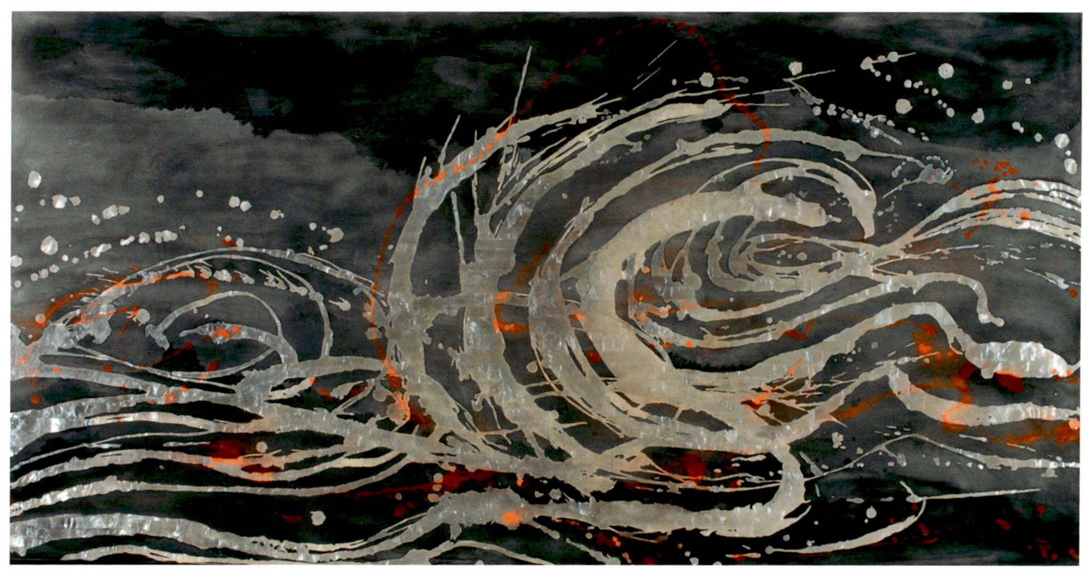

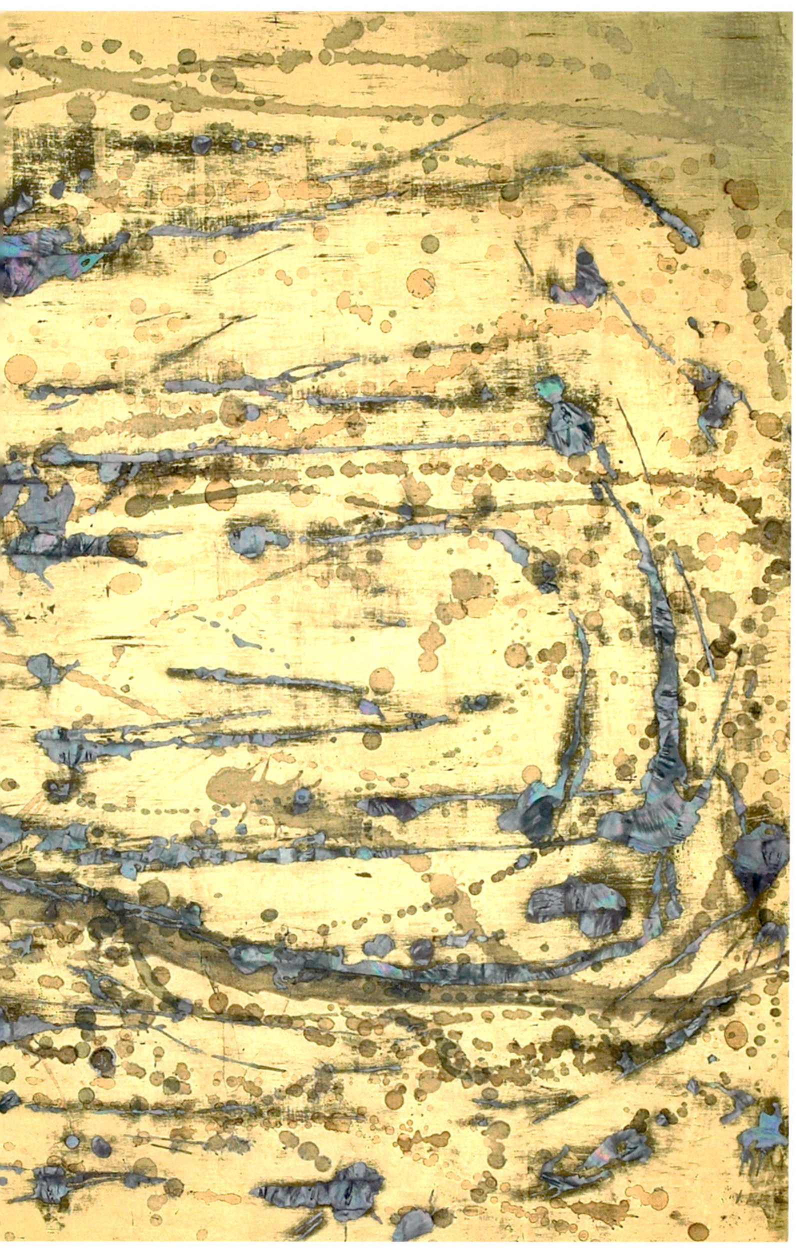

(top) Nancy Lorenz, **Wave II**, 2006. Mother-of-pearl, pigment, and shellac on panel, 36 × 72 in. Private collection
Courtesy of the artist and Morgan Lehman Gallery, New York

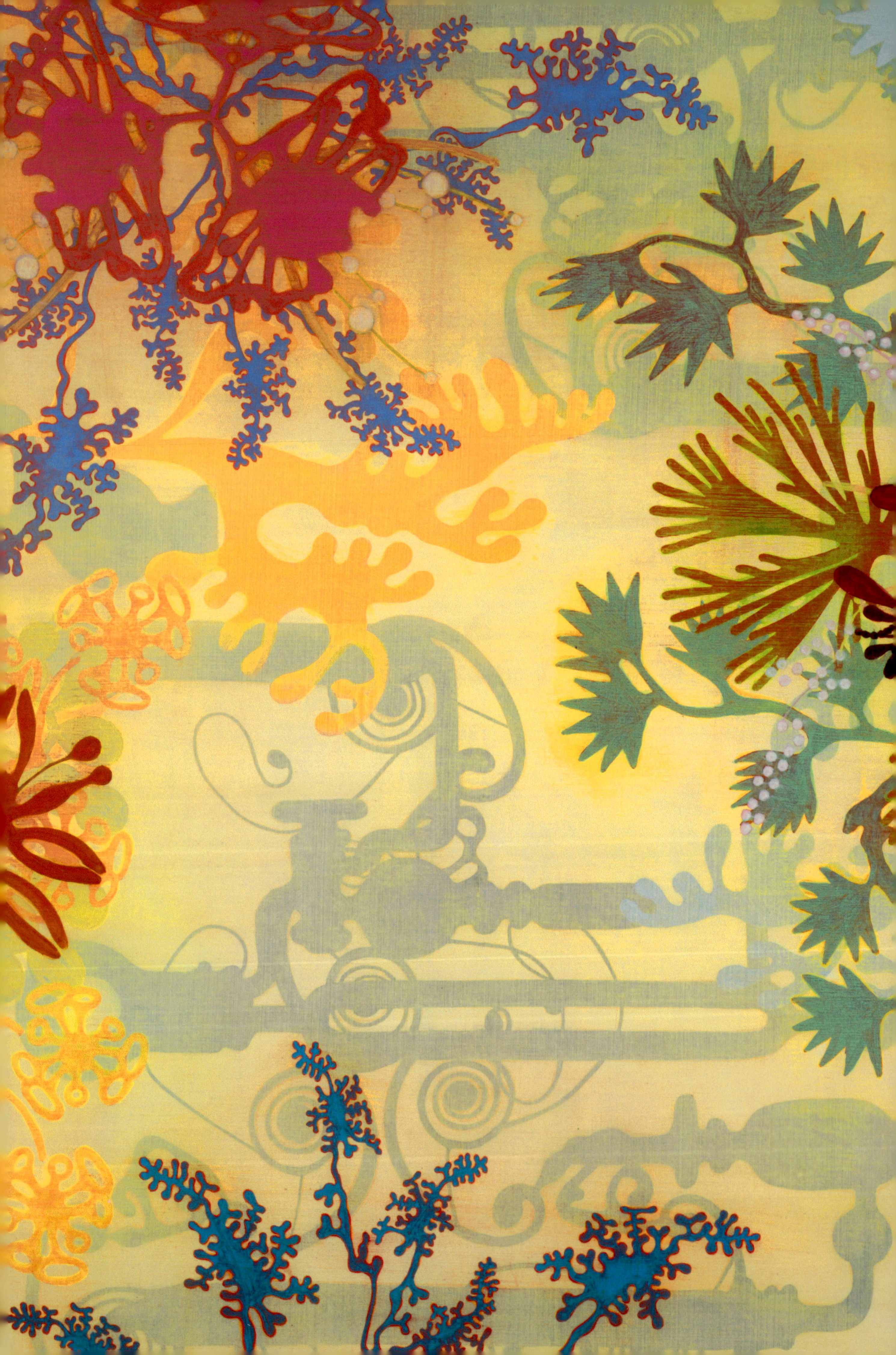

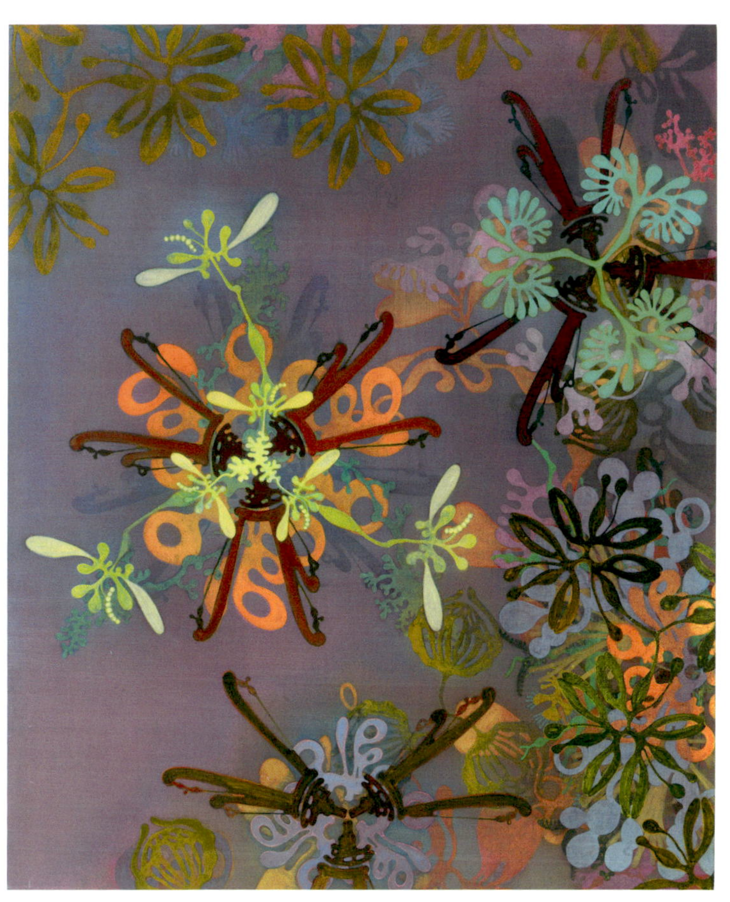

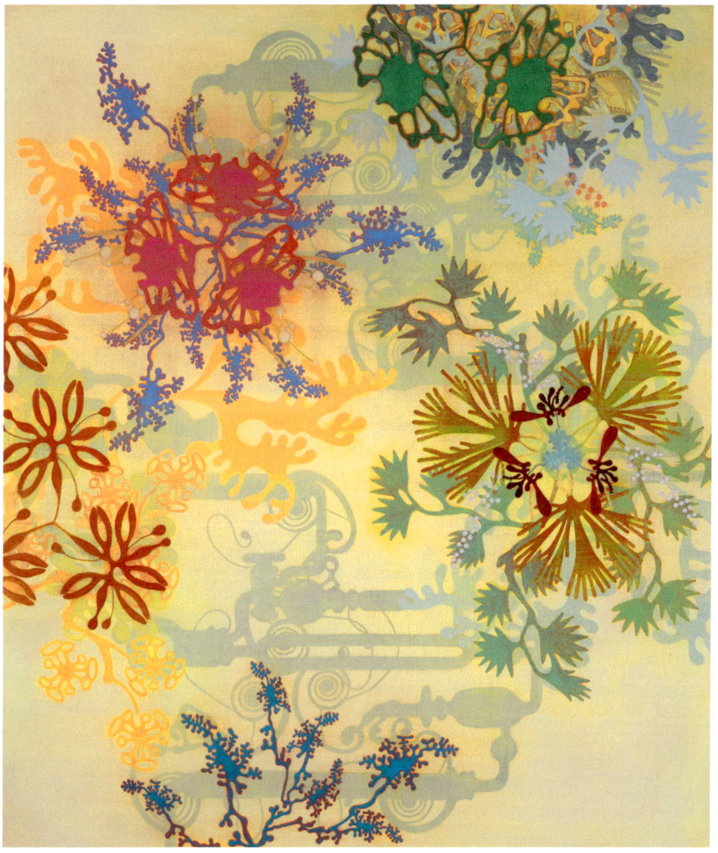

Annette Davidek, **Untitled**, 2010. Oil on birch panel, 38 × 32 in. Courtesy of the artist and Littlejohn Contemporary, New York

Annette Davidek, **Untitled**, 2012. Oil on birch panel, 48 × 42 in. Courtesy of the artist and Littlejohn Contemporary, New York

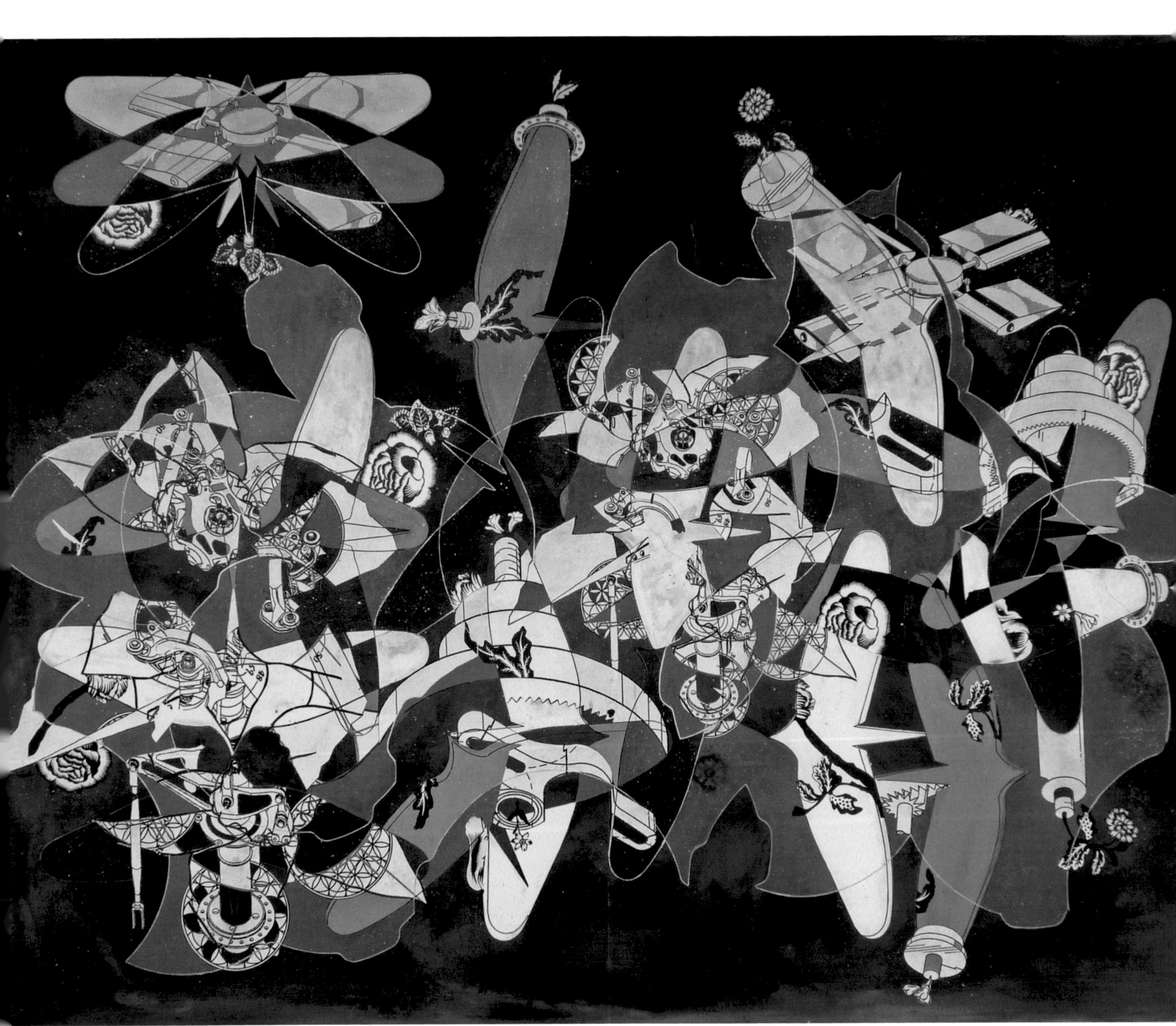

 Fausto Fernandez, **Modern Advances Adapting to Nature**, 2011. Collage and acrylic on canvas, 74 × 96 in. Courtesy of the artist

Nancy Lorenz, **Ribbons**, 2012. Moon gold leaf, mother-of-pearl, and pigment on panel, 20 × 15 in. Courtesy of the artist and Tiffany & Co., New York

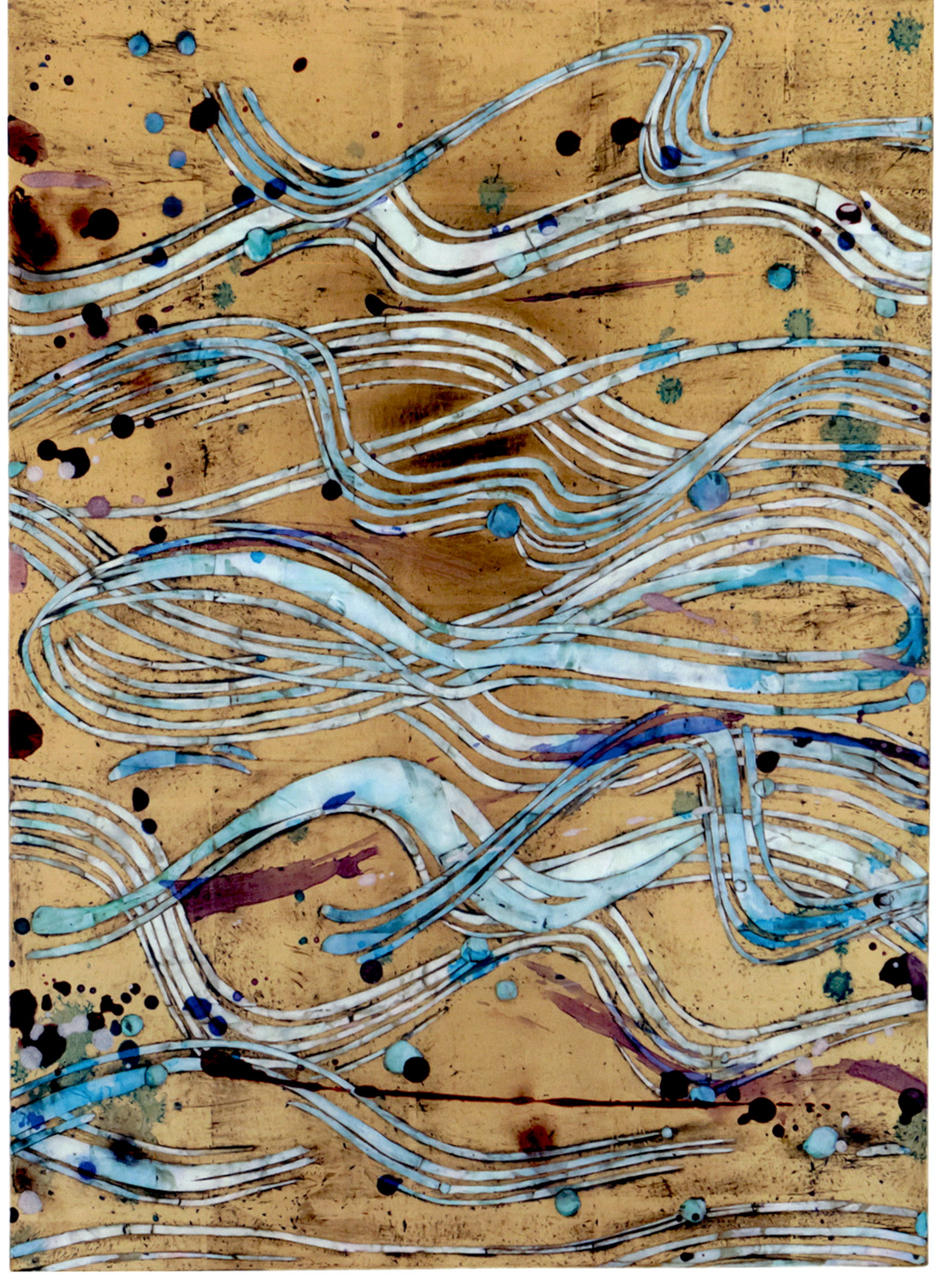

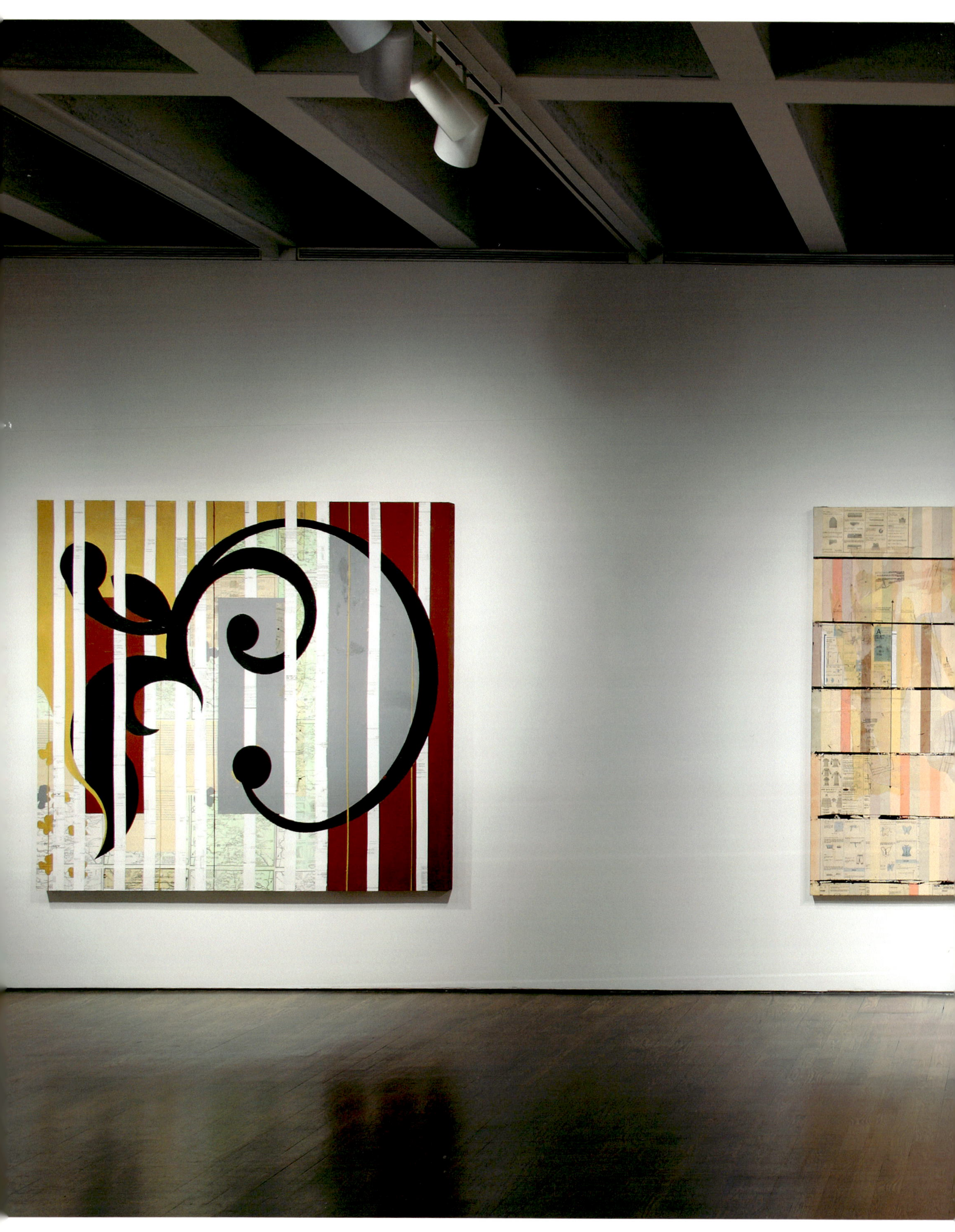

Fausto Fernandez, Installation view: **Remix: New Modernities in a Post-Indian World**, Art Gallery of Ontario, Toronto, Canada, 2008
Courtesy of Art Gallery of Ontario

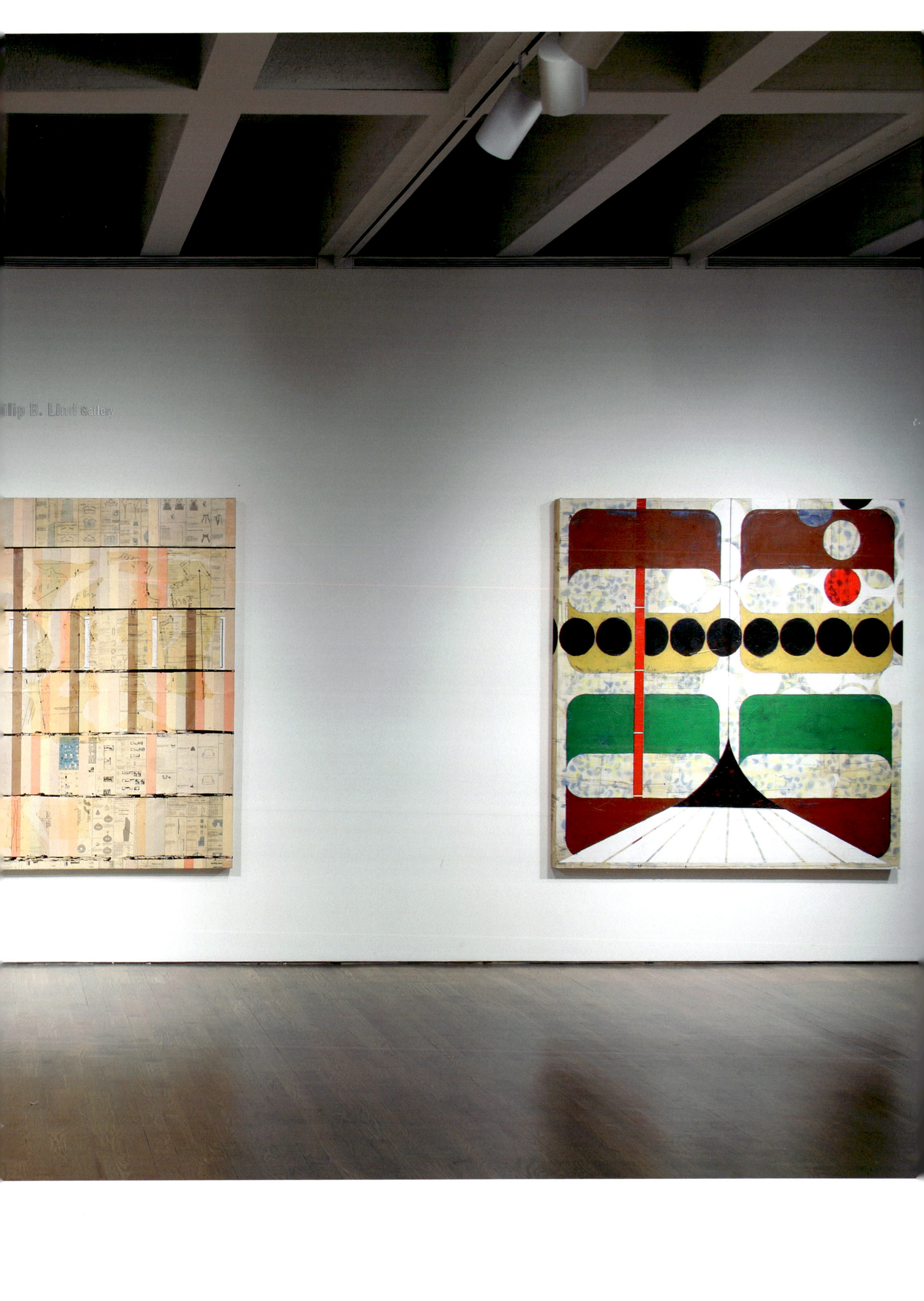
B. Lind Gallery

Annette Davidek, **Untitled**, 2010. Oil on birch panel, 48 × 42 in. Courtesy of the artist and Littlejohn Contemporary, New York

Annette Davidek, **Untitled**, 2012. Oil on birch panel, 48 × 42 in. Courtesy of the artist and Littlejohn Contemporary, New York

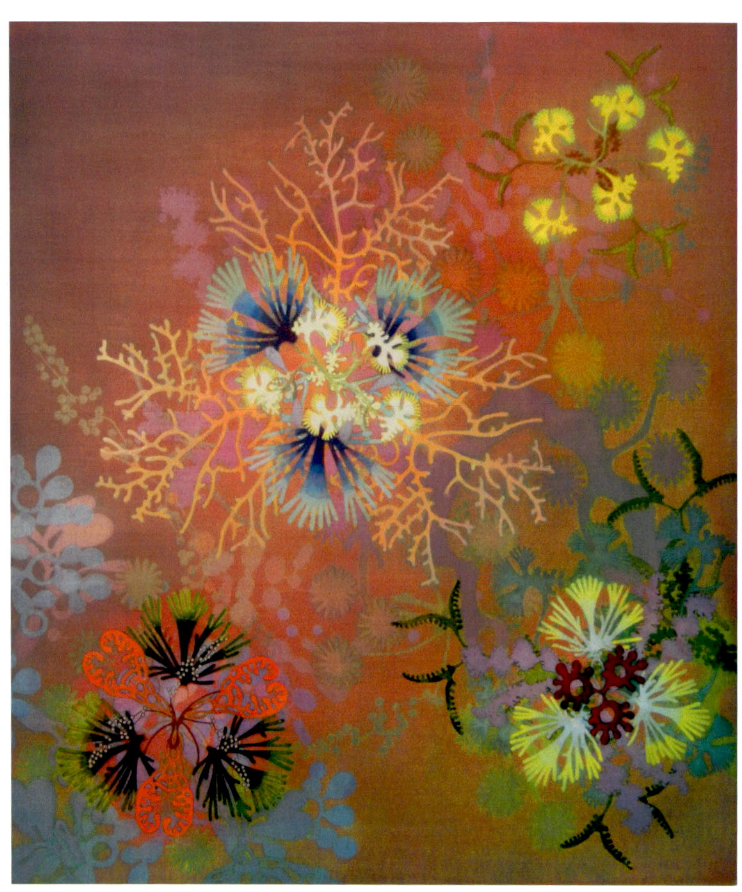

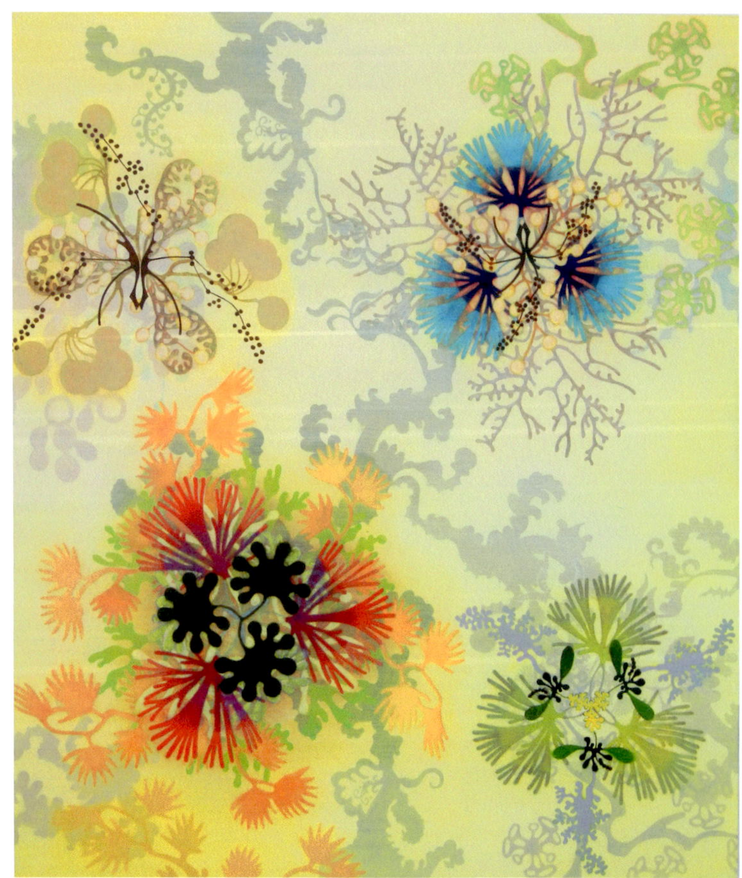

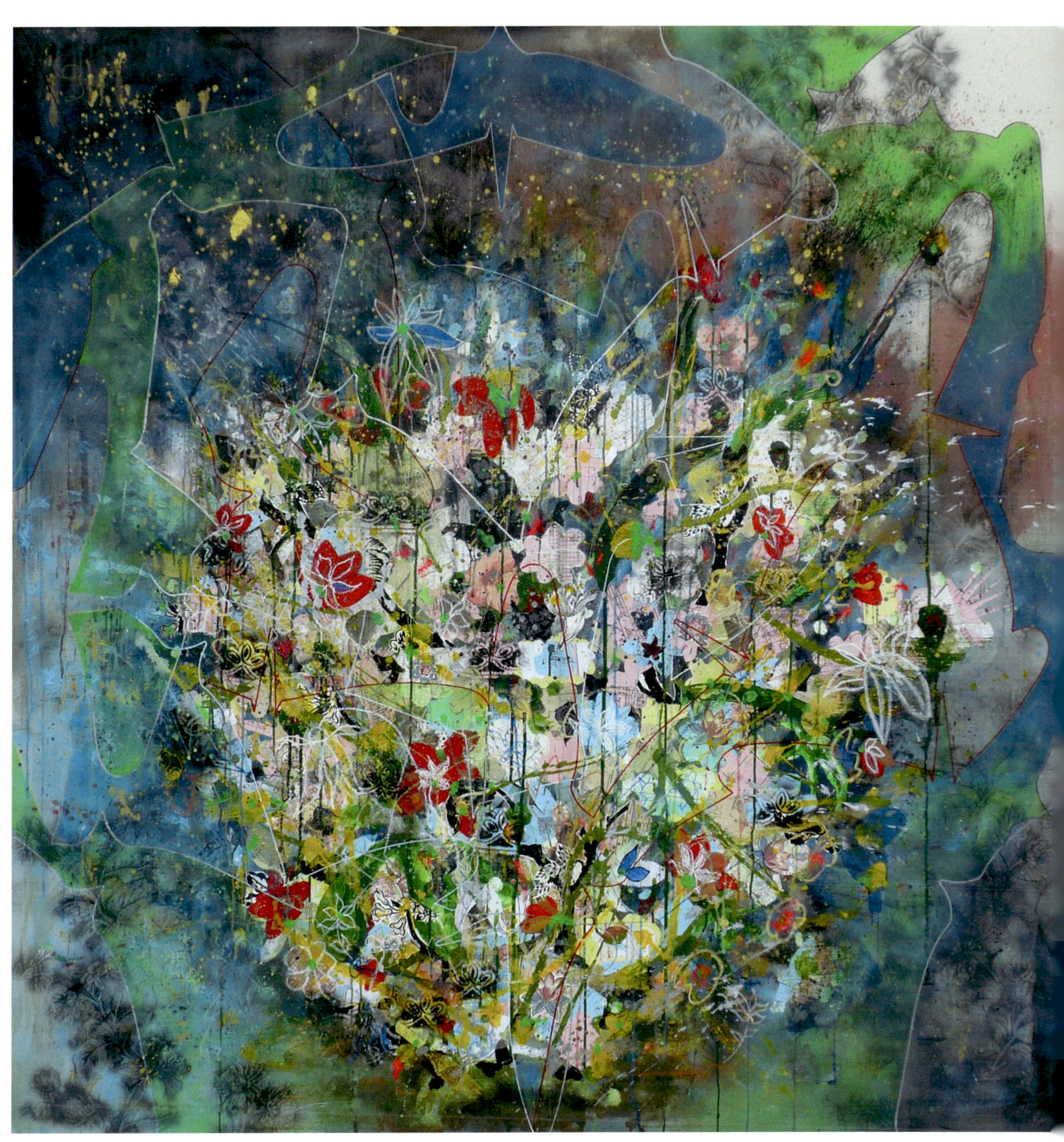

Fausto Fernandez, **All Flowers In Time Bend Towards The Sun**, 2013. Collage, architectural plans, maps, acrylic, oil pastel, and spray paint on canvas, 72 × 72 in.
Collection of Tammi Westfall. Courtesy of the artist

Nancy Lorenz, **Palladium X**, 2013. Gesso, black clay, palladium leaf, and pigment on panel, 6¾ × 9 in. Collection of Adrian Schwalbe. Courtesy of the artist

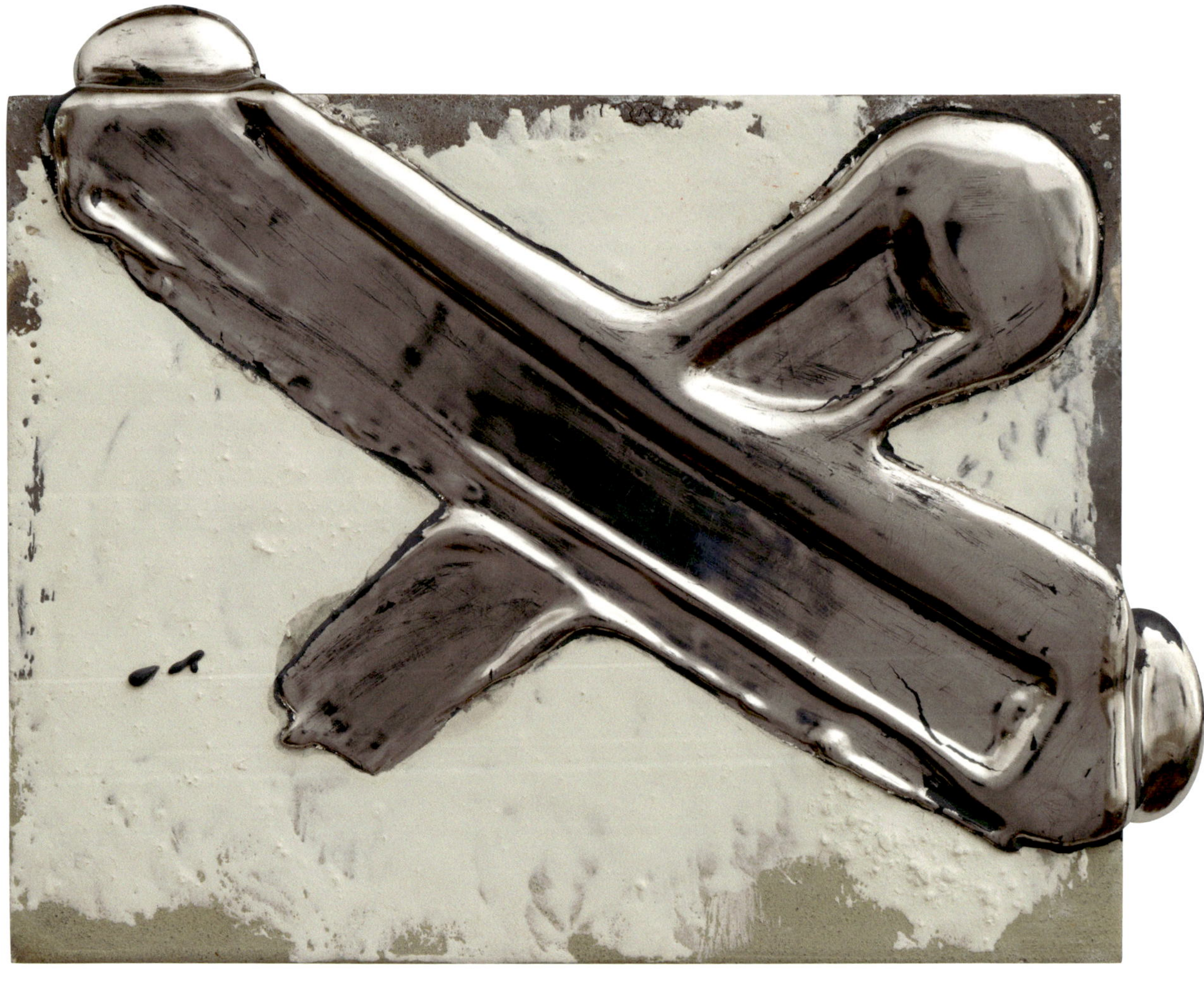

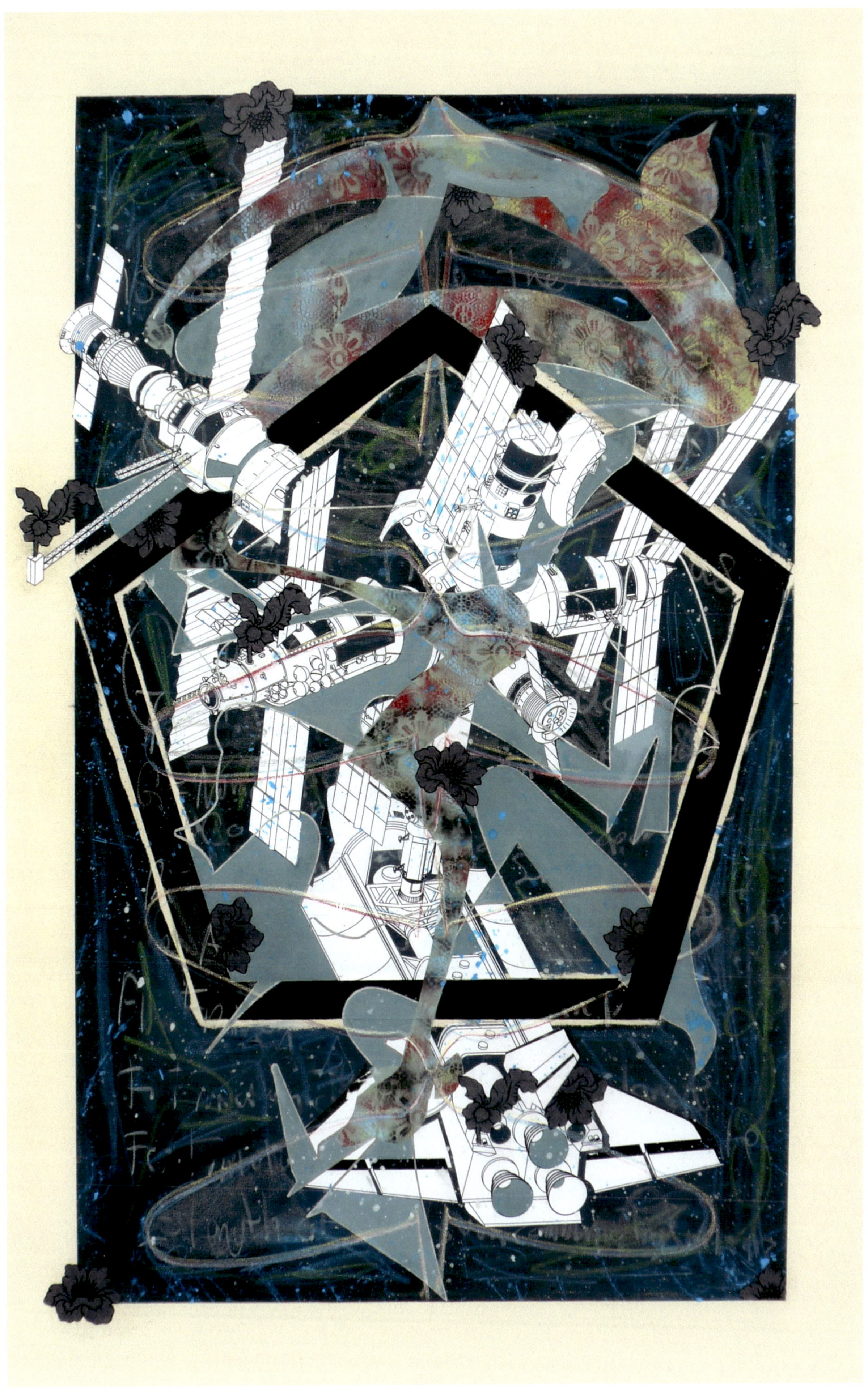

Fausto Fernandez, **The Drake Equation**, 2012. Collage, acrylic, oil pastel, and spray paint on canvas, 72 × 48 in. Courtesy of the artist

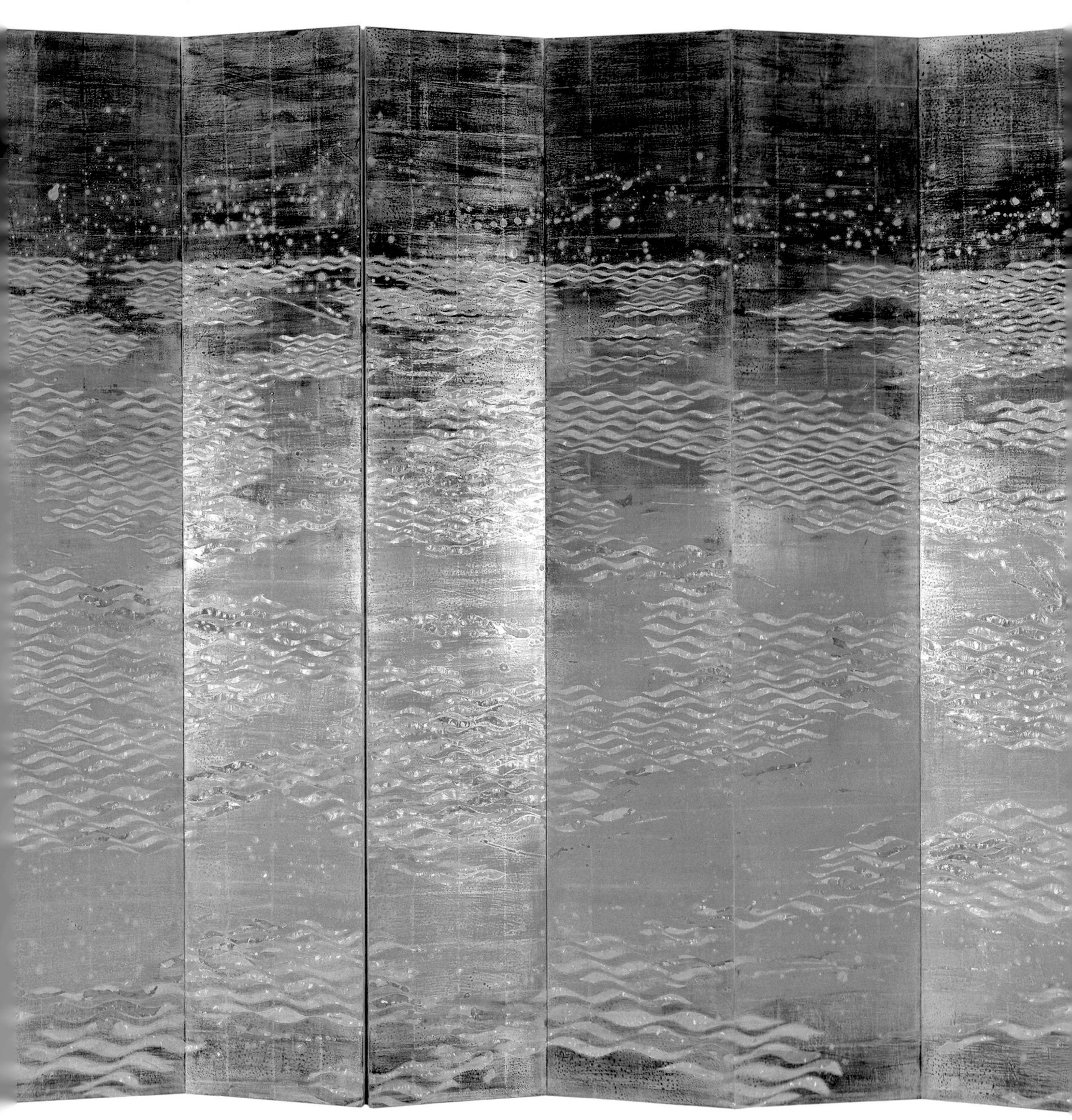

Nancy Lorenz, **Silver Water Screen**, 2009. Silver leaf, mother-of-pearl, and gilder's clay on panels, 104 × 222 in. Courtesy of the artist

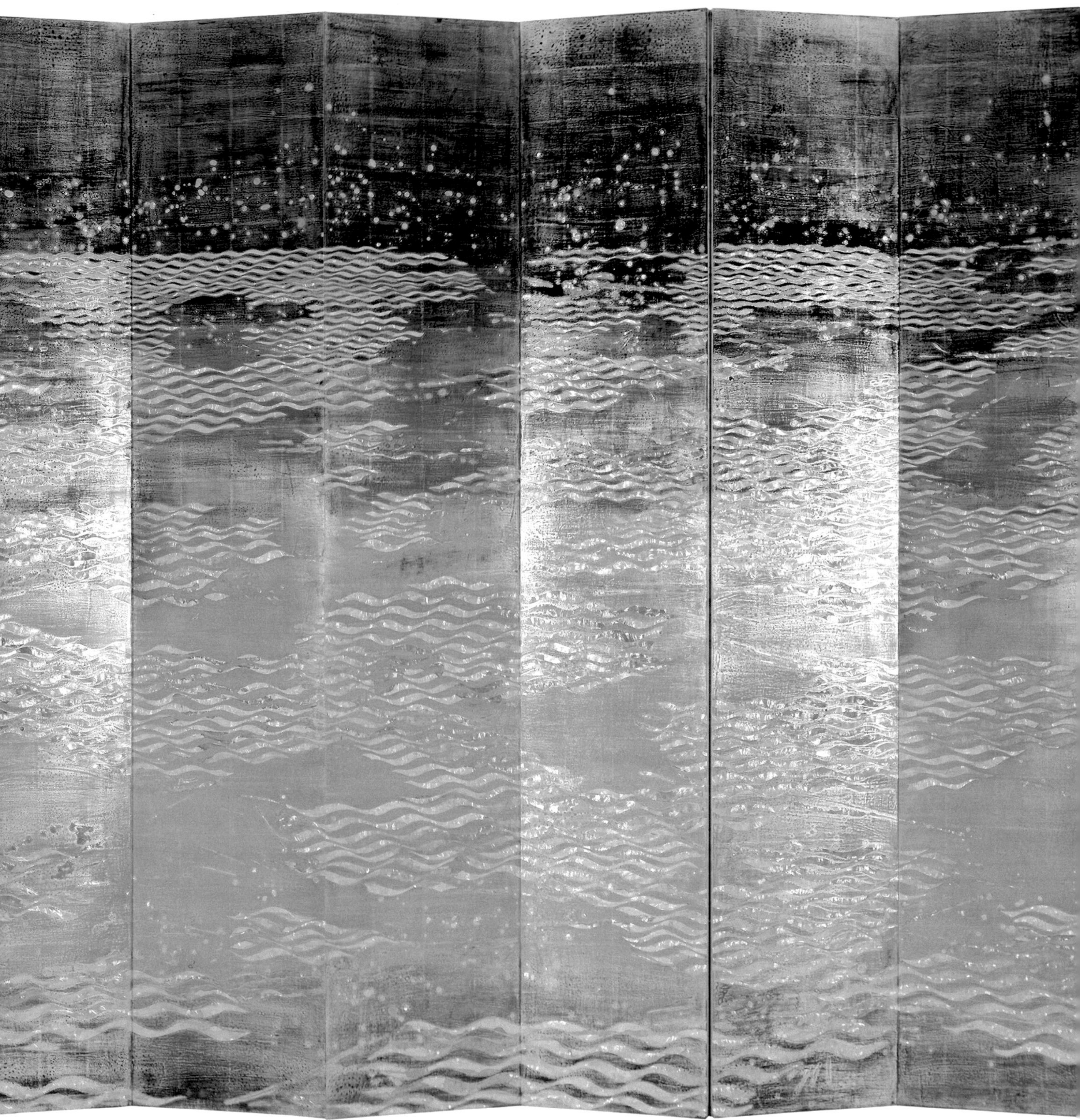

Fausto Fernandez, **Love Is What You Make It Out To Be**, 2013. Collage, architectural plans, maps, acrylic, oil pastel, and spray paint on canvas, 72 × 72 in. Courtesy of the artist

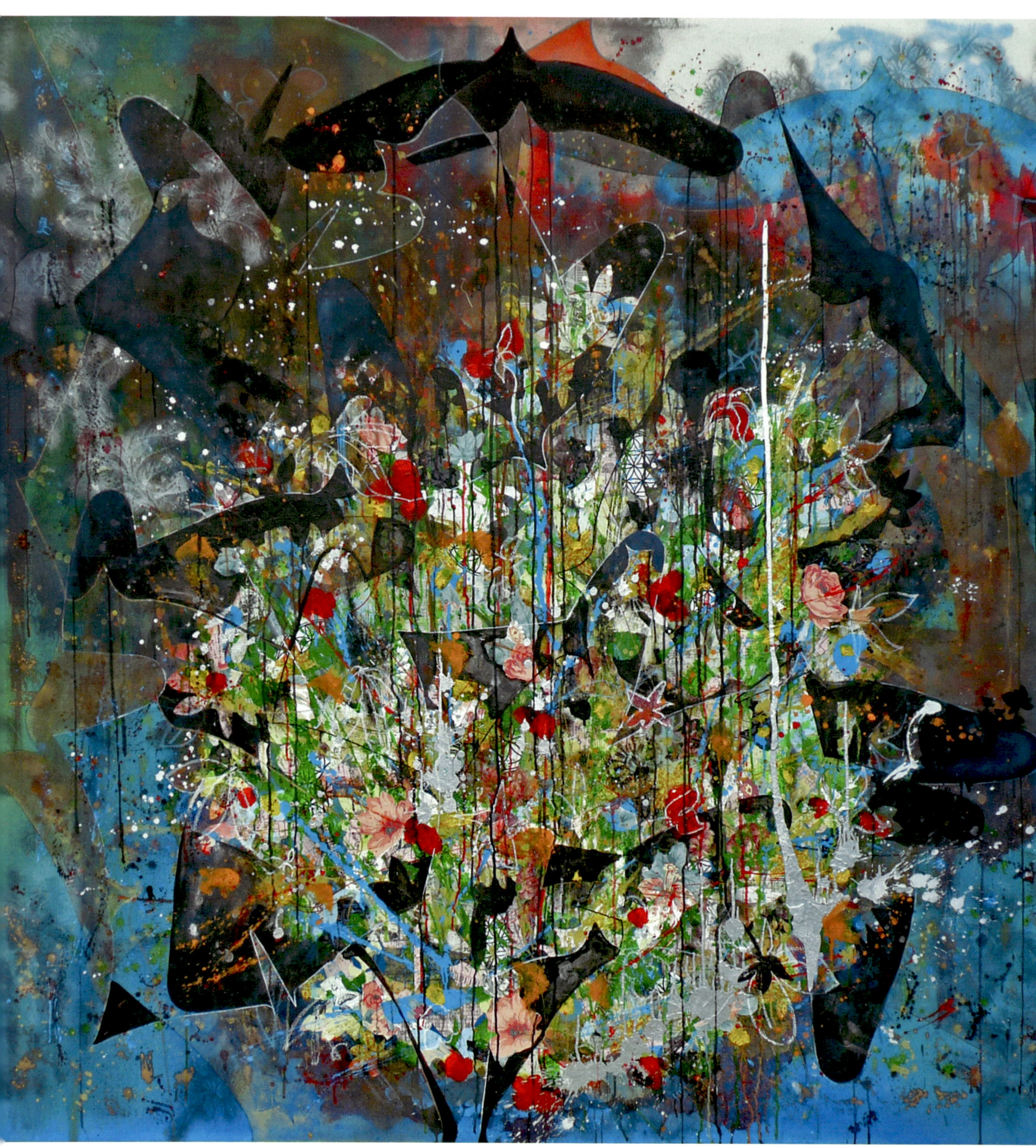

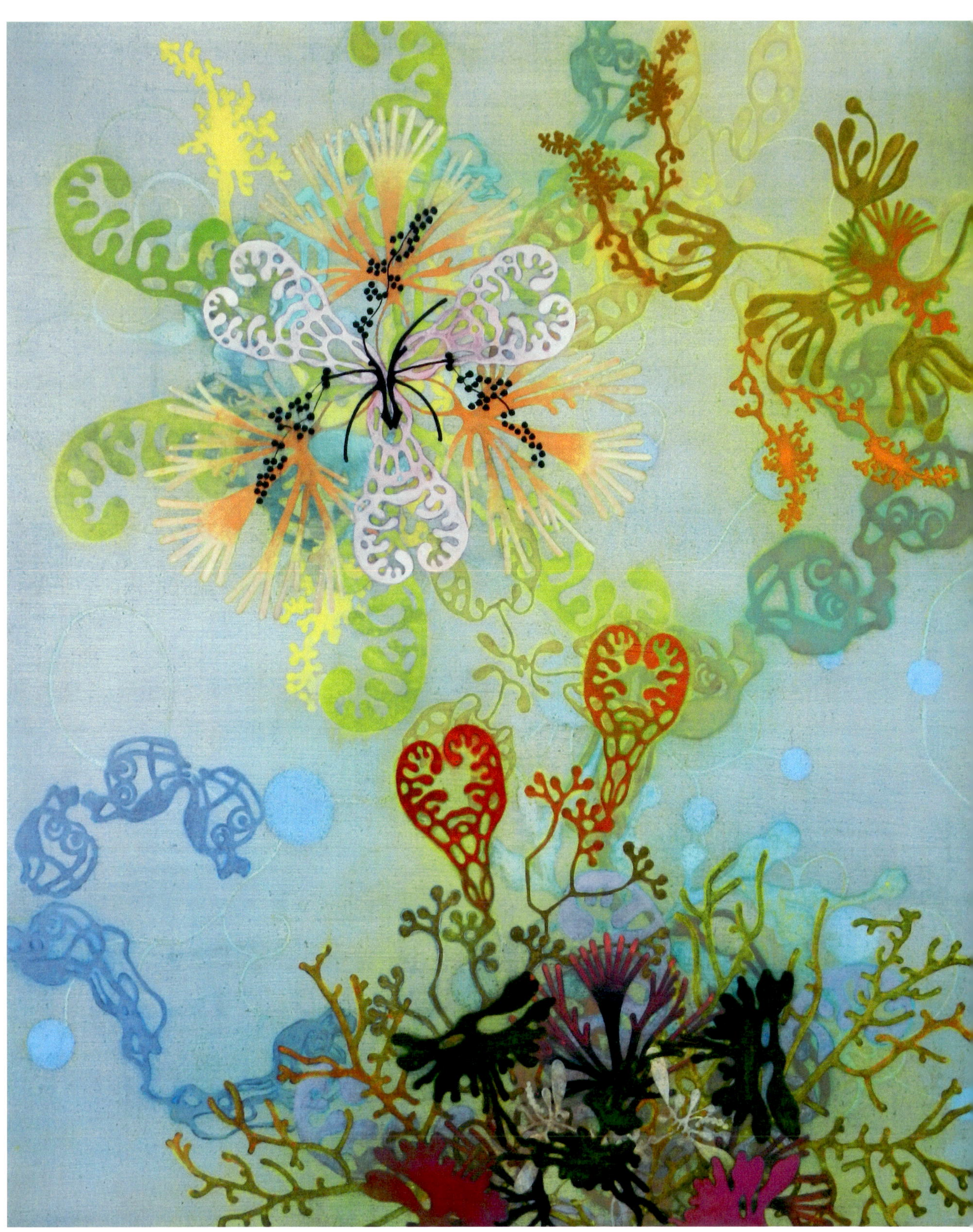

Annette Davidek, **Untitled**, 2008. Oil on birch panel, 38 × 32 in. Courtesy of the artist and Littlejohn Contemporary, New York

# Ryan McGinness

Born 1972

On initial encounter, the imagery in many of Ryan McGinness' paintings has the overall qualities one might associate with the Abstract Expressionist Jackson Pollock or commercially printed fabrics and wallpaper. On closer inspection, however, a host of specific and precise elements are discernible, including stylized human figures, abstract motifs, logos, and symbols. These elements are built up as layers of vividly colored images that create a dynamic sense of deep space. The flat application of paint physically contradicts the works' convincing illusion of depth. This flatness, combined with McGinness' high-key palette, produces cool yet seductive visual effects.

Armed with a design background, McGinness merges the worlds of fine art, graphic design, popular culture, and advertising. His approach moves beyond the traditions of easel painting to encompass sculpture, installation, books, and consumer products. With seemingly little effort, he moves from one form to another, tying together myriad images, materials, and techniques in a Warhol-like way. Not surprisingly, McGinness worked as a curatorial assistant at the Andy Warhol Museum in Pittsburgh, Pennsylvania. Connections between the two artists are clearly evident.

The dizzying optical effects and complex surface layering that characterize McGinness' work belie the artist's highly structured approach to artmaking. Working in series, he packages his various productions in a consumer-friendly and democratic way—from paintings, prints, and sculptures, to notecards, t-shirts, and skateboards. Lines are blurred between fine art and fine design, and in many cases, such distinctions are erased altogether. In the end, some example of McGinness' wide-ranging output can be acquired by most anyone.

Ryan McGinness is a native of Virginia Beach, Virginia, and is based in New York. He earned a Bachelor of Fine Arts from Carnegie Mellon University in Pittsburgh, Pennsylvania, in 1994. His work has been shown in numerous solo and group exhibitions at museums and galleries for the past decade, including at San Antonio's Blue Star Contemporary Art Museum. His works are found in collections including the Albright-Knox Art Gallery, Buffalo, New York; Cincinnati Art Museum, Ohio; the Metropolitan Museum of Art, New York; Museum of Contemporary Art San Diego, California; the Museum of Modern Art, New York; and the Virginia Museum of Fine Arts, Richmond. Reviews of the artist's exhibitions regularly appear in *Art in America*, *Artforum*, *Artnews*, and the *New York Times*.

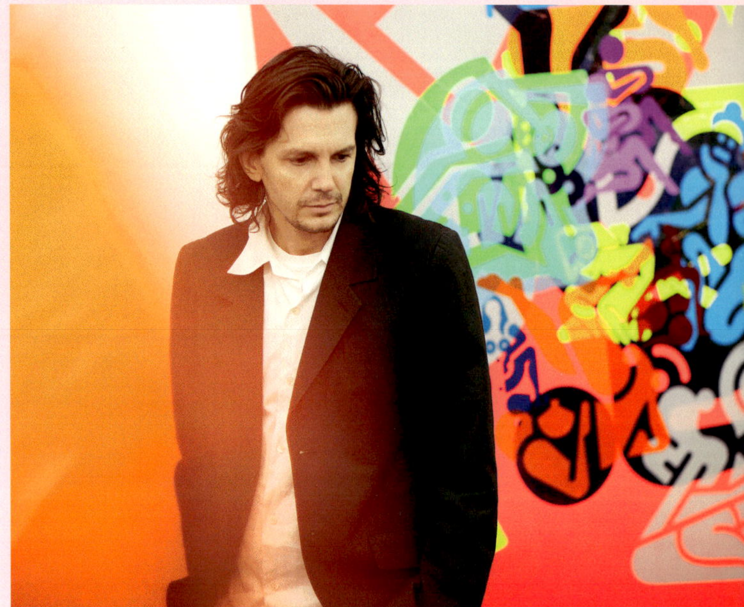

Courtesy of Ryan McGinness Studios, Inc./Art Resource, NY.

# Beatriz Milhazes

Born 1960

Beatriz Milhazes' vibrant compositions reflect the energy and theatre of her native Brazil. Using dense, overlapping images; familiar shapes and motifs; and a pulsating color palette, Milhazes constructs large paintings that encourage —even demand—that the viewer's eyes move swiftly in order to drink in their visual excess. Specific subjects are often identifiable as the mind begins to deconstruct the numerous layers and complex arrangements of subjects such as the sun, roses, and pearls. In addition to large canvas works, Milhazes makes striking prints, dense layered collages, three-dimensional objects, and site-based works.

Milhazes has even ventured into the performing arts, specifically in set design. Whether working on canvas or paper, with volumes in space, or within the realm of theatre, she always uses her characteristic strategy of juxtaposing several signature elements in order to seduce the viewer and offer striking visual rewards.

Subtle references to nature weave in and out of Milhazes' highly structured compositions, grounding these abstractions in the world of reality. The works' intense colors push the imagery backward and forward, playing with illusionistic space in confounding ways. By combining organic forms, geometric shapes, and decorative patterning, Milhazes makes an art that is optimistic and celebratory. She offers the viewer a rare opportunity to attend a visual feast, a bountiful spread which emphasizes seductive beauty over conceptual rigor.

Born in 1960, Beatriz Milhazes resides in her native Rio de Janeiro, Brazil. In the early 1980s she studied at the Curso de Comunicacao Social, FACHA, and the School of Visual Arts, both in Rio de Janeiro. Her paintings and prints have been exhibited internationally; she was included in biennial exhibitions in Sydney, Australia, 1998; Sao Paolo, Brazil, 1998 and 2004; Venice, Italy, 2003; and Shanghai, China, 2006. Milhazes's work is found in the collections of the Carnegie Museum of Art, Pittsburgh, Pennsylvania; Museo Nacional Centro de Arte Reina Sofia, Madrid, Spain; and in New York's Metropolitan Museum of Art, Museum of Modern Art, and Solomon R. Guggenheim Museum. Reviews of the artist's work regularly appear in *Art in America*, *Artforum*, *Artnews*, and the *New York Times*.

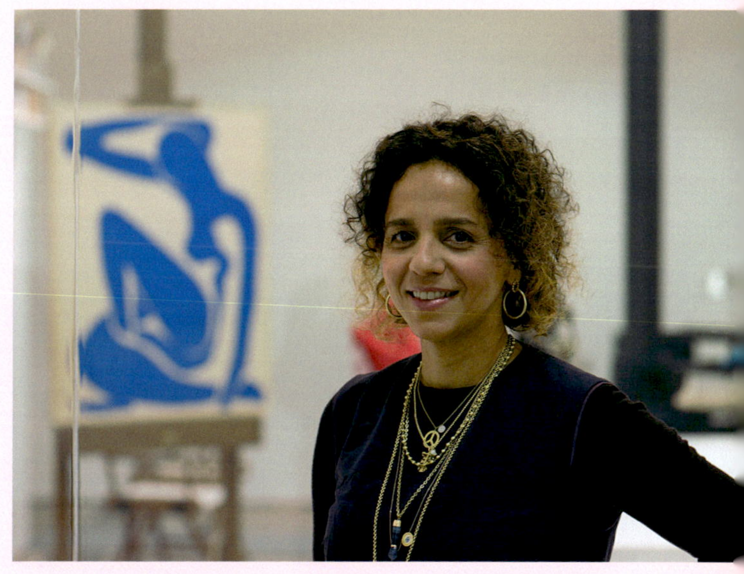

Courtesy of the artist and James Cohan Gallery, New York.

# *Jiha Moon*

Born 1973

Korean-born Jiha Moon fuses elements of Asian and American cultures in her deceivingly delicate works, in much the same way that her life combines aspects of both. Somewhat parallel, her art teeters between figuration and abstraction, generally combining both on the surface of a single work. Images drawn from everyday life and popular culture—Pac-Man, peonies, butterflies, Georgia peaches, Alice in Wonderland—are set tumbling across stylized landscapes or swirling within tumultuous waters.

Moon emphasizes the works' Eastern connections through motifs such as a fan shape or materials such as *hanji* paper and silk. However, her bold, striking palette and confident graphic style prevent Moon's art from becoming a clichéd hybrid of her Korean birthplace and her adopted American home.

The sources for and influences on Moon's paintings and prints also draw on these two historically distinct cultures. More apparent are references to Chinese landscape paintings, popular graphic design, American abstraction, and Japanese prints, while less evident are traces of Korean folk art and folk quilts, Renaissance etchings, and the art of Netherlandish painter Hieronymus Bosch. By drawing on these widely varied points of origin and allowing them to come crashing together, Moon has developed a highly personal and unique vocabulary with which to express her sometimes conflicting, sometimes harmonious sensibilities.

A native of Dae-Gu, South Korea, Moon was born in 1973 and moved to the United States at the age of 26 in 1999. She studied at Korea University in Seoul, earning a Bachelor of Fine Arts in 1996, after which she received a Master of Fine Arts from Ewha Womans University, also in Seoul, in 1999. In 2001 Moon received a Master of Arts, followed by a Master of Fine Arts in 2002, both from the University of Iowa, Iowa City. For more than a decade she has exhibited her paintings and collages in solo and group exhibitions, receiving reviews in *Art in America*, *Artforum*, and the *New York Times*, among other publications. Her work is found in museum collections including the High Museum of Art, Atlanta, Georgia; Hirshhorn Museum and Sculpture Garden, Washington, D.C.; Mint Museum, Charlotte, North Carolina; Smith College Museum of Art, Northampton, Massachusetts; and Virginia Museum of Fine Arts, Richmond. Moon lives in Atlanta, Georgia.

Courtesy of the artist and RYAN LEE, New York.

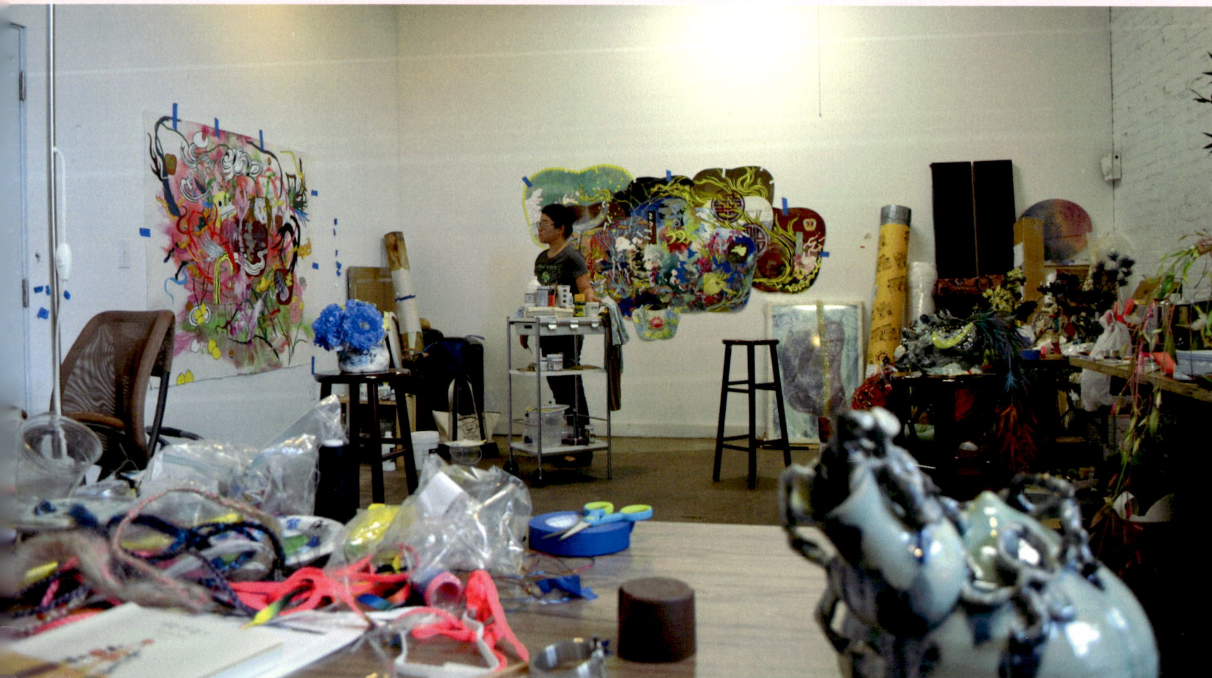

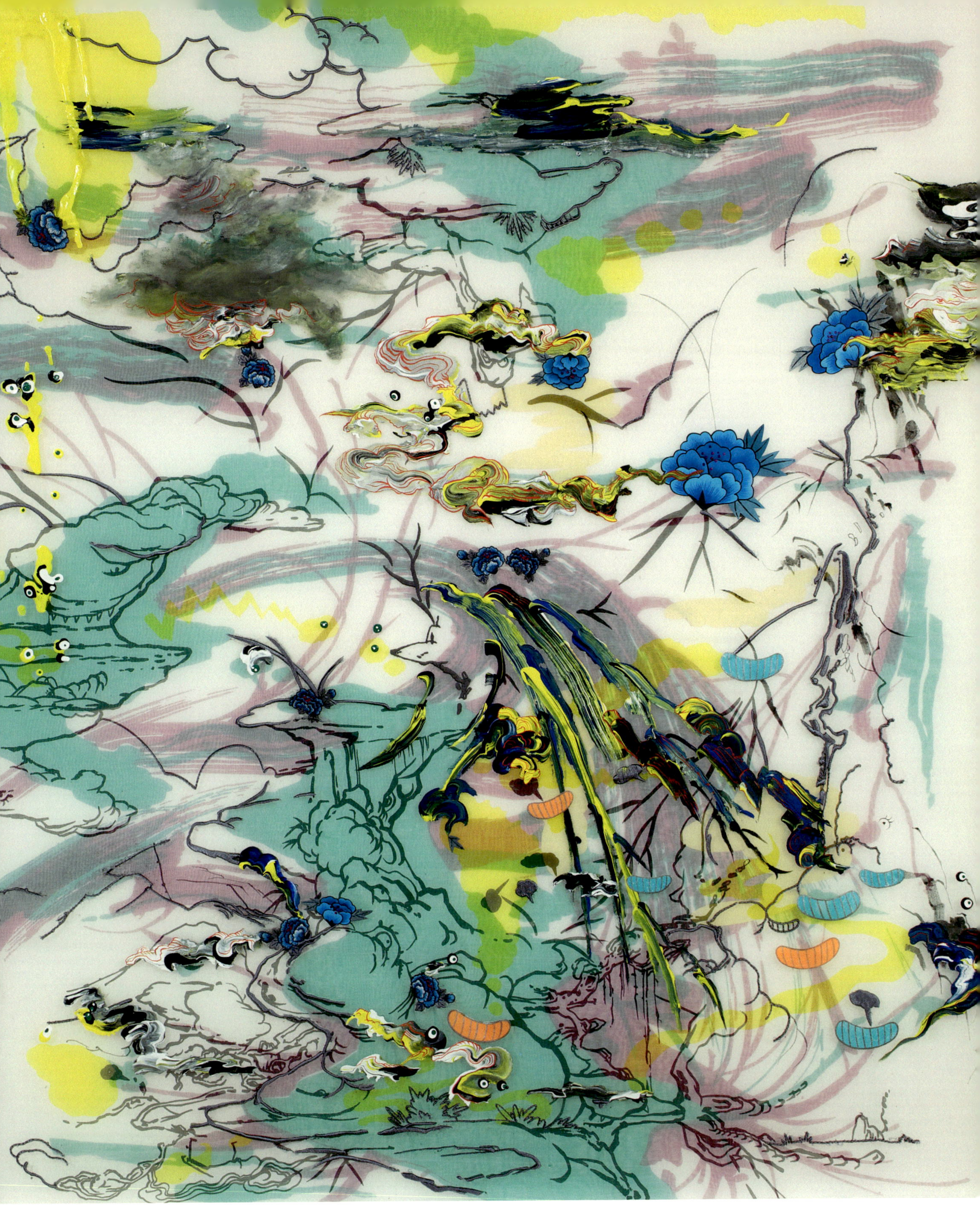

Jiha Moon, **Springfield II—Cheshire Creek**, 2010, in collaboration with The Fabric Workshop and Museum, Philadelphia, Pennsylvania. Hand screen-print on silk organza, hand embroidery, acrylic, and collage with hanji paper, 37½ × 33½ in. Courtesy of the artist and RYAN LEE, New York

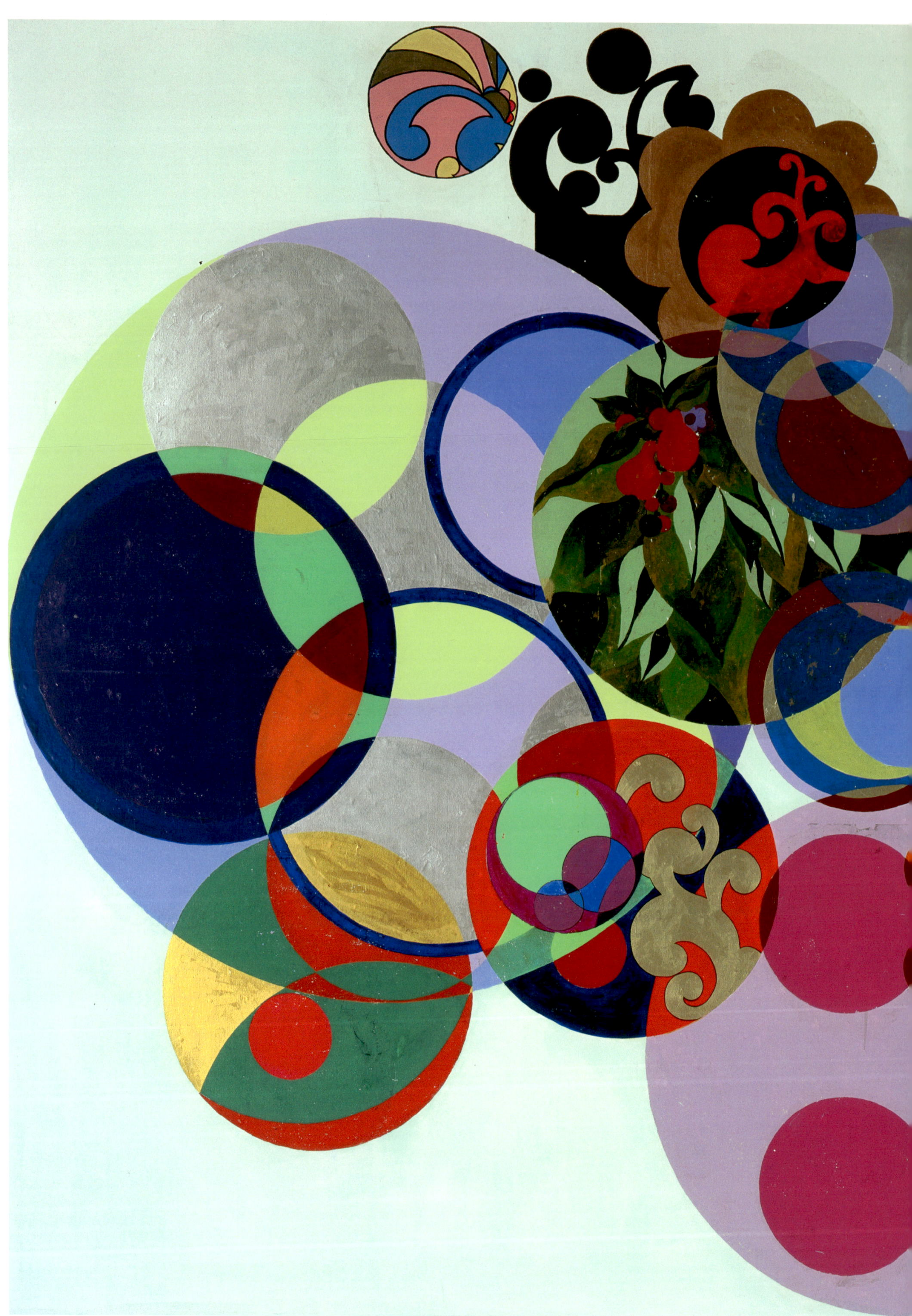

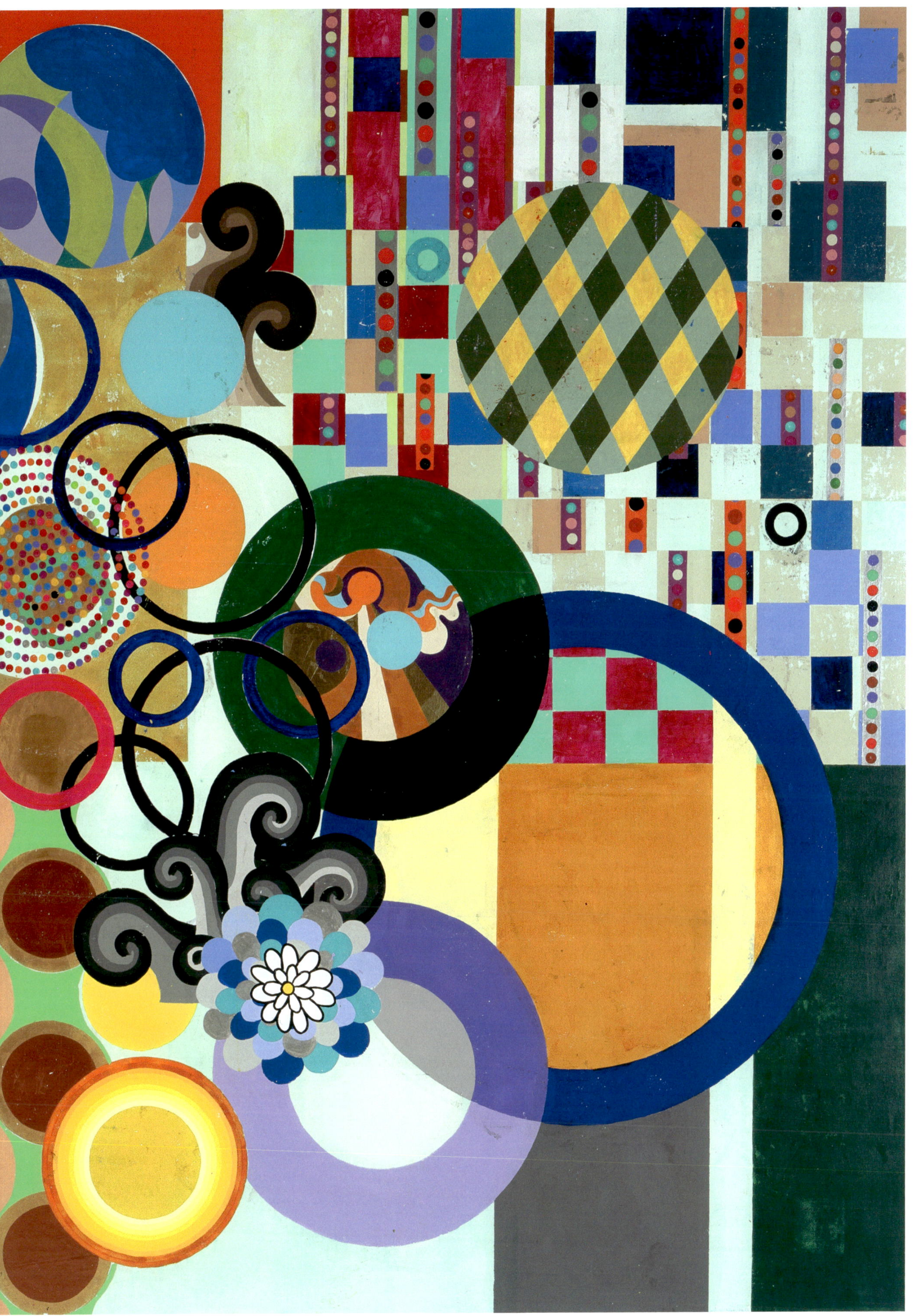

Beatriz Milhazes, **Sinfonia Nordestina**, 2008. Acrylic on canvas, 96⅞ × 144⅞ in. Courtesy of the artist and James Cohan Gallery, New York

Jiha Moon, **American Halfie**, 2010. Ink and acrylic on hanji paper mounted on canvas, 22 × 28 in. Courtesy of the artist and RYAN LEE, New York

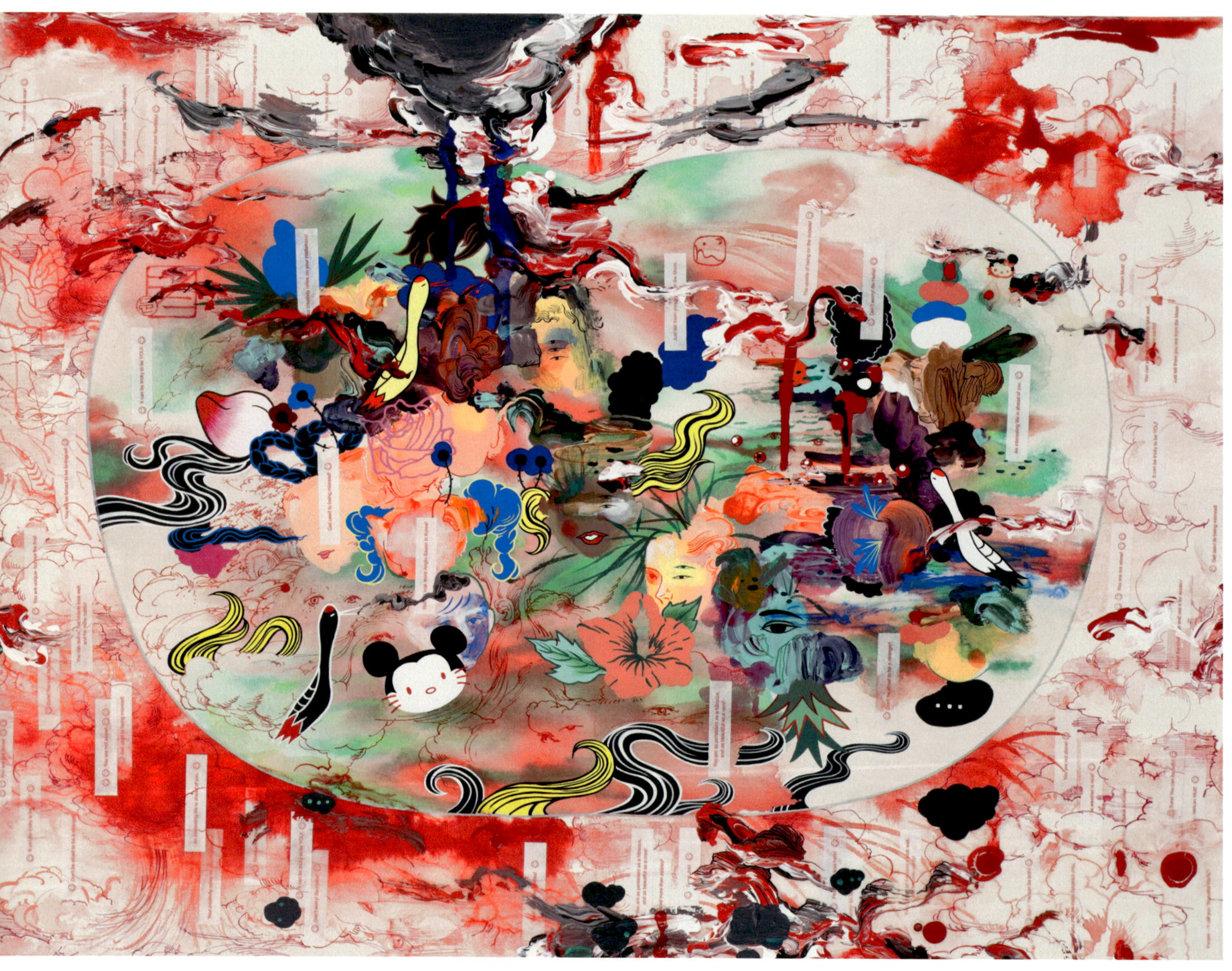

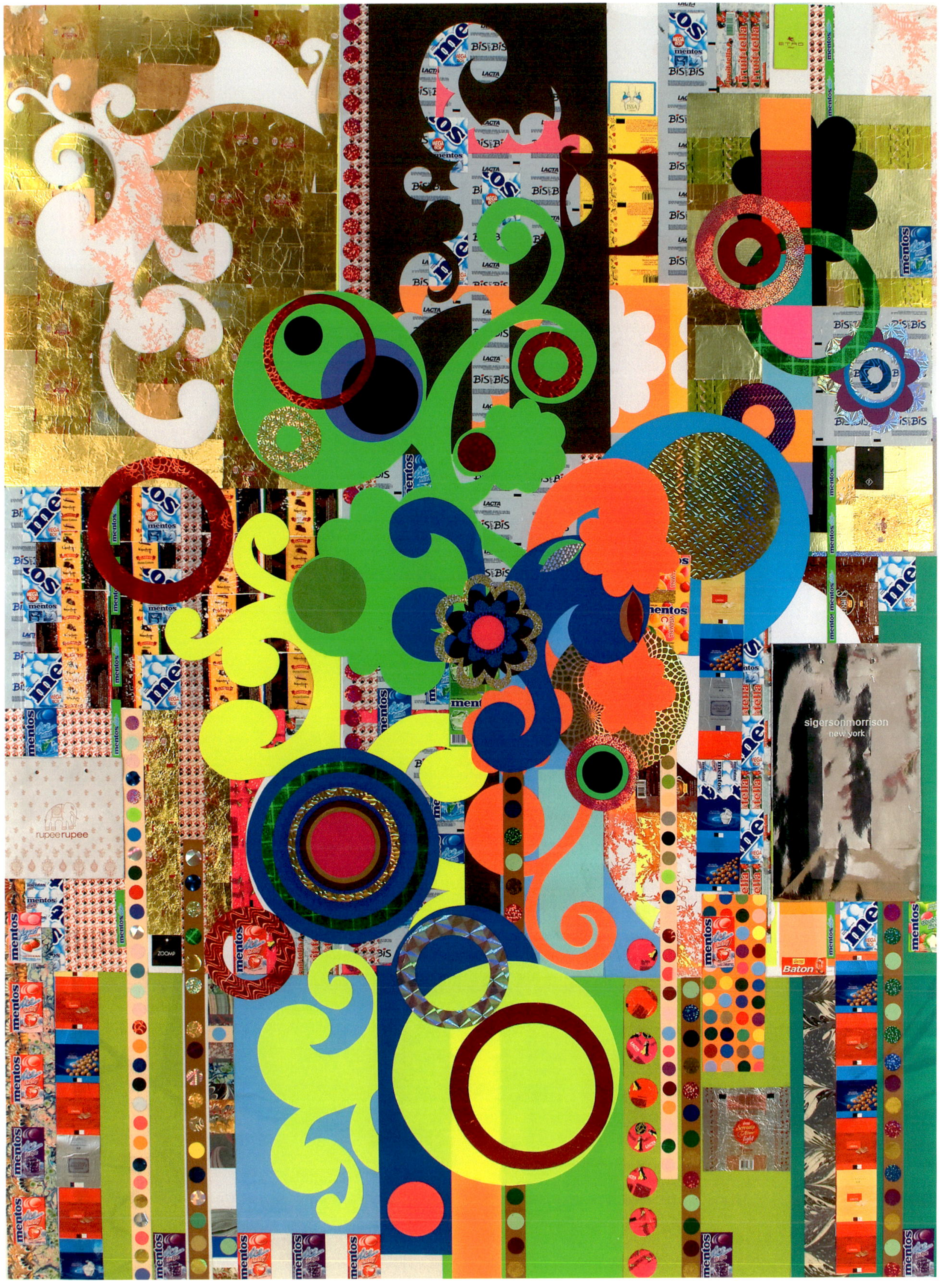


Beatriz Milhazes, **Yogurt**, 2008. Mixed media on paper, 73 × 55½ in. Courtesy of the artist and James Cohan Gallery, New York

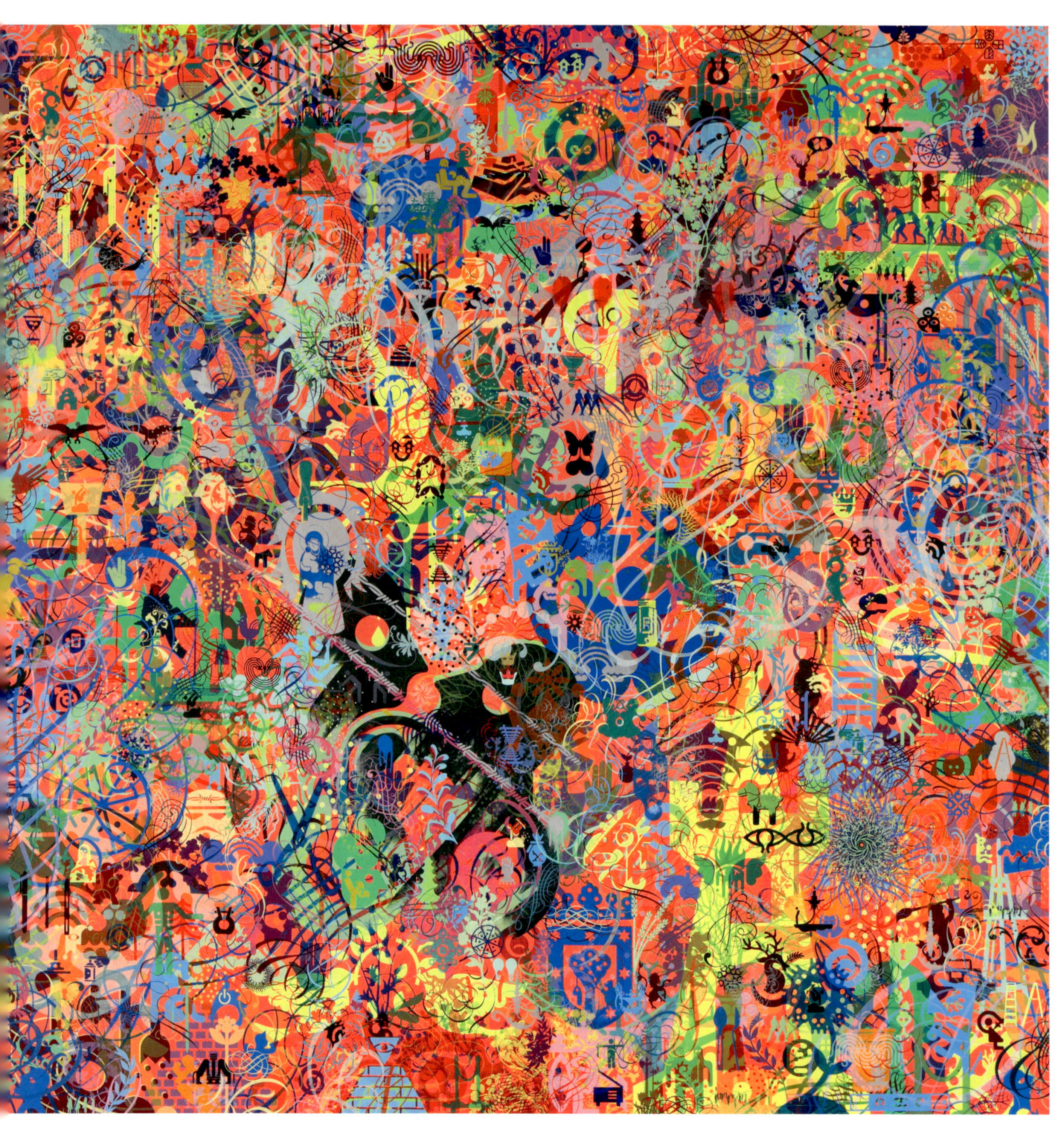

Ryan McGinness, **Mutual Information**, 2008. Acrylic on canvas, 96 × 96 in. Private collection
Courtesy of Ryan McGinness Studios, Inc./Art Resource, NY. 

Ryan McGinness, **Moshi Moshi**, 2007. Acrylic on canvas, 96 × 96 in. Private collection


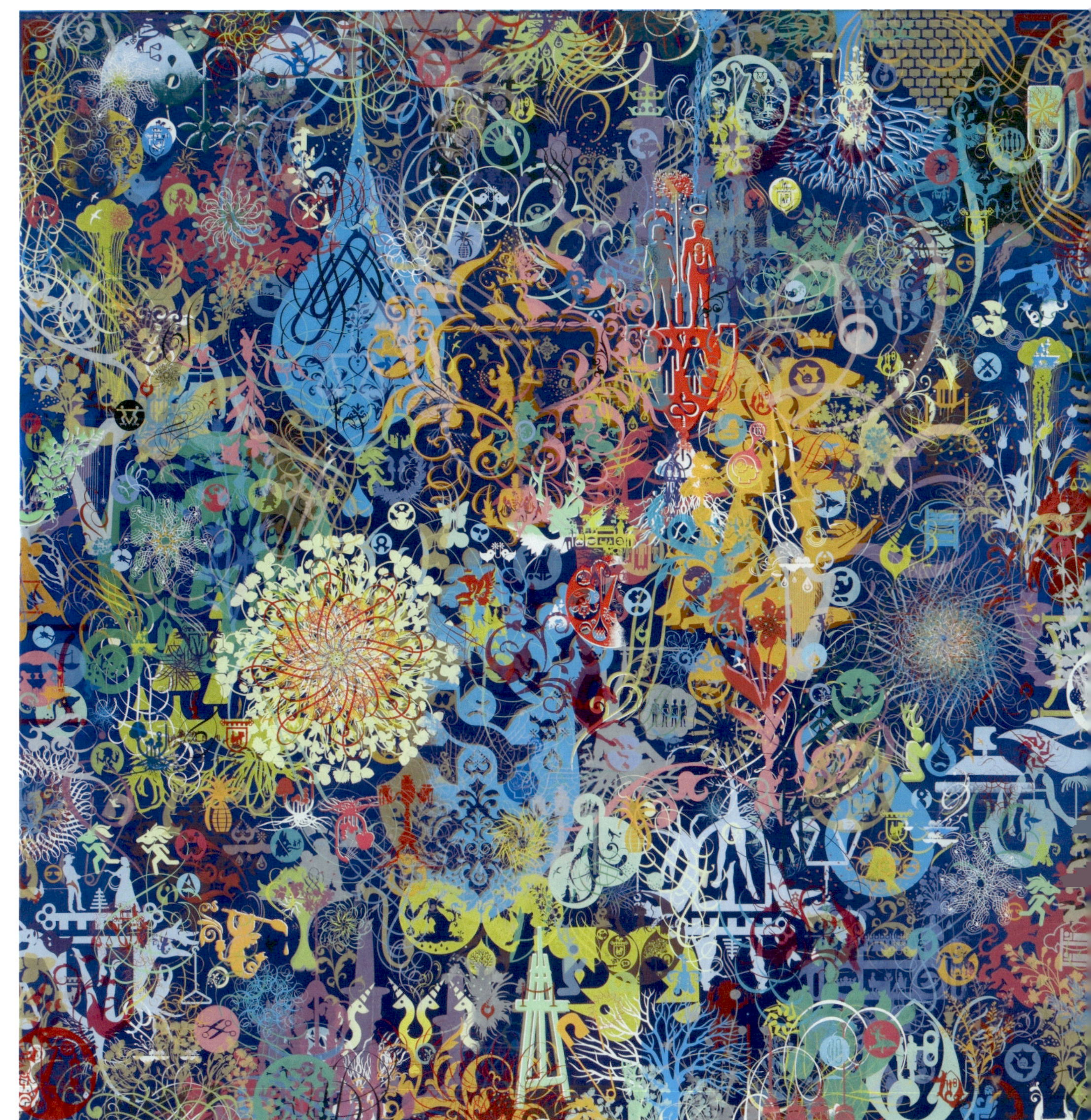

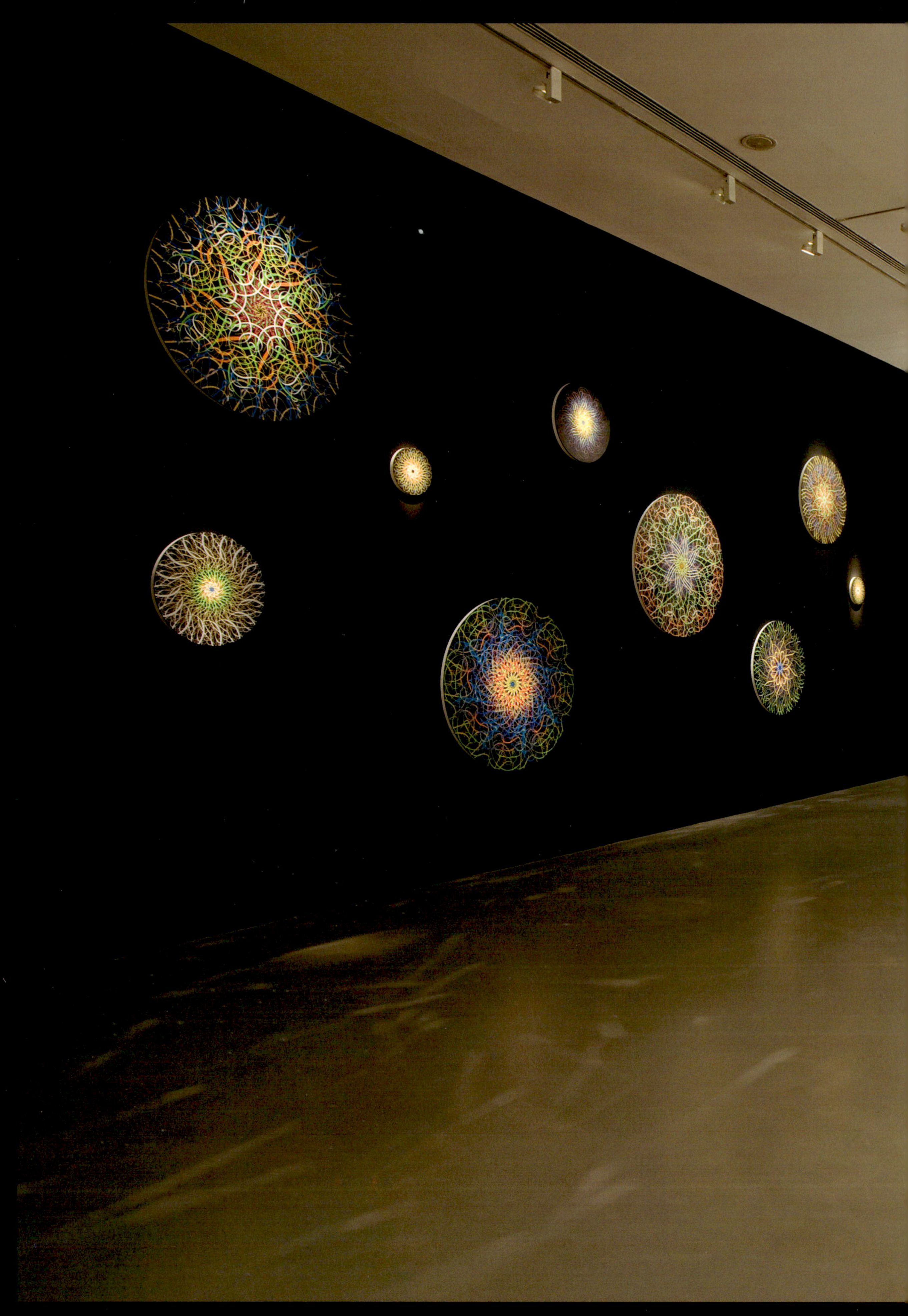

Ryan McGinness, **Studio Franchise**, 2010. Installation view: La Casa Encendida, Madrid, Spain
Courtesy of Ryan McGinness Studios, Inc./Art Resource, NY. © Ryan McGinness/Artists Rights Society (ARS), New York

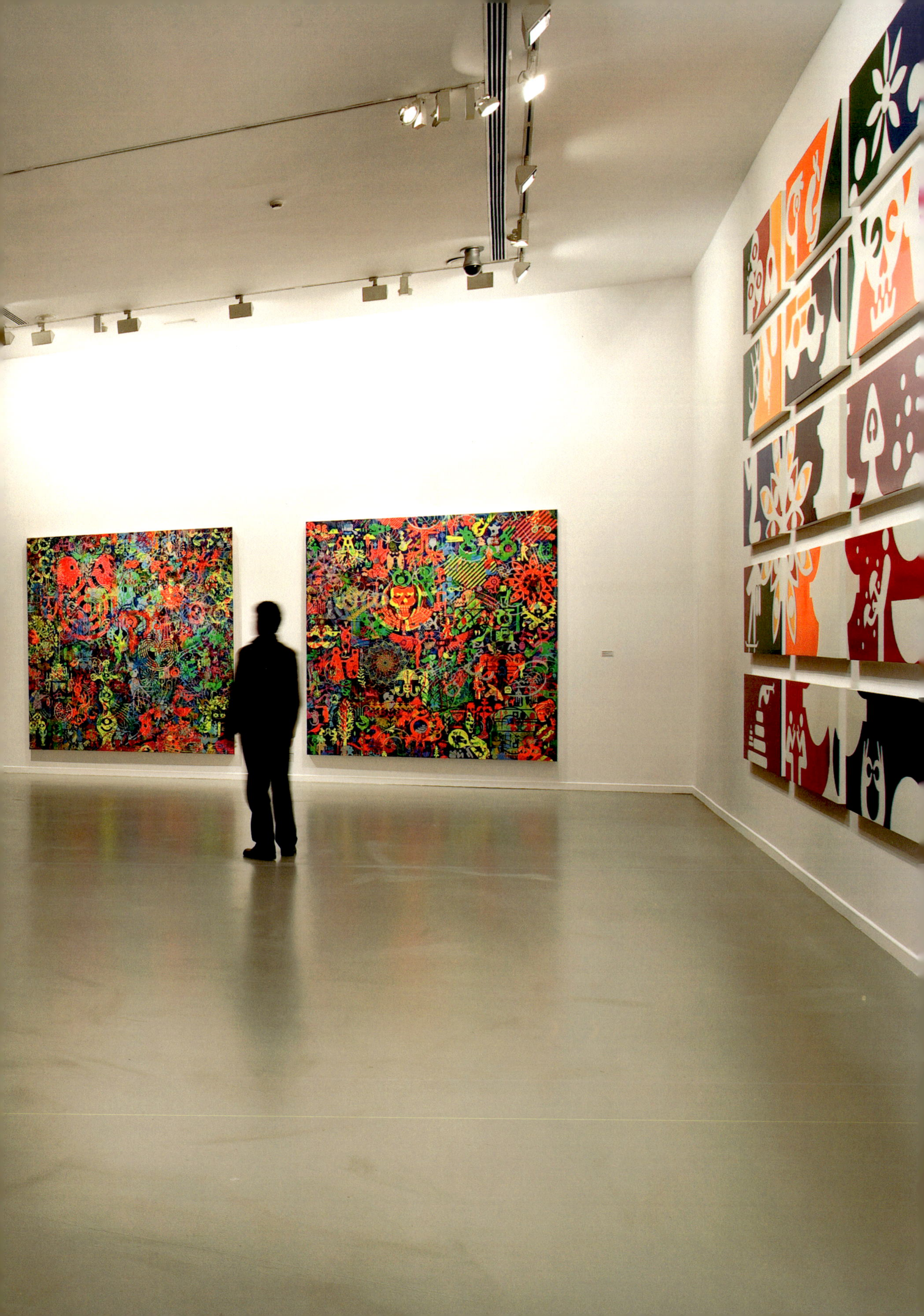

Jiha Moon, **Pied de Grue**, 2012. Ink, acrylic, fabric, and embroidery patches on hanji paper, 47 × 72 in.
Courtesy of the artist and RYAN LEE, New York

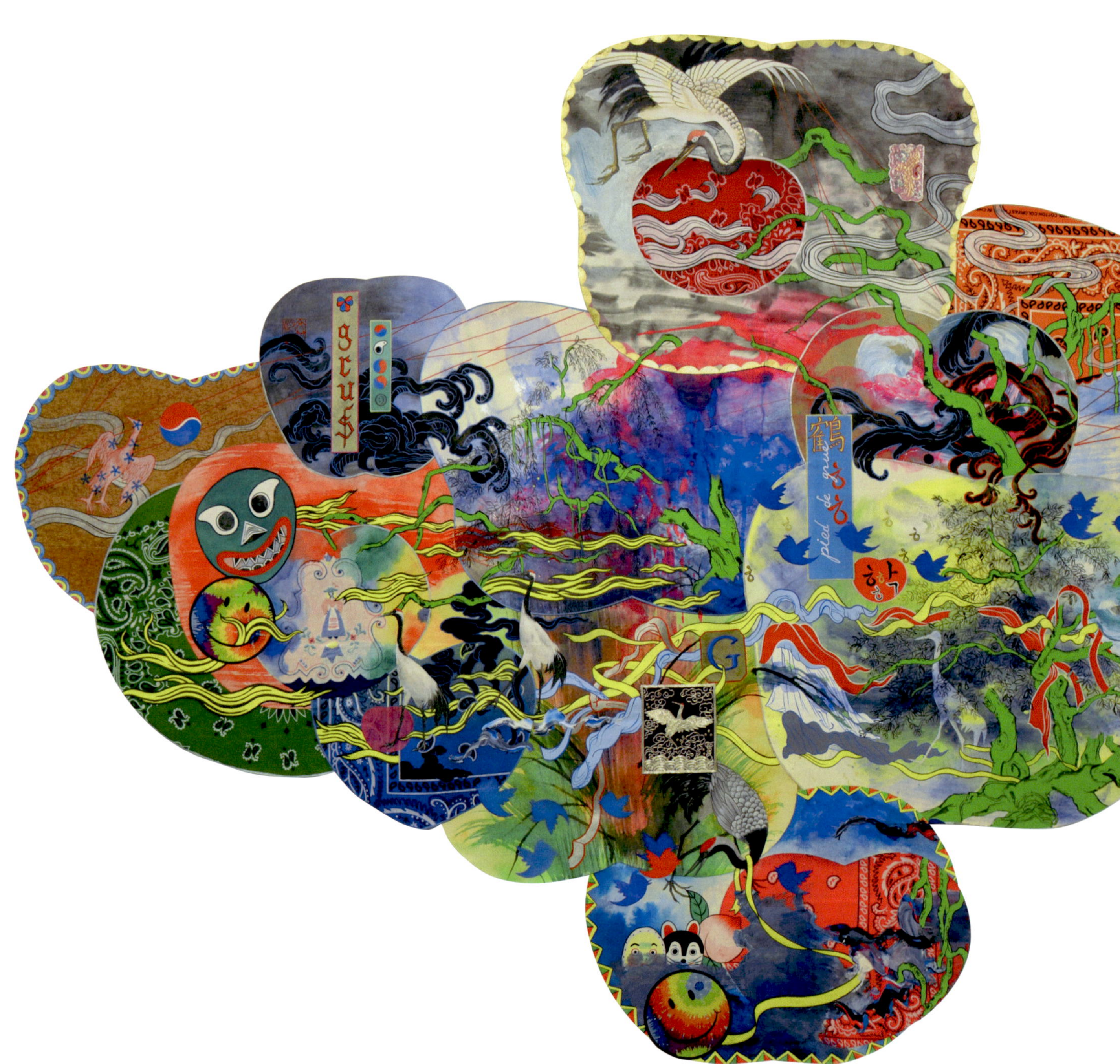

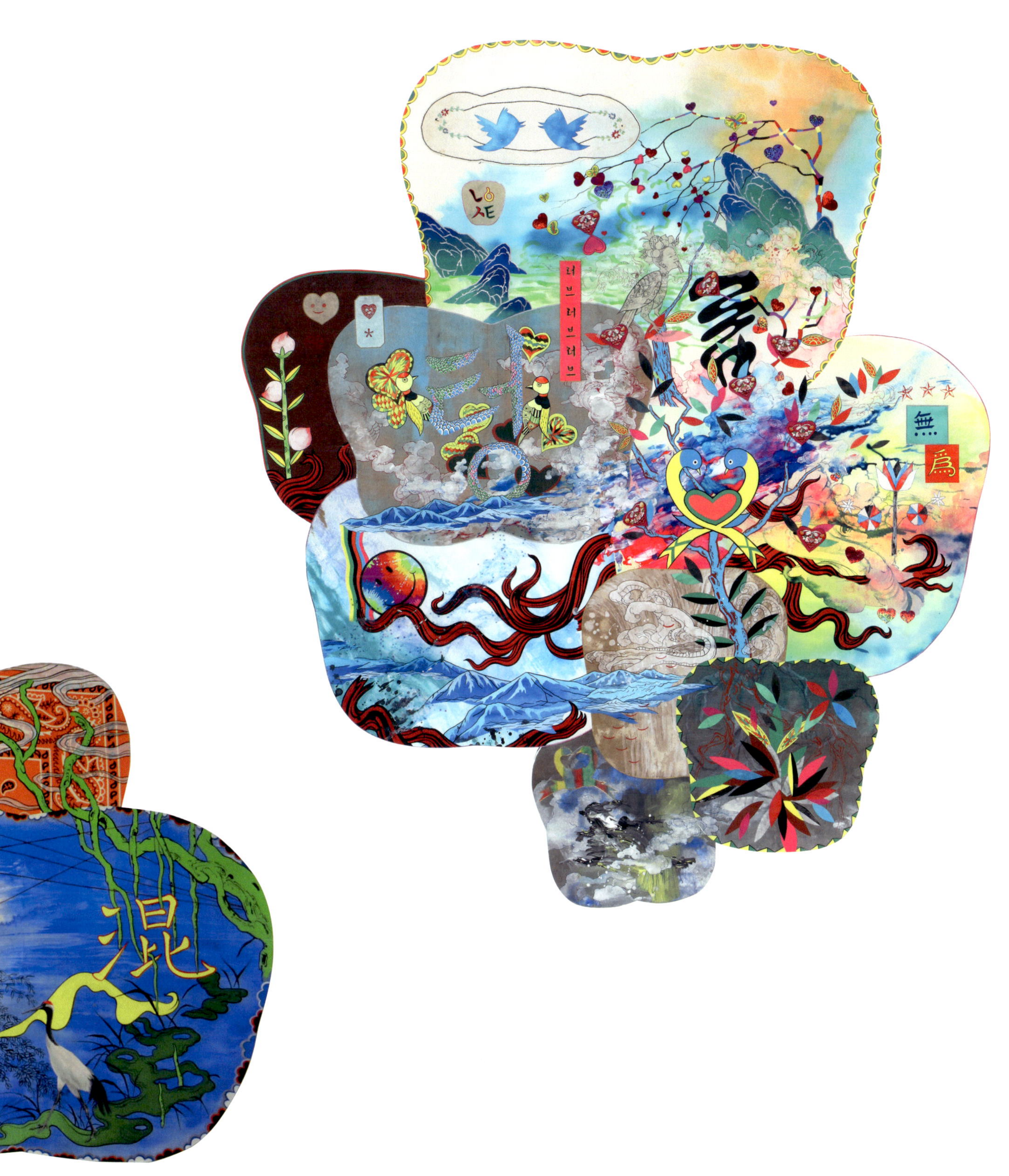


Jiha Moon, **Tongue (Love, Love, Love)**, 2011. Ink, acrylic, fabric, and embroidery patches on hanji paper, 62 × 46 in.
Courtesy of the artist and RYAN LEE, New York

Beatriz Milhazes, **Carambola**, 2008. Acrylic on canvas, 54⅞ × 50⅝ in. Courtesy of the artist and James Cohan Gallery, New York

Beatriz Milhazes, **Mulatinho**, 2008. Acrylic on canvas, 97⅝ × 97⅝ in. Courtesy of the artist and James Cohan Gallery, New York

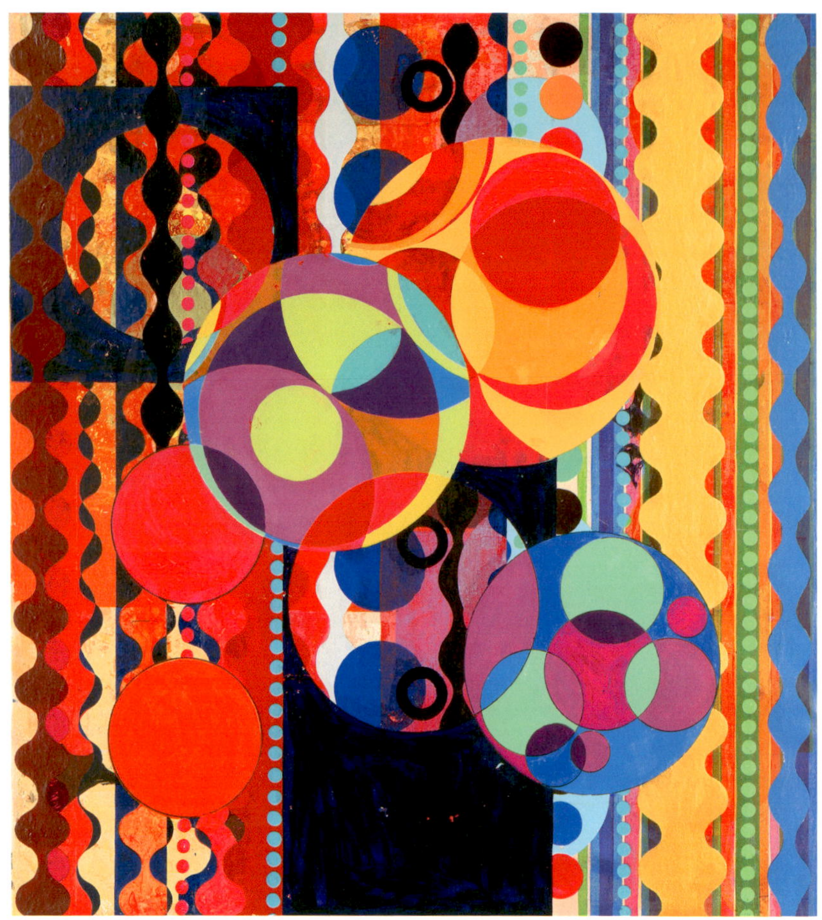

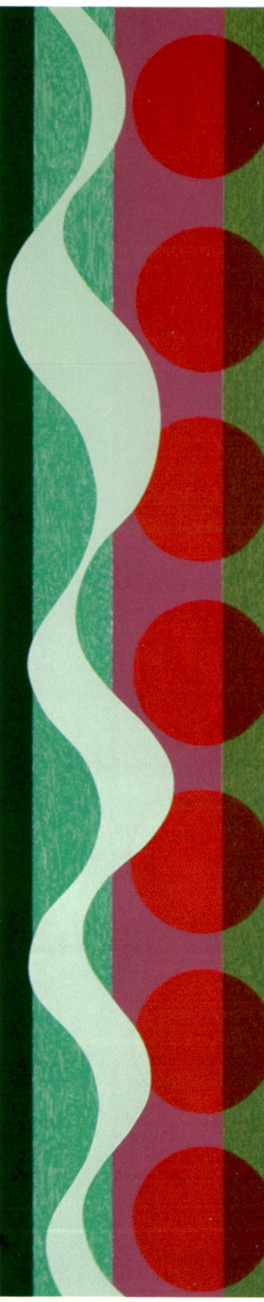

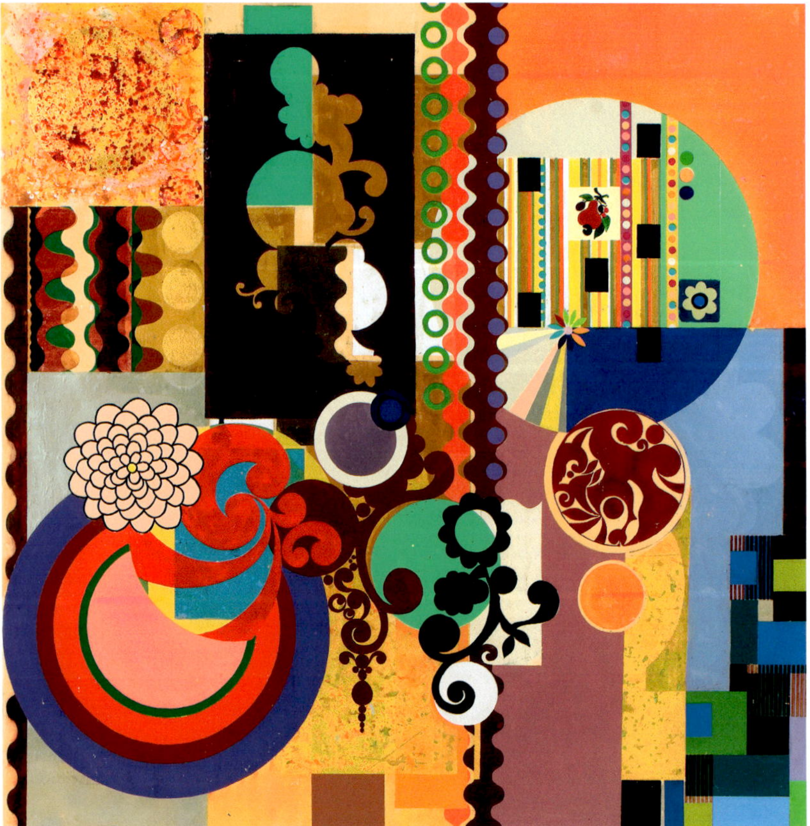

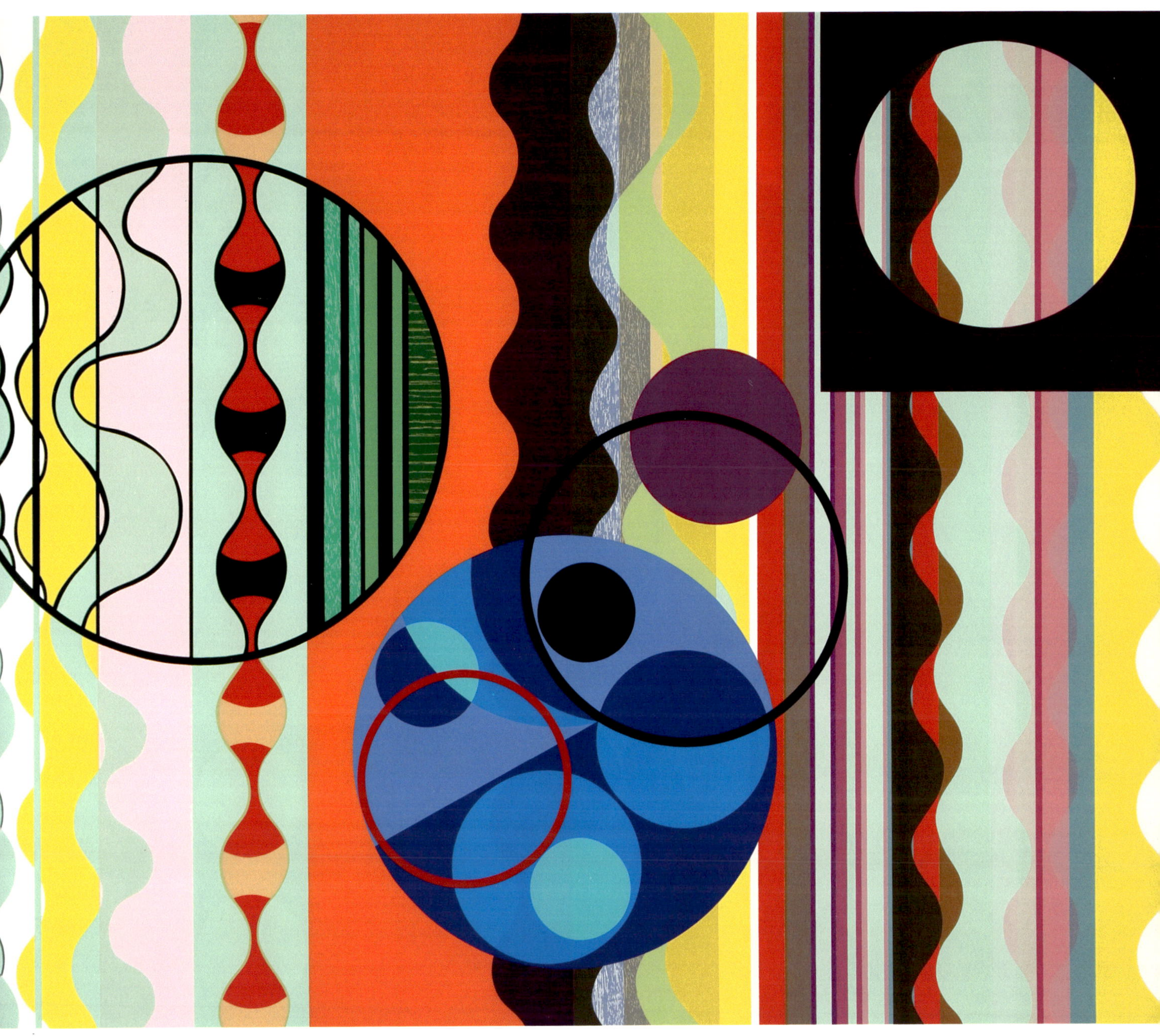

Beatriz Milhazes, **Açúcar (Sugar)**, 2010. Woodblock and screenprint, 31½ × 47¼ in. Courtesy of the artist and James Cohan Gallery, New York

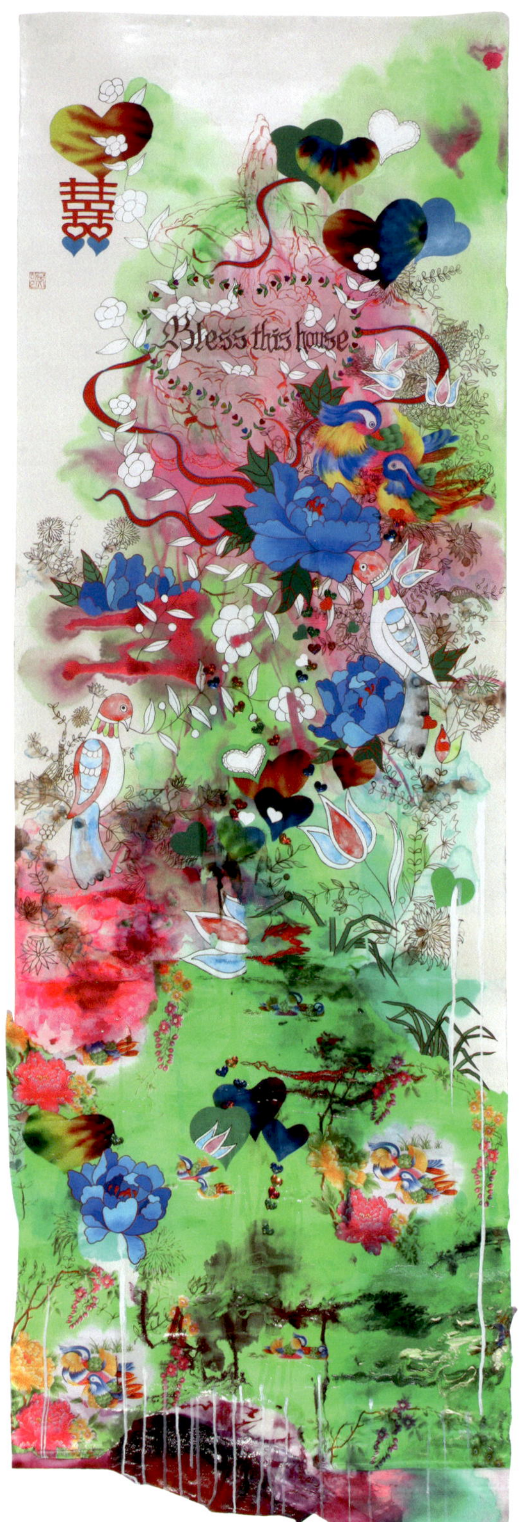


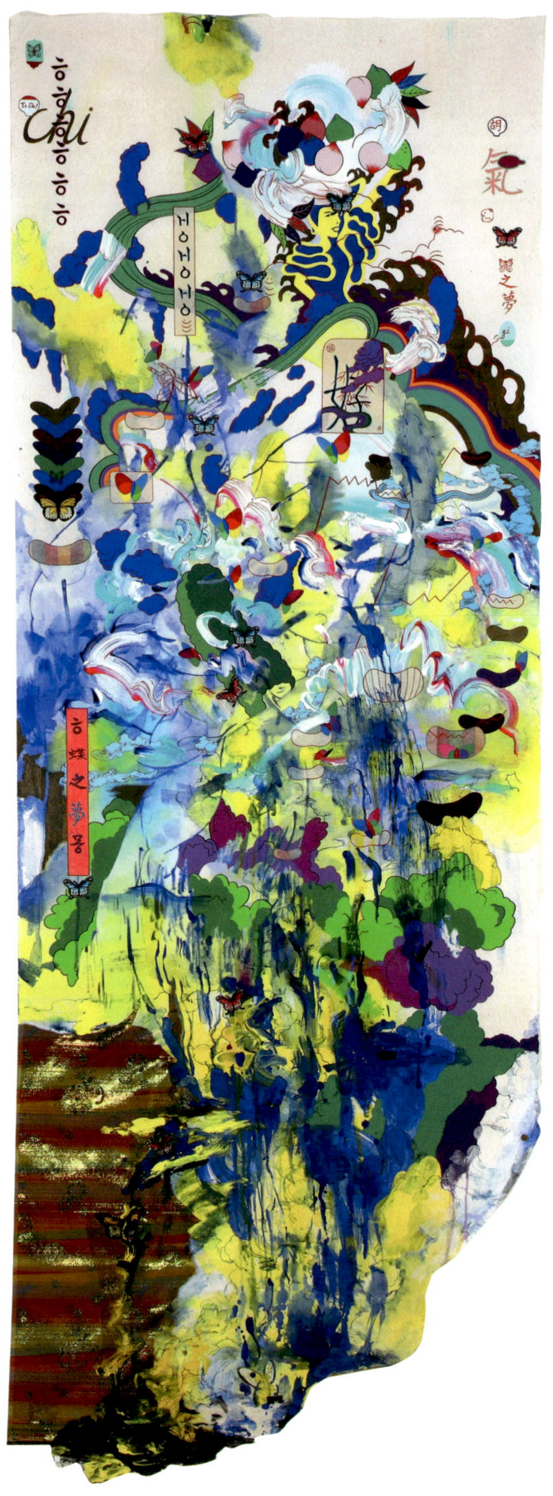


Jiha Moon, **Bless This House**, 2010. Ink, acrylic, fabric, and embroidery patches on hanji paper, 90 × 30 in.
Courtesy of the artist and RYAN LEE, New York

Jiha Moon, **Springfield—Butterfly Dream**, 2010. Ink, acrylic, fabric, and embroidery patches on hanji paper, 81½ × 30 in.
Courtesy of the artist and RYAN LEE, New York

Ryan McGinness, **The True Knowledge of Things**, 2007. Acrylic on canvas, 96 × 96 in. Collection of The Museum of Contemporary Art San Diego, California. Courtesy of Ryan McGinness Studios, Inc./Art Resource, NY. 

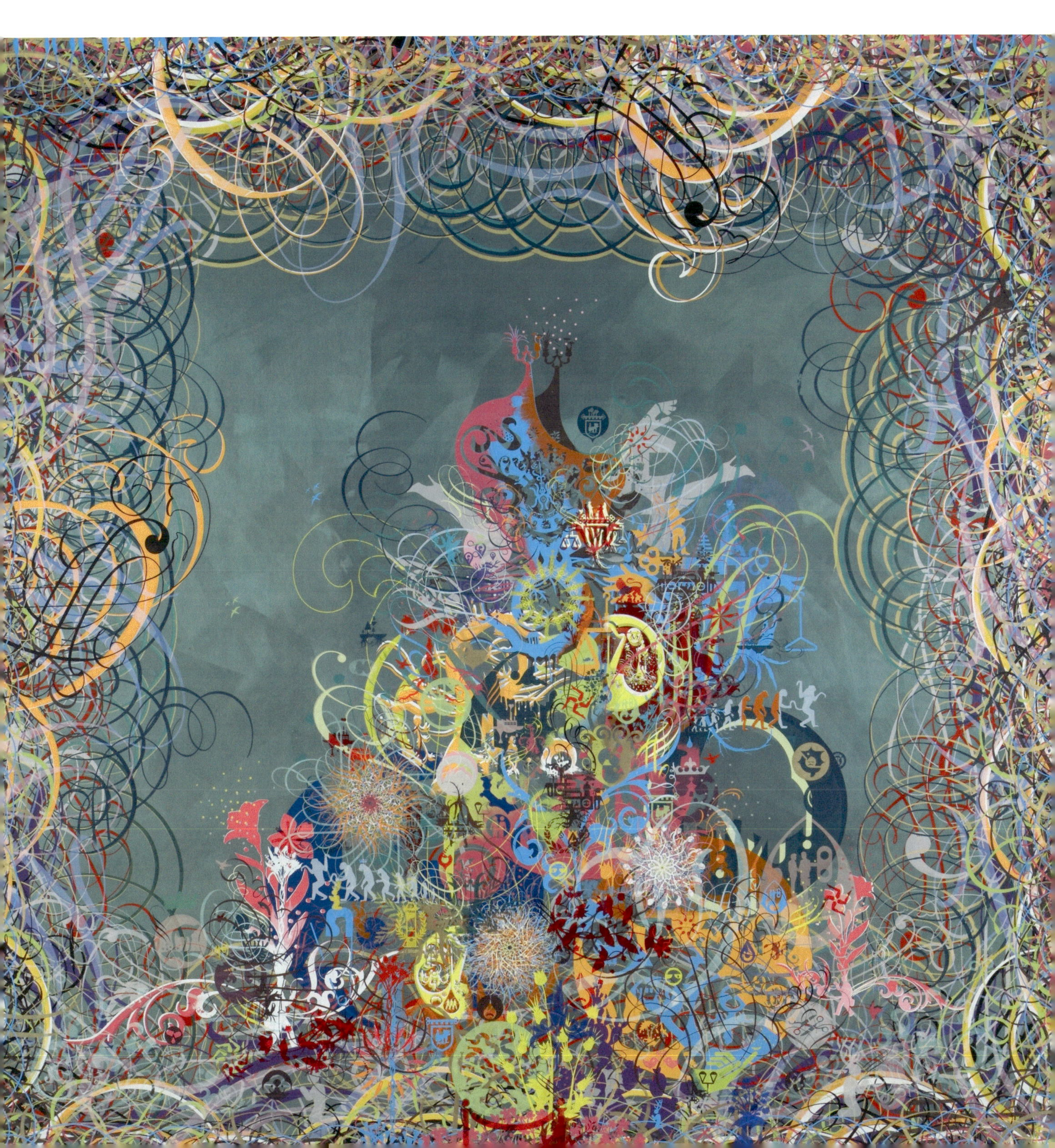

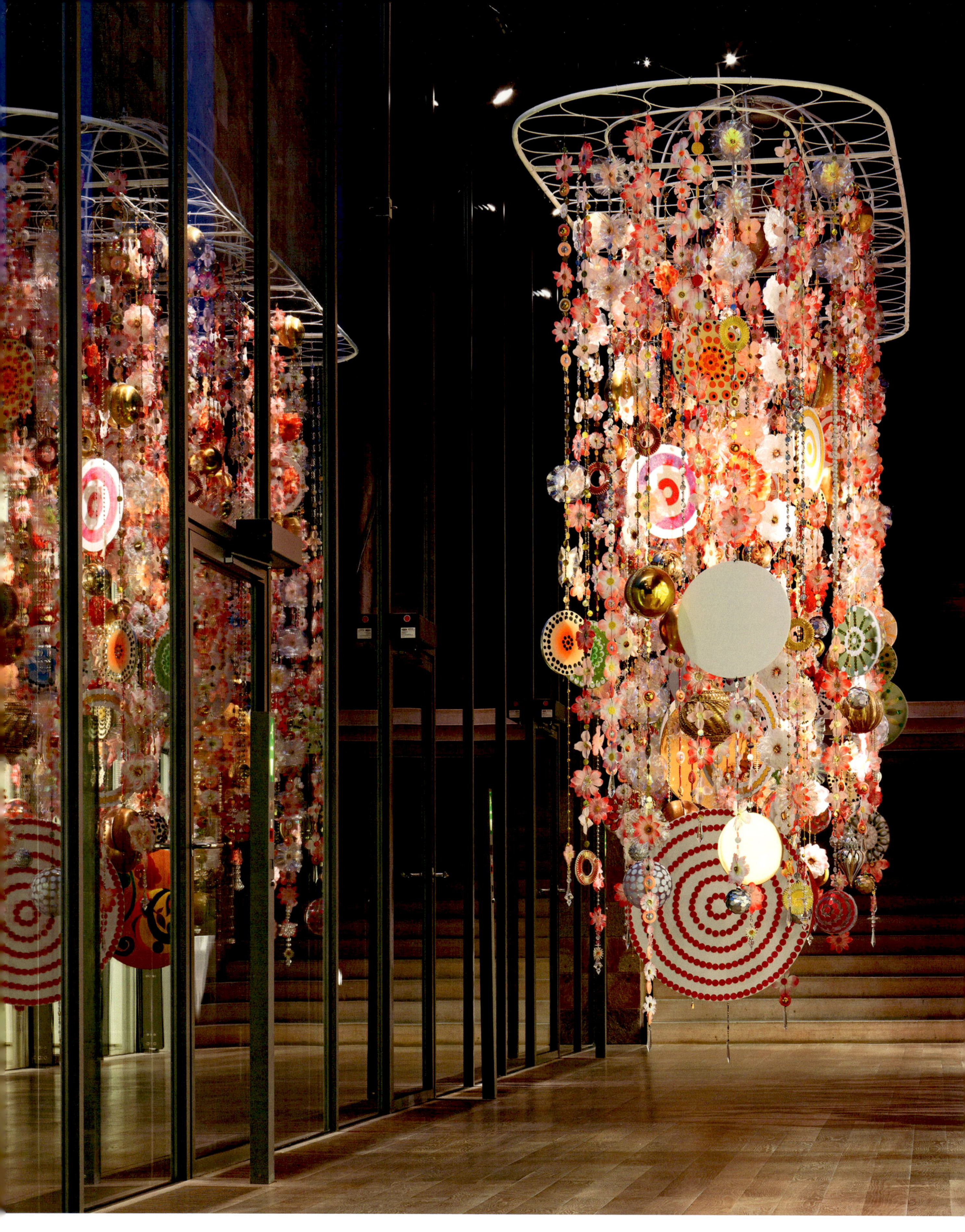

Beatriz Milhazes, **Gamboa**, 2008. Mixed media, 275½ × 59 × 157½ in. Courtesy of the artist and James Cohan Gallery, New York

Ryan McGinness, **A Rich Fantasy Life**, 2007. Installation view: Quint Contemporary Art, La Jolla, California.
Courtesy of Quint Contemporary Art


Ryan McGinness, **A Rich Fantasy Life**, 2007. Installation view: Quint Contemporary Art, La Jolla, California.
Courtesy of Quint Contemporary Art


Ryan McGinness, **Pain-free Kittens**, 2005. Installation view: Quint Contemporary Art, La Jolla, California.
Courtesy of Quint Contemporary Art


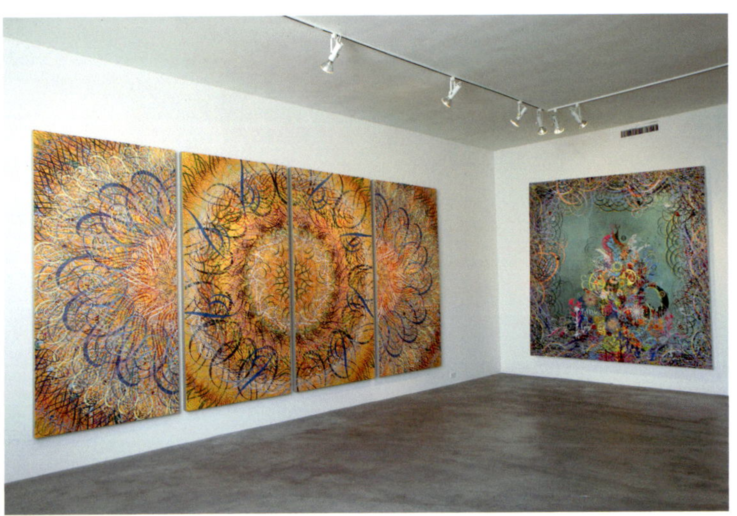

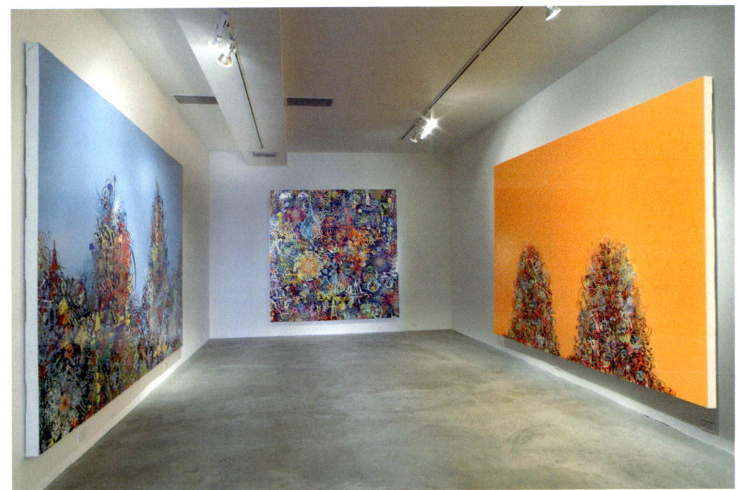

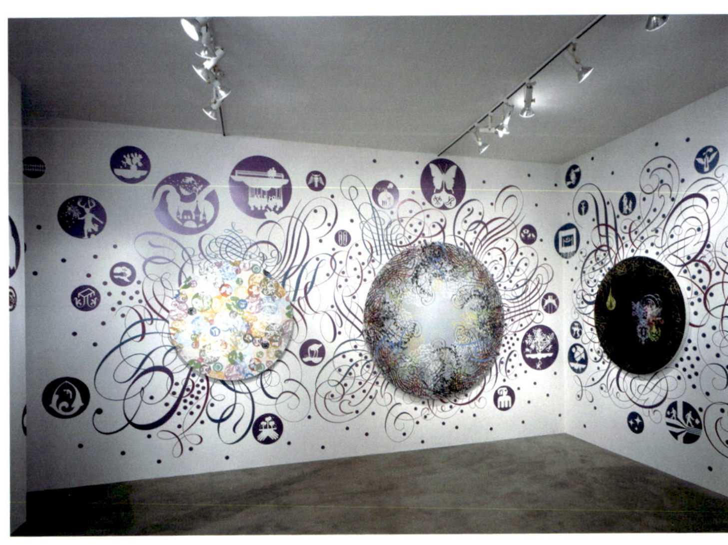

# *Paul Henry Ramirez*

Born 1963

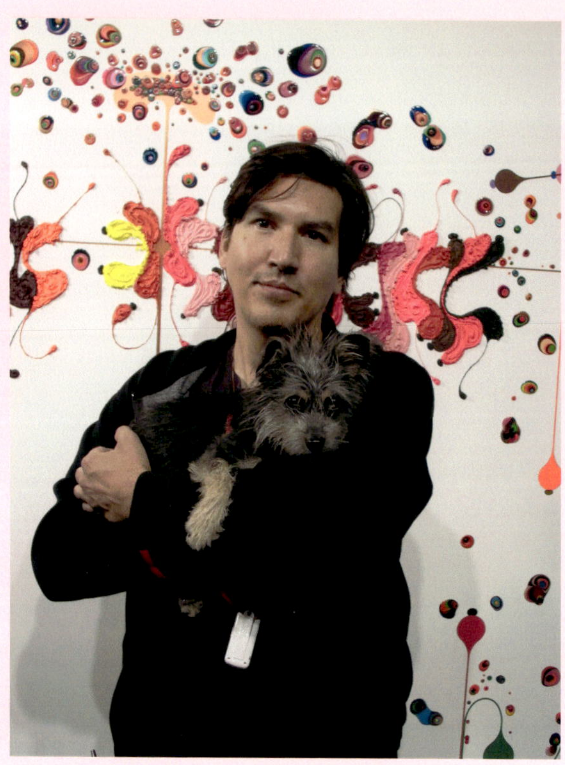

Courtesy of the artist.

Paul Henry Ramirez incorporates eccentric shapes and quirky designs in his cool, elegant abstract paintings. For some viewers, the playful imagery might belie the sophisticated color relationships, precisely conceived compositions, and sensitive paint handling that play important roles in their creation as well as in their appreciation by an audience. Ramirez extends the works' physical size and conceptual weight by combining canvases and works on paper with painting done directly on the walls of a museum or gallery, resulting in lush environments that surround and absorb the viewer. In these installations, a quiet conversation slowly emerges among the various elements.

In his native El Paso, Texas, Ramirez designed retail window displays for department stores. After moving to New York in the early 1990s, he continued to create window displays, including those for Henri Bendel in midtown Manhattan. His experiences working with upscale fashion and fine design influenced the artist's sense of presentation and aesthetics. By comparison, Ramirez's paintings, drawings, and installations developed in a restrained, even sparse, way. However, they retain the fine details, visual sophistication, and understated elegance associated with luxury goods.

An important and unique aspect of Ramirez's practice is the fact that his paintings can stand alone or be incorporated into site installations. Working with a defined site, he considers the architecture and architectural details of the space, the movement of viewers, and the relationships between the canvases or works on paper and the painting done directly on the gallery walls. This approach echoes the considerations involved in designing window displays and connects these seemingly unrelated activities. Yet all are creative products of the same artist.

Paul Henry Ramirez was born in El Paso in 1963. Shortly after graduating from high school Ramirez co-founded *Juntos 1985, The First Hispanic Invitational Art Exhibition,* in Texas. Before attending the University of Texas at El Paso, he had his first international solo exhibition at Museo de Arte in Ciudad Juárez, Chihuahua, Mexico. For over a decade his work has been featured in solo and group exhibitions nationally and internationally, and it is found in collections including the El Paso Museum of Art; Hirshhorn Museum and Sculpture Garden, Washington D.C.; Newark Museum, New Jersey; Smithsonian American Art Museum, Washington D.C.; and Whitney Museum of American Art, New York, among others. The artist lives and works in Pennington, New Jersey.

# Rex Ray

Born 1956

Rex Ray straddles the worlds of fine art and commercial design, both in his life and in his work. His intricate collaged panels are built layer upon layer from painted and printed papers that he meticulously hand cuts and assembles into eye-popping compositions. Ray's intuitive sense of patterning, juxtapositions of brilliant colors, and use of subtle surface textures result in exotic explosions on canvas and wood. Essentially abstractions, the works present stylized images that allude to a host of subjects, ranging from flowering-plant forms to ornate jewelry to hip mid-twentieth-century design. Perhaps it is their elusive familiarity that captivates viewers, or more likely, the immediate visual pleasure and buoyant feeling experienced when encountering Ray's art.

Despite a labor-intensive working process, Ray is a prolific artist whose San Francisco, California, studio is packed with work in every state of creation, from blank surfaces awaiting bright paper cutouts to glistening finished panels propped against the walls. Years working as a graphic designer provide the artist with many of the skills that he transfers to fine art, skills that form the backbone of his current practice. Ray's collages are highly dependent on his design aptitude, yet transcend pure decoration through the complex interweaving of fanciful forms that create the illusion of three-dimensional space.

A unique dimension of Ray's work is the various functional products that he designs for the consumer market. In many ways his approach is similar to Pop art icon Andy Warhol, who also moved freely between the worlds of fine art, commerce, and popular culture. Floor rugs, silk scarves, wallpaper, throw pillows—even iPod and iPad cases—bear Ray's signature imagery. Together with his unique collages on canvas and wood, his mass-produced objects in diverse materials demonstrate the artist's unified vision and widen the audience for his work. Nearly anyone can own something that he has touched, adding an inclusive, democratic spirit to this art.

Rex Ray was born on a military base in Germany. He received a Bachelor of Fine Arts from the San Francisco Art Institute, California, in 1988, and has exhibited his work for the past two decades, including a 2009 solo presentation at the Museum of Contemporary Art Denver, Colorado. As a graphic designer, Ray has created items for Apple, Dreamworks, Sony Music, Warner Brothers, and numerous other clients. He designed over 100 "Bill Graham Presents" concert posters for performers including the Rolling Stones, Patti Smith, and R.E.M.

Courtesy of the artist.

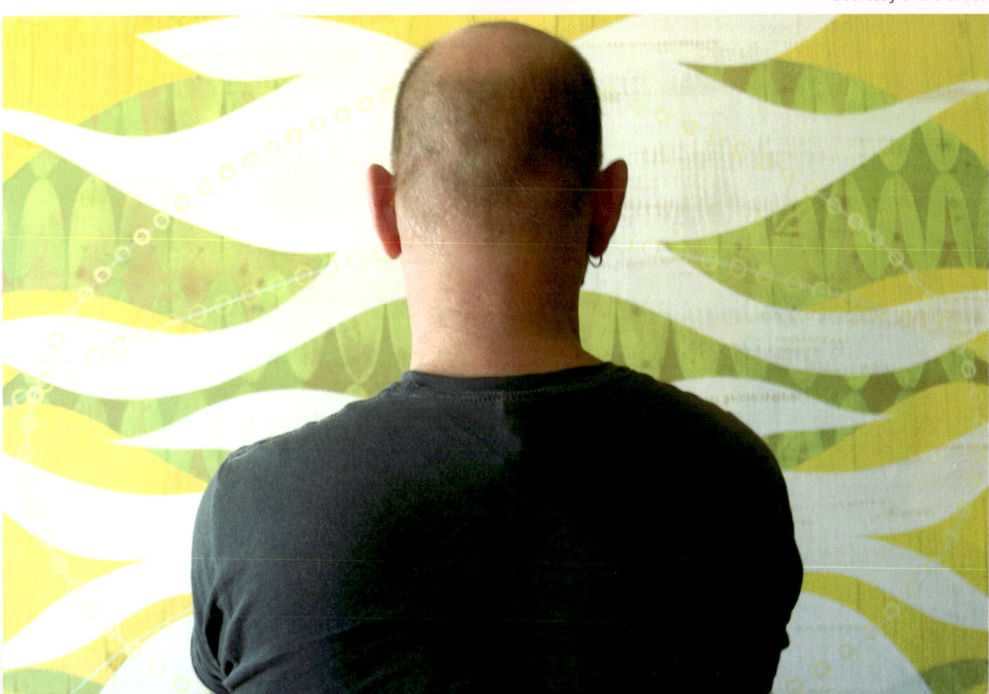

# Rosalyn Schwartz

Born 1952

Questions about beauty, taste, and style are at the heart of Rosalyn Schwartz's paintings and collages. The daughter of an interior designer, Schwartz grew up surrounded by luxurious fabrics and exquisite antiques. In creating her work, the artist draws inspiration not only from this personal history of abundance and visual excess, but also from art history, popular culture, and kitsch, borrowing freely from acknowledged masters and masterpieces, vintage photographs and magazine illustrations, and mass-produced decorative objects.

Although the imagery in Schwartz's art varies widely, an underlying concern with beauty ties the works together. In one direction, this concern manifests itself as visual interpretations of paintings by artists including French Rococo painter Francois Boucher and Spanish romantic Francisco Goya. Schwartz repaints these existing works using inventive brushwork and dissonant colors, altering the scale of her sources and inverting or eliminating aspects of the original compositions. Sometimes the result appears far from the original, and only Schwartz's title offers a clue to her interpretation's origin. In another approach, she bases her paintings in traditional subjects such as landscape and still life, again employing painting techniques and a palette that teeters between sophistication and bad taste. These works call into question just who decides what is quality—how the same art can be praised by some and detested by others.

Another large body of work is the intimate collages that sandwich photographs, magazine pages, wallpaper snippets, illustrations, and Mylar tape together with paint, drawing materials, and cut paper. The found images incorporated in the collages range from botanical prints to architectural elements to portraits of French sex symbol Brigitte Bardot. Like the works on canvas, the collages show clear evidence of the artist's touch with their spontaneous, textured surfaces. In an opposing direction, Schwartz recently began to experiment with digital imaging, and the results are by contrast cooler and more distanced than her paintings and collages.

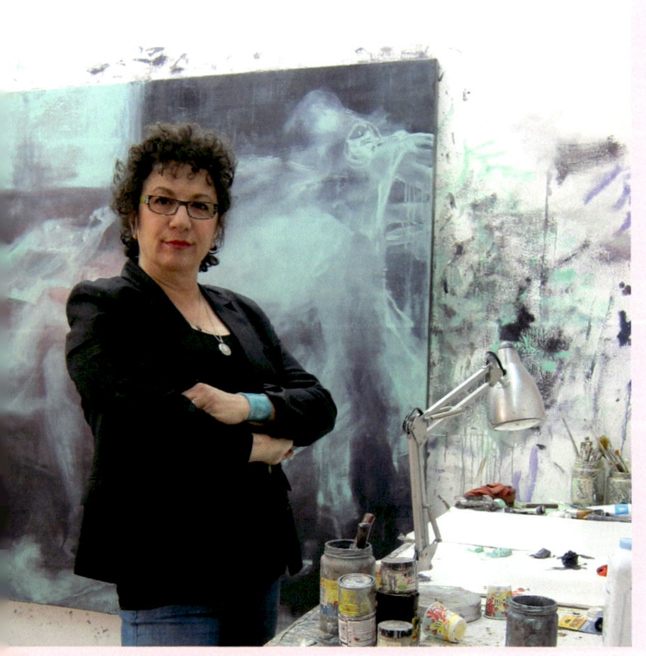

Courtesy of the artist.

Rosalyn Schwartz was born in 1952, in St. Louis, Missouri. After receiving a Bachelor of Arts from Washington University in St. Louis, in 1975, Schwartz received a Master of Fine Arts in 1979 from Fontbonne College, also in St. Louis. Her work has been featured in solo and group exhibitions nationally and internationally; in 2013 she presented *A Brief History of Seduction*, a solo project at the McNay Art Museum. Schwartz lives and works in Urbana, Illinois.

# *Susan Chrysler White*

Born 1954

Susan Chrysler White manipulates paint so that it appears simultaneously intuitive and methodical. Working on both flat surfaces and in three-dimensional space, she derives her imagery from the tangible world of the human figure and nature, and the unseen worlds of faith and the spiritual. Trained as a painter, White expands her creative vocabulary by forcing her abstract subjects off the two-dimensional surfaces of paper and canvas and into the viewer's space.

White carefully organizes her compositional structures to create an arresting sense of deep space that mimics the mystery of her mystical sources. Decorative elements and complex patterning hover over and within amorphous fields, ranging from symmetrical shapes resembling Rorschach images, to jewel-like striated forms, to lacy silhouettes of delicate fern fronds, and most everything in between. White's vivid palette vacillates between seduction and repulsion, escalating the visual tension inherent in the work. Tension is also created when some of the paintings burst from their rectangular confines to form irregular perimeters, or hurl elements into the viewer's space, attached to the work's surface yet appearing to come from within.

White even takes the elements in her paintings into full three-dimensional space. Painted on shaped pieces of glass and plexiglass, they are assembled and hang from above. The same vivid palette and vocabulary of marks and motifs adorn the surfaces. Alone or in clusters, these constructions allude to everything from fantastic plant forms to oversized wind chimes to Rococo excess. In a rare gesture, White fashioned a large, monochromatic white sculpture which radiates a restrained elegance.

Susan Chrysler White was born in Chico, California, in 1954. In 1977 she received a Bachelor of Arts in painting from the University of California, Berkeley, and in 1980, a Master of Fine Arts in painting and drawing from the University of California, Davis. For over two decades, her work has been exhibited in solo and group exhibitions, and she has completed a number of public commissions. Since 2000 White has taught painting and drawing at the University of Iowa, Iowa City.

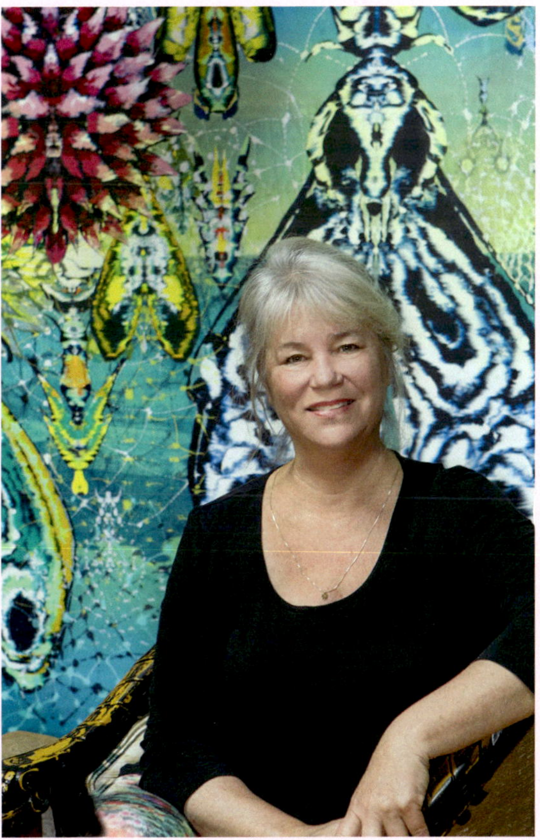

Courtesy of the artist.

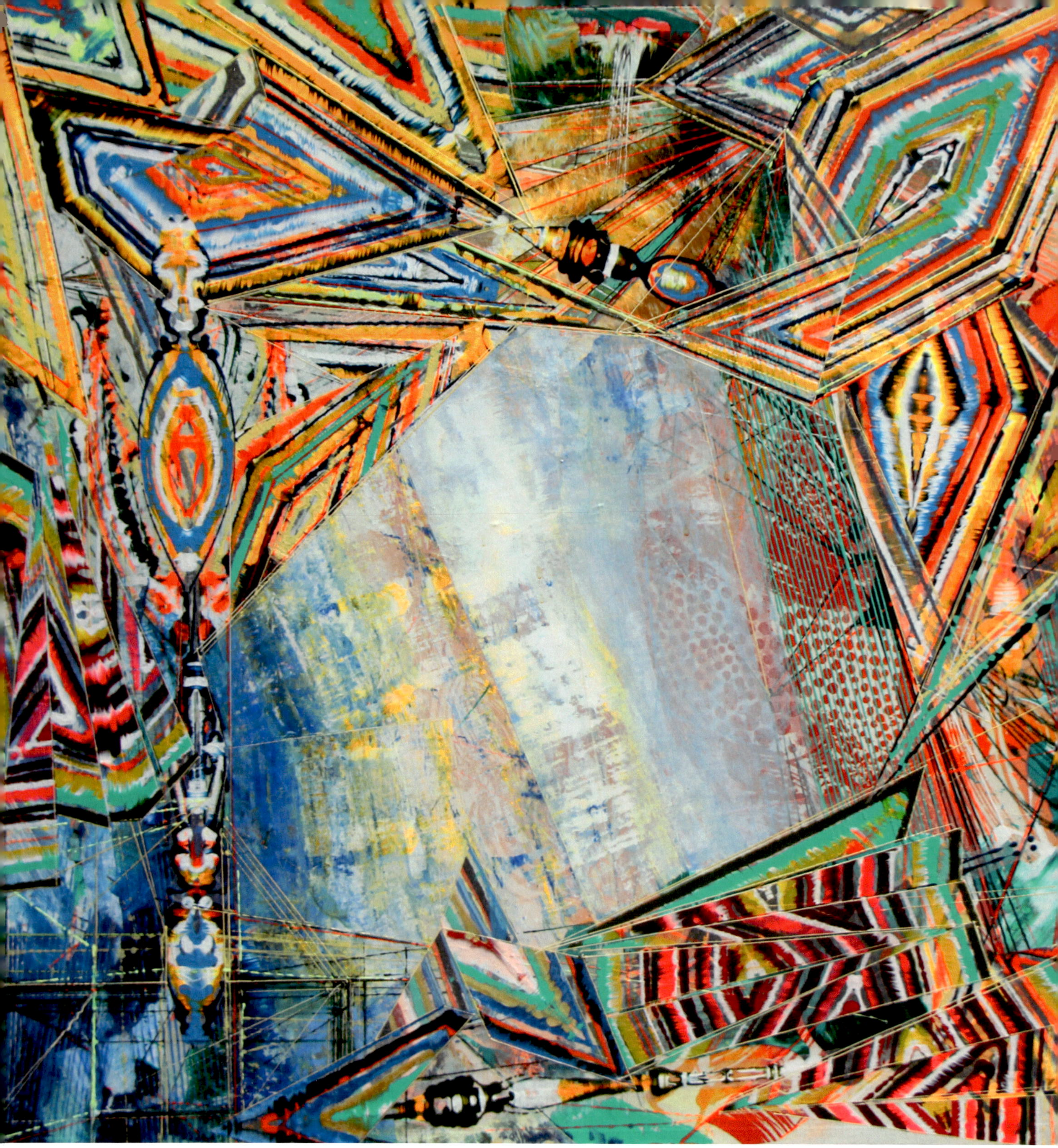



Susan Chrysler White, **Portal**, 2012. Acrylic on canvas, 30 × 30 in. Courtesy of the artist

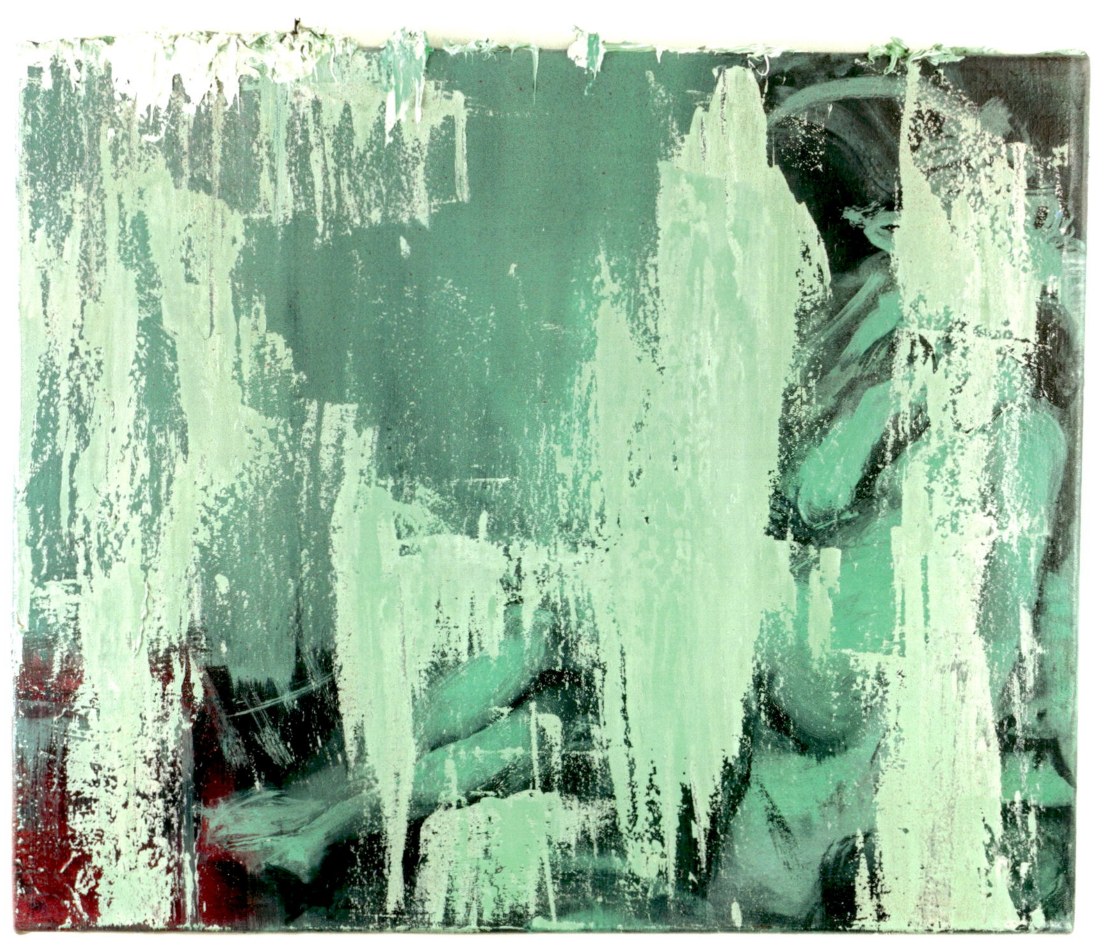

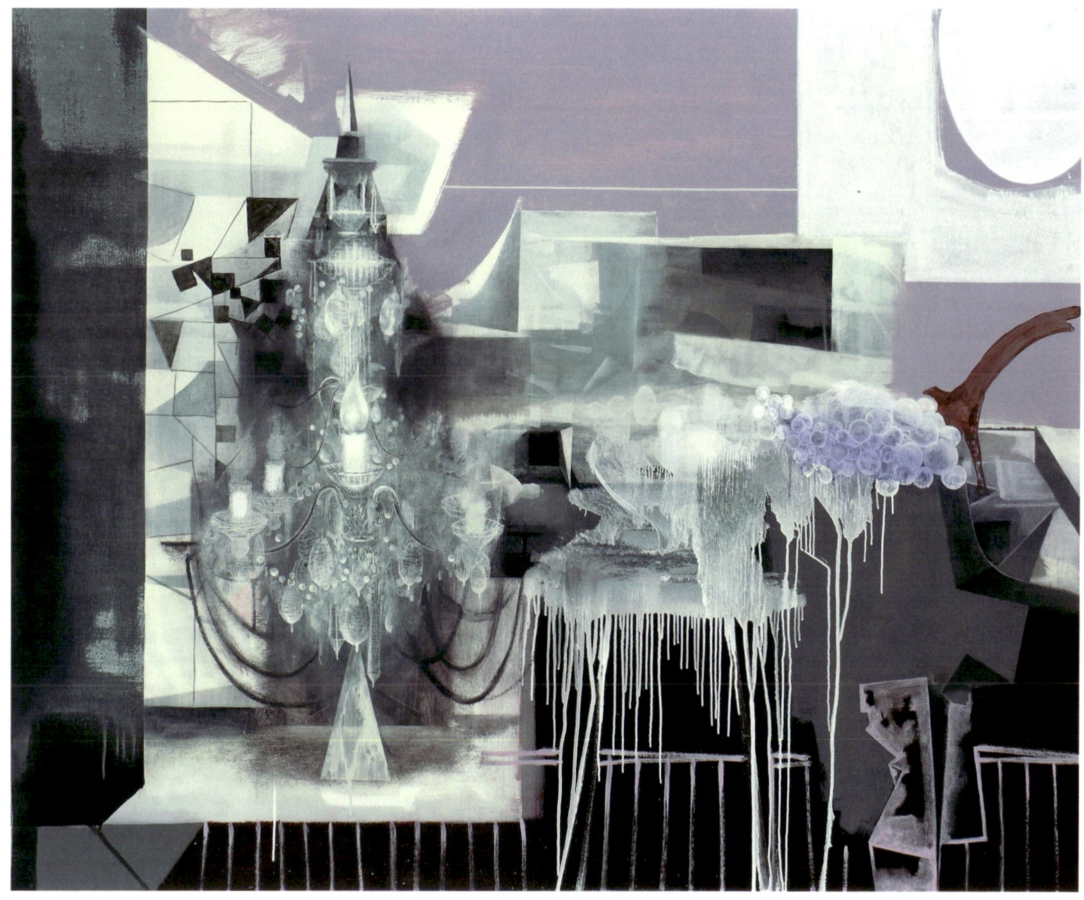

Rosalyn Schwartz, **After Boucher 2**, 2013. Oil on canvas, 11 × 14 in. Courtesy of the artist

Rosalyn Schwartz, **Kafka**, 2006. Oil on canvas, 52 × 66 in. Courtesy of the artist

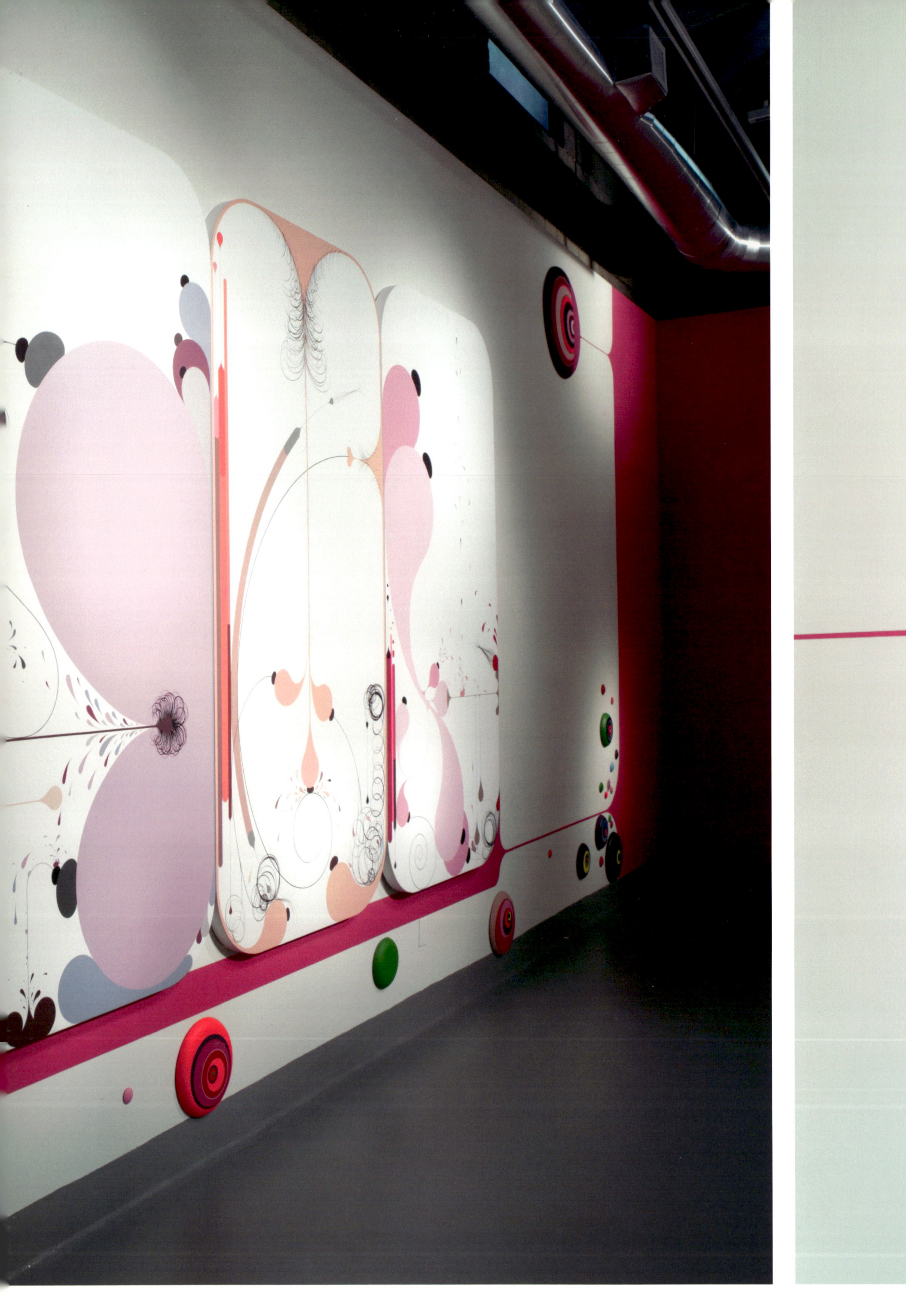

Paul Henry Ramirez, **Untitled**, 1999. Acrylic and flashe on panel, 96 × 144 × 2 in.
From the **Edging into Excess** series. Collection of the Whitney Museum of American Art, New York
Installation view: **Seriously Playful: Paul Henry Ramirez 1995–2004**, Stanlee and Gerald Rubin Gallery, The University of Texas at El Paso, 2004
Acrylic on canvas, Formica, and wall painting, approximately 216 × 600 × 1440 in. Courtesy of the artist

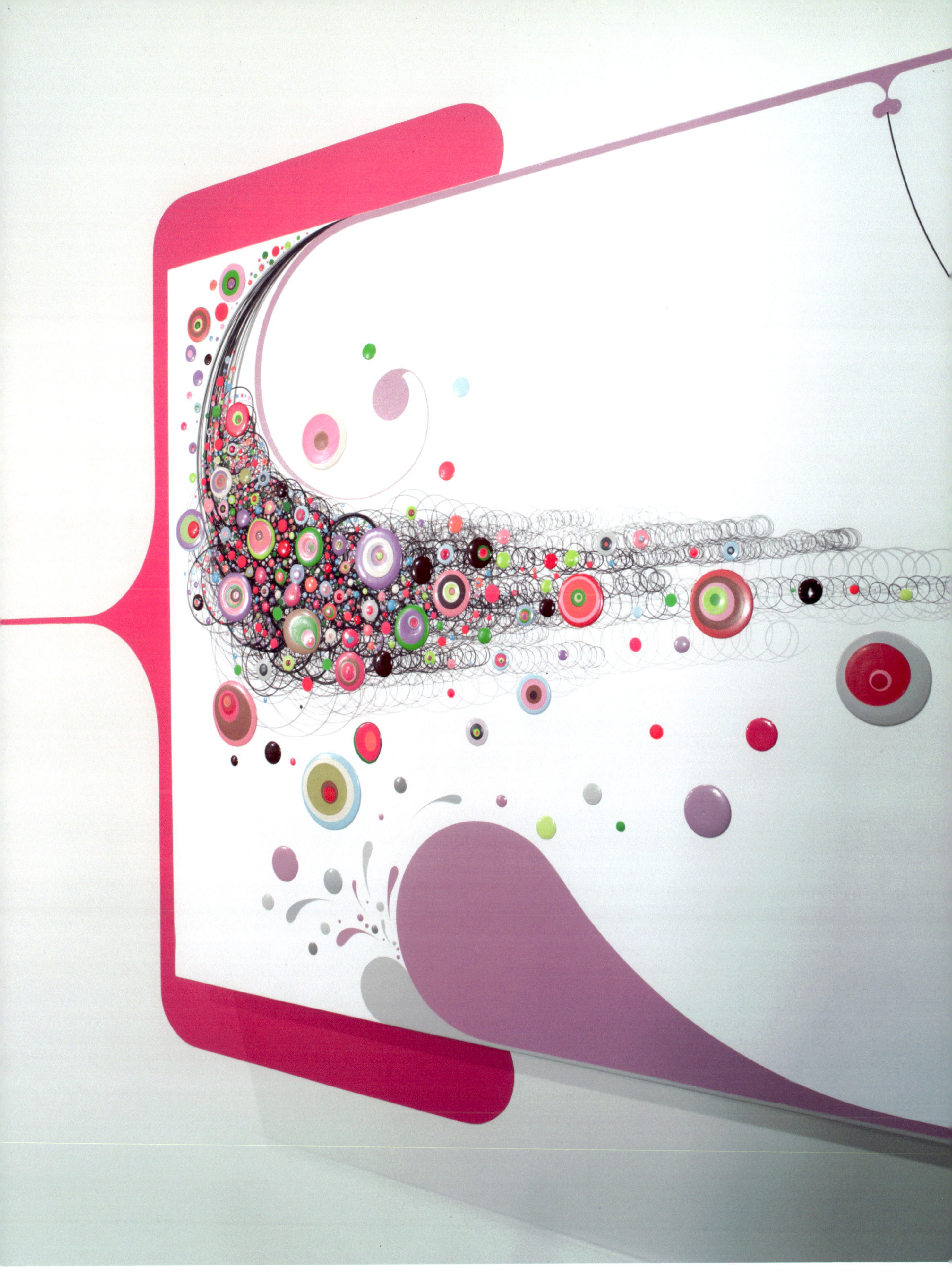

Paul Henry Ramirez, **Elevatious Transcendsualistic 5** (detail), 2001. Acrylic, enamel, and flashe on canvas on panel, 24 × 96 × 2 in.
Collection of the El Paso Museum of Art, Texas
Installation view: **Seriously Playful: Paul Henry Ramirez 1995–2004**, Stanlee and Gerald Rubin Gallery, The University of Texas at El Paso, 2004.
Courtesy of the artist

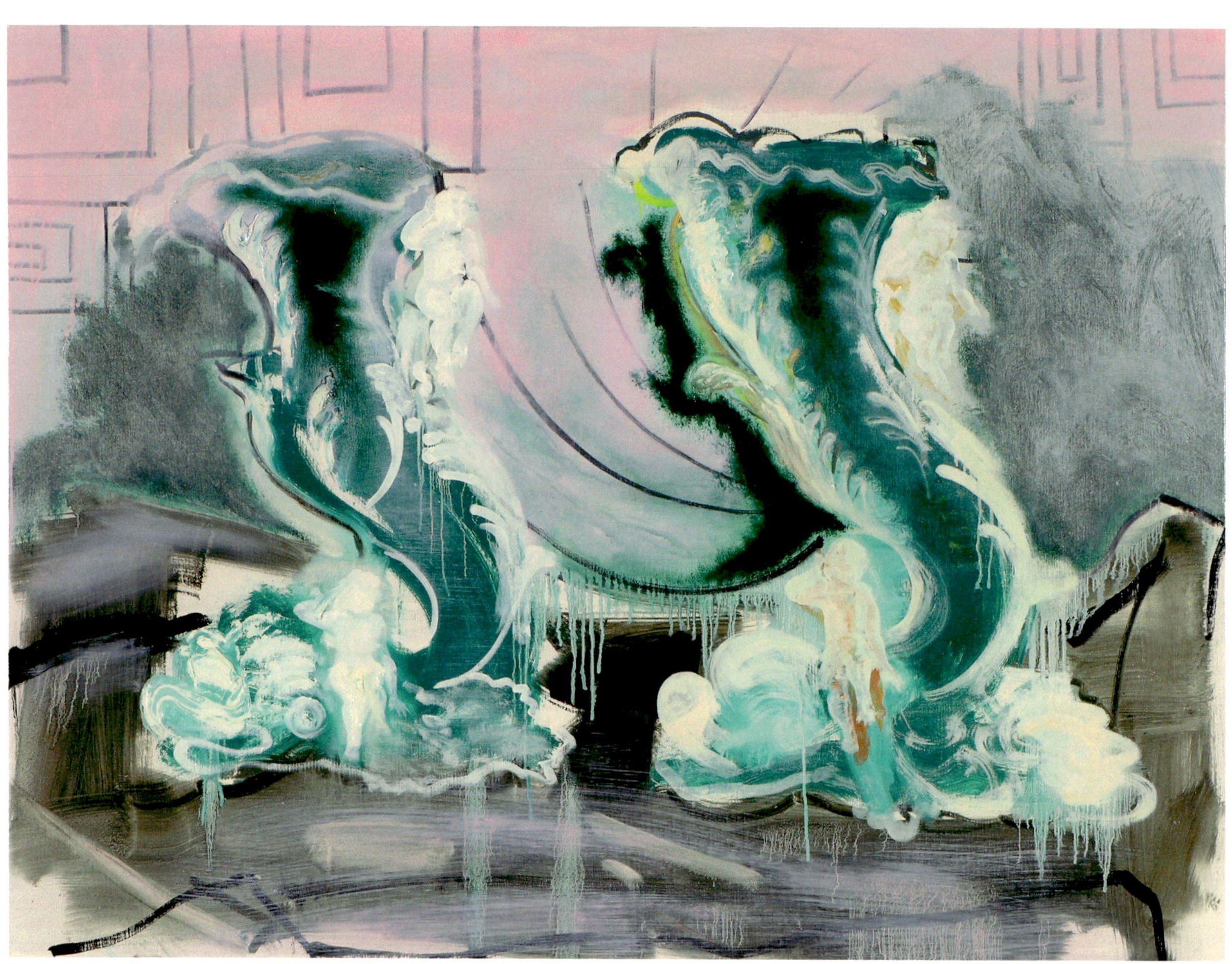

 Rosalyn Schwartz, **Rococo Vases 1 (eBay)**, 2008. Oil on canvas, 30 × 40 in. Courtesy of the artist

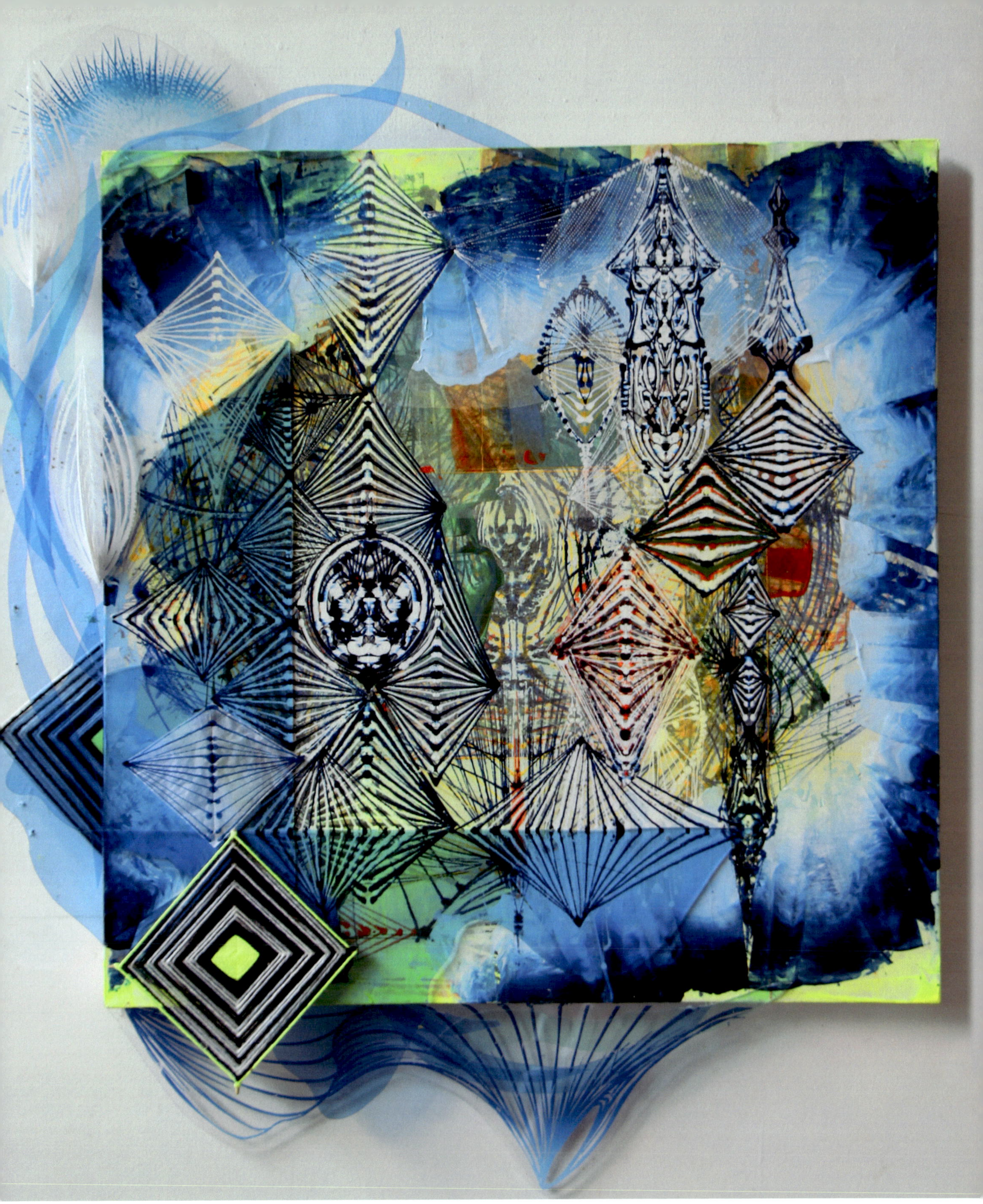

Susan Chrysler White, **Watermark**, 2013. Acrylic, cotton, and plexiglass on canvas, 38 × 42 in. Courtesy of the artist

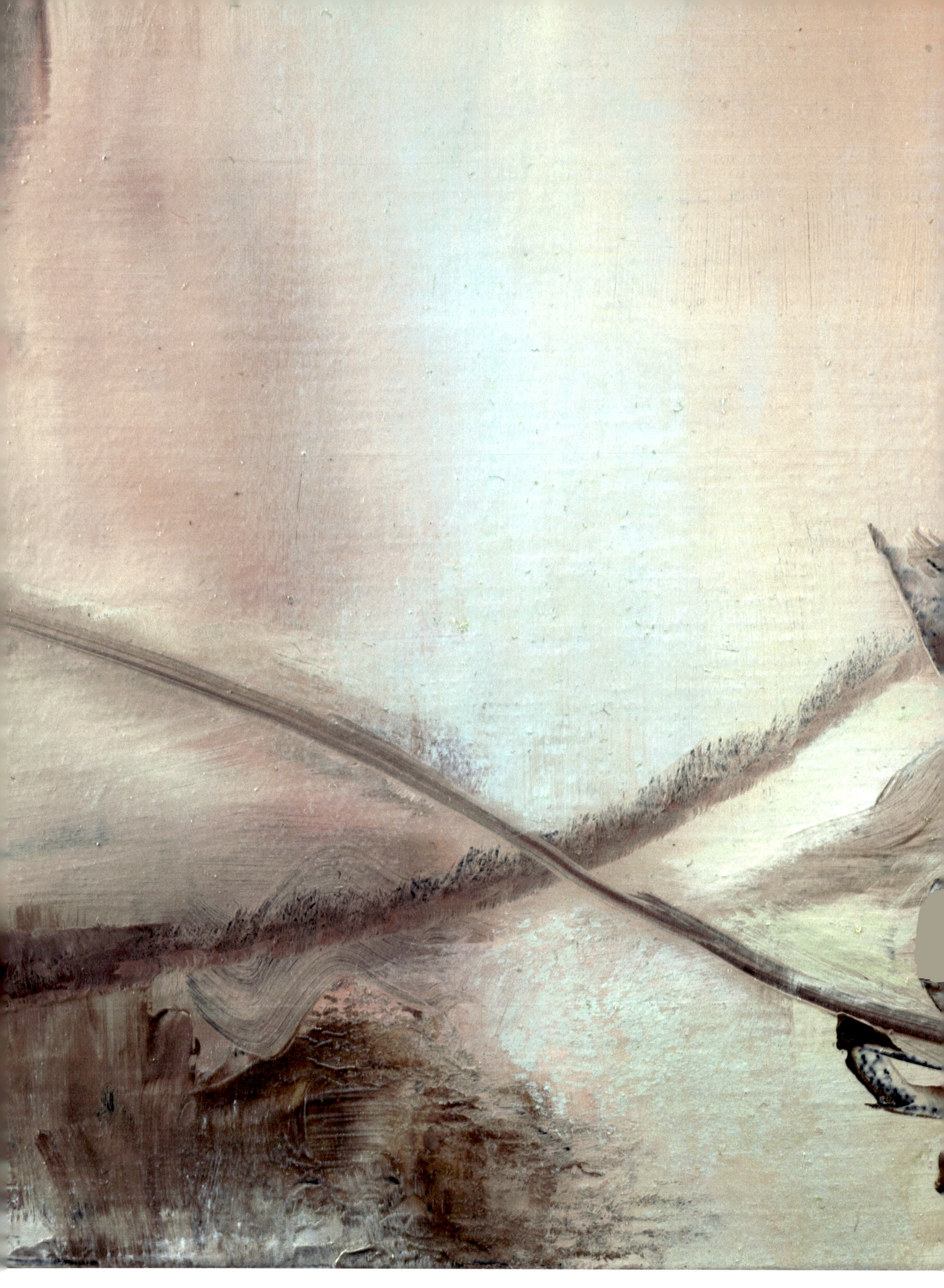

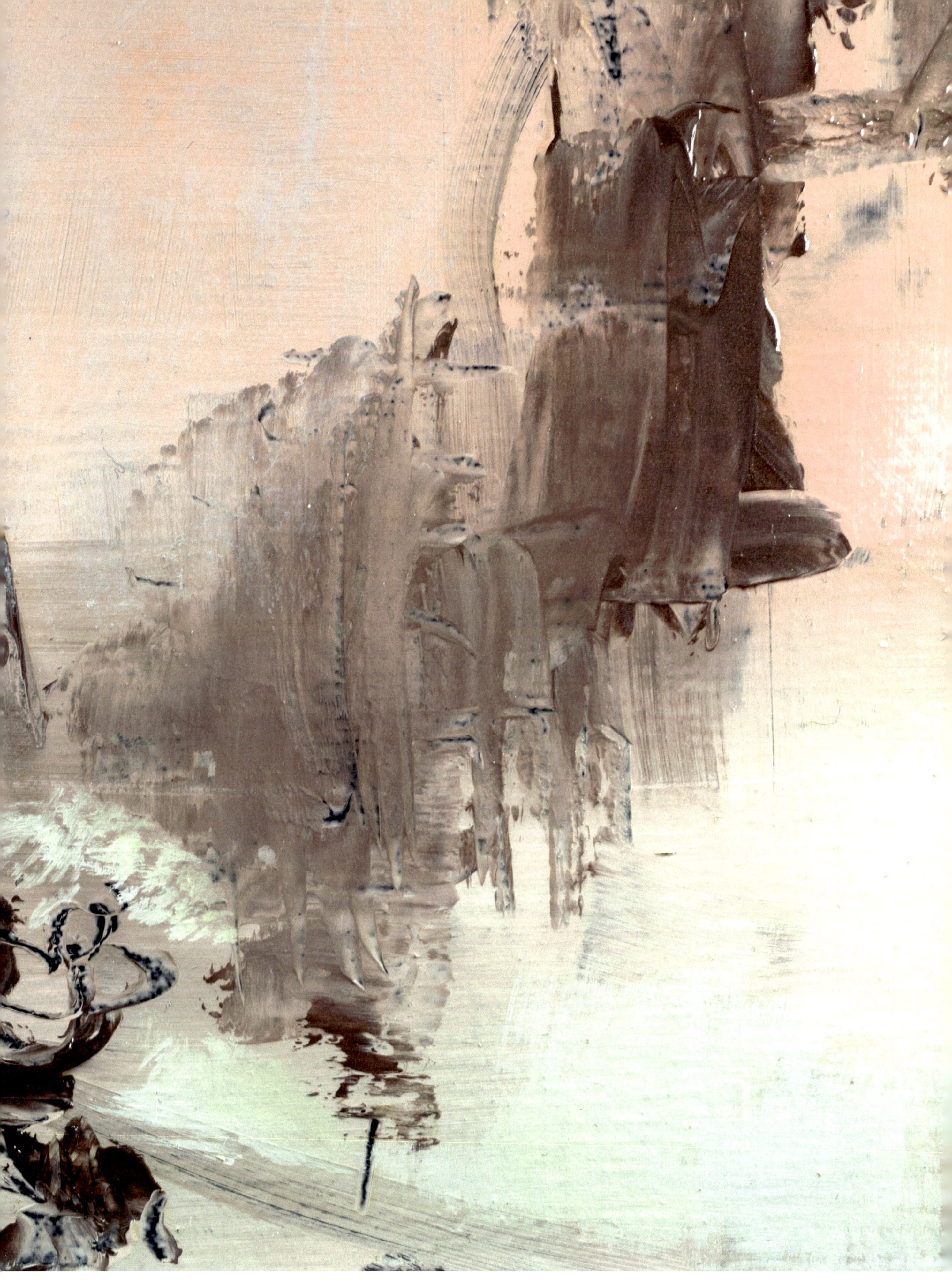

Rosalyn Schwartz, **Landscape 2 (blush)** (detail), 2012. Oil on canvas, 28 × 22 in. Courtesy of the artist

Paul Henry Ramirez, **PLAYCONICS 4**, 2011. Acrylic on canvas, 66 x 66 in. Courtesy of the artist

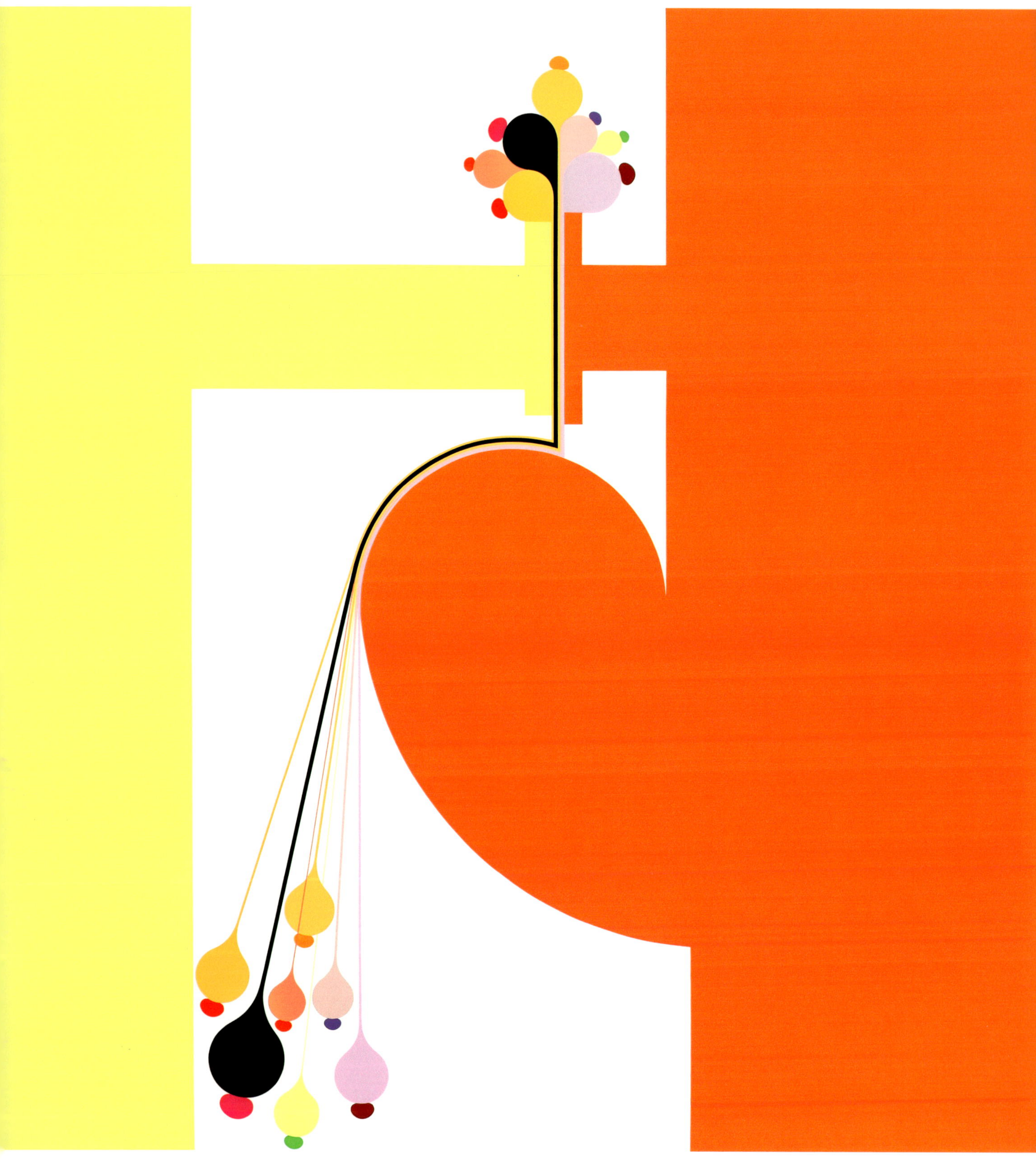

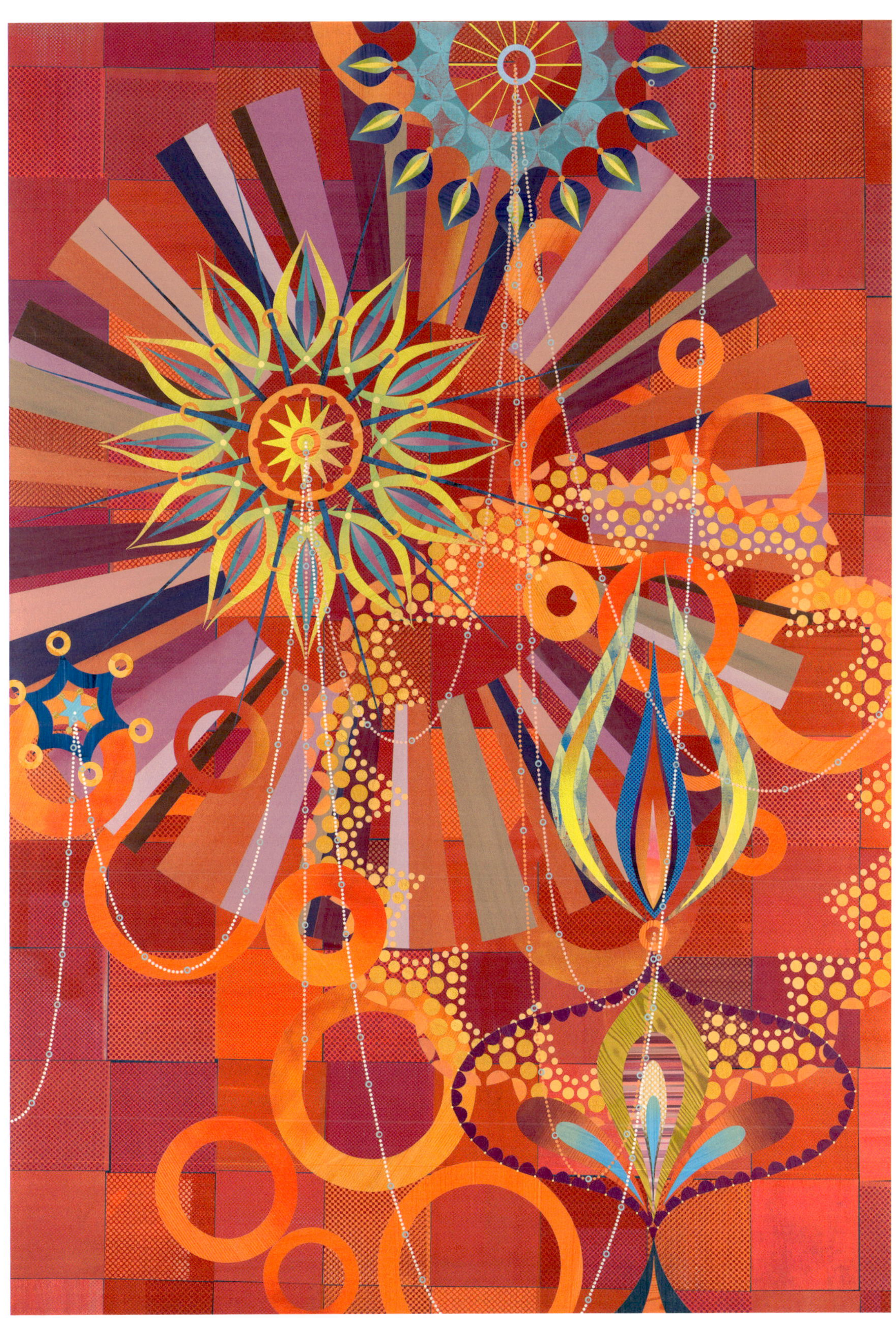

Rex Ray, **Haemolysis**, 2010. Oil, acrylic, and mixed media on linen, 108 × 76 in. Courtesy of the artist and Gallery 16, San Francisco, California

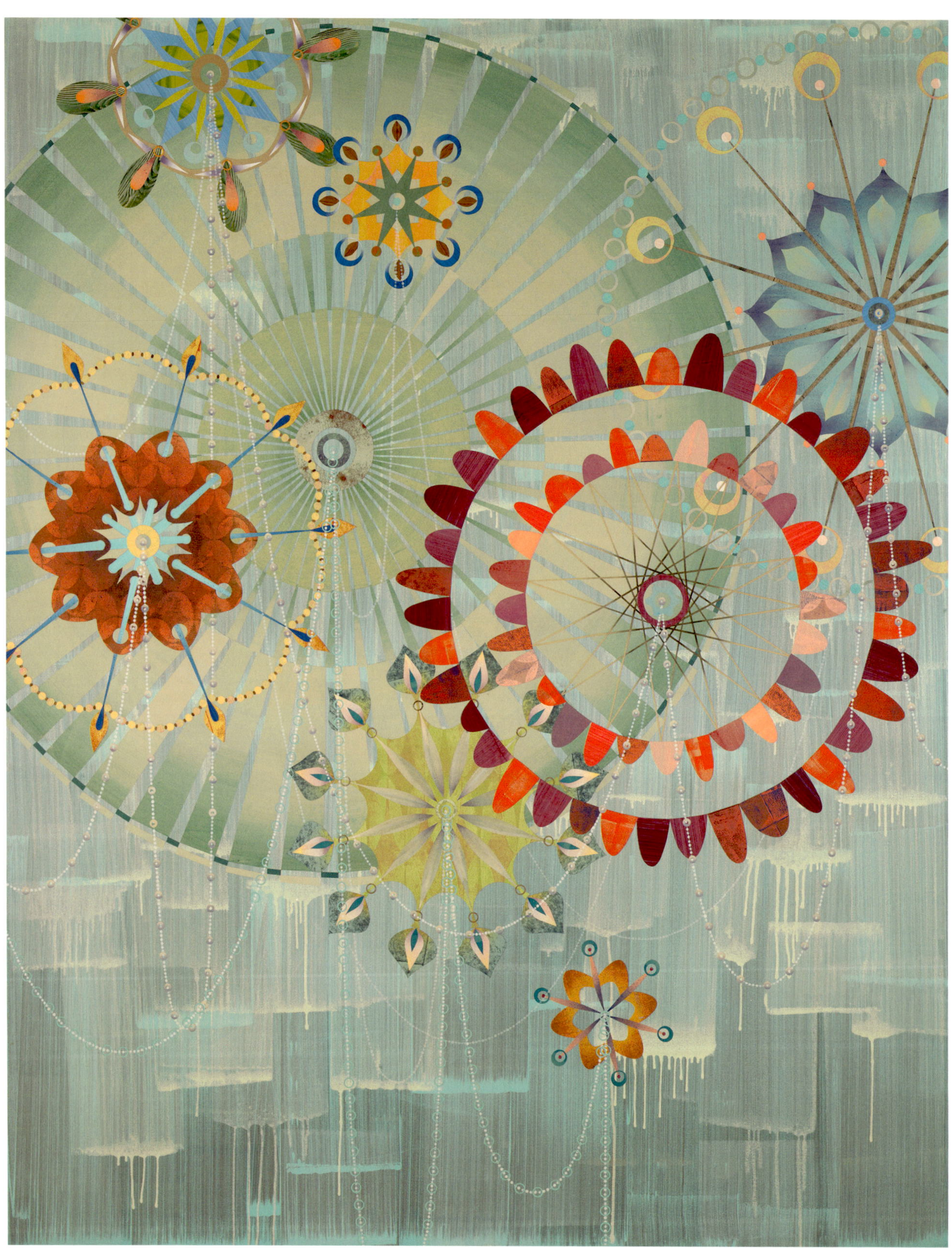

 Rex Ray, **Thelidium**, 2006. Oil, acrylic, and mixed media on linen, 84 × 76 in. Courtesy of the artist and Conduit Gallery, Dallas, Texas

Rosalyn Schwartz, **Corot**, 2012. Mixed media on paper, 8 × 8 in. Courtesy of the artist

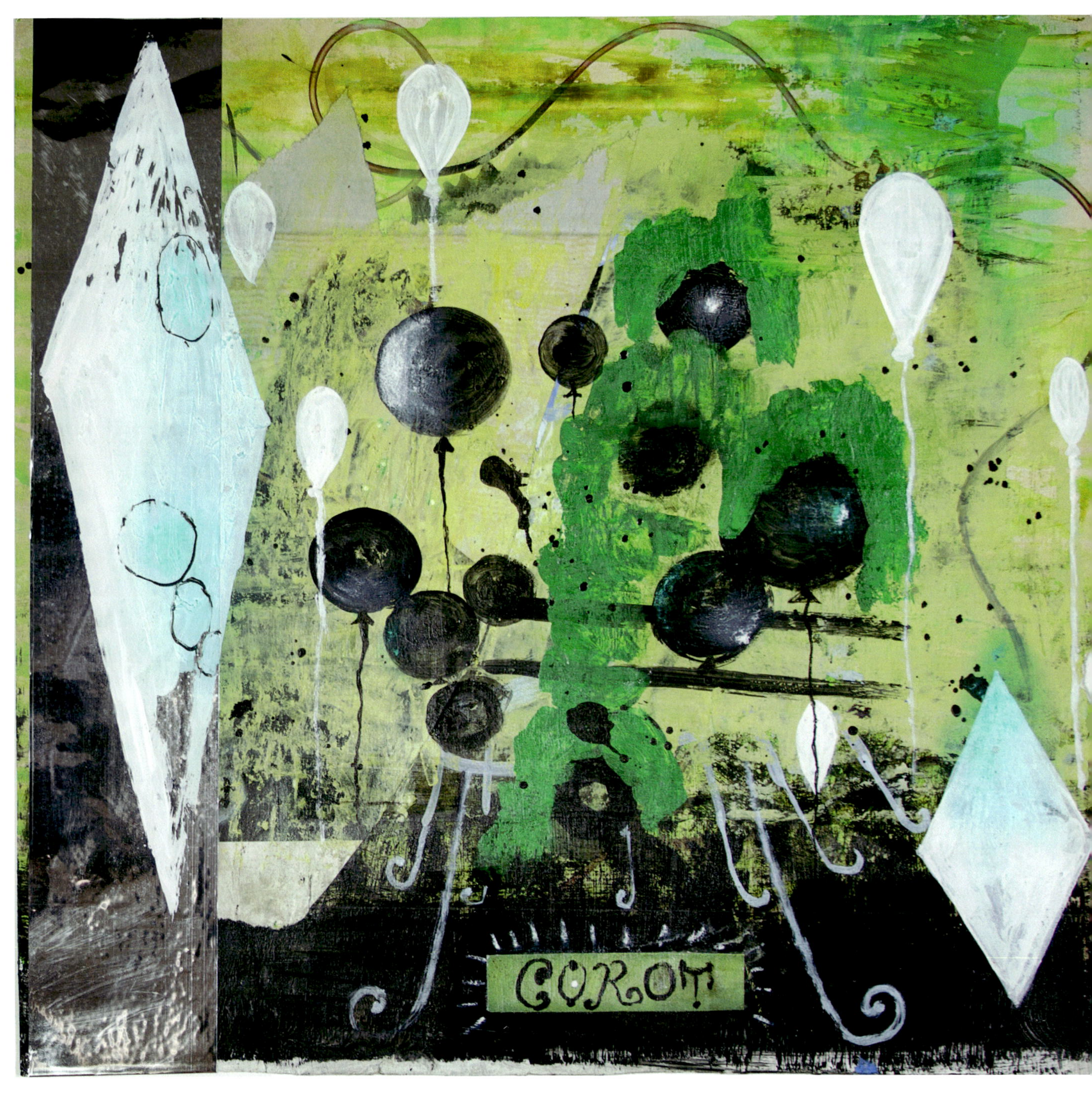

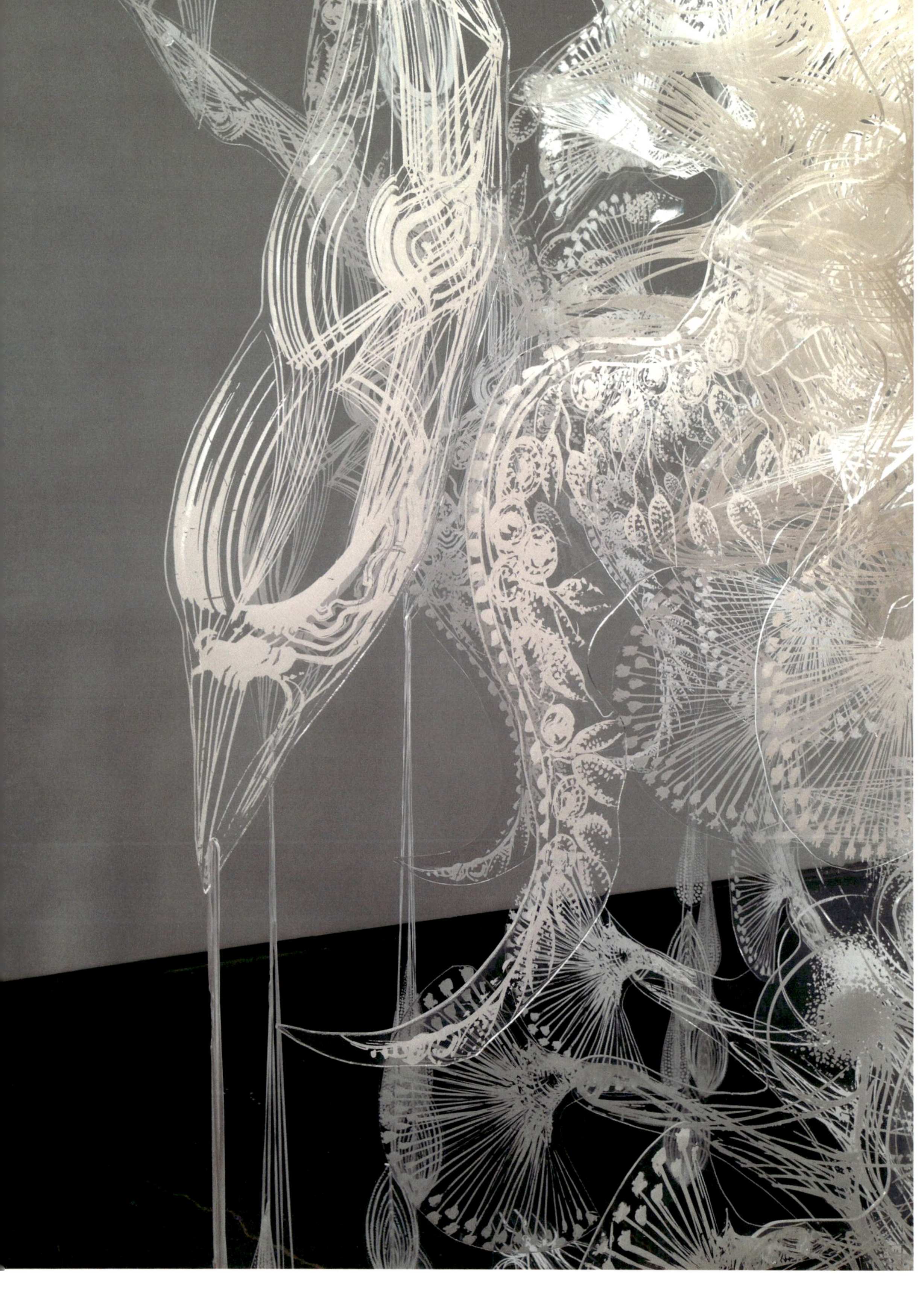

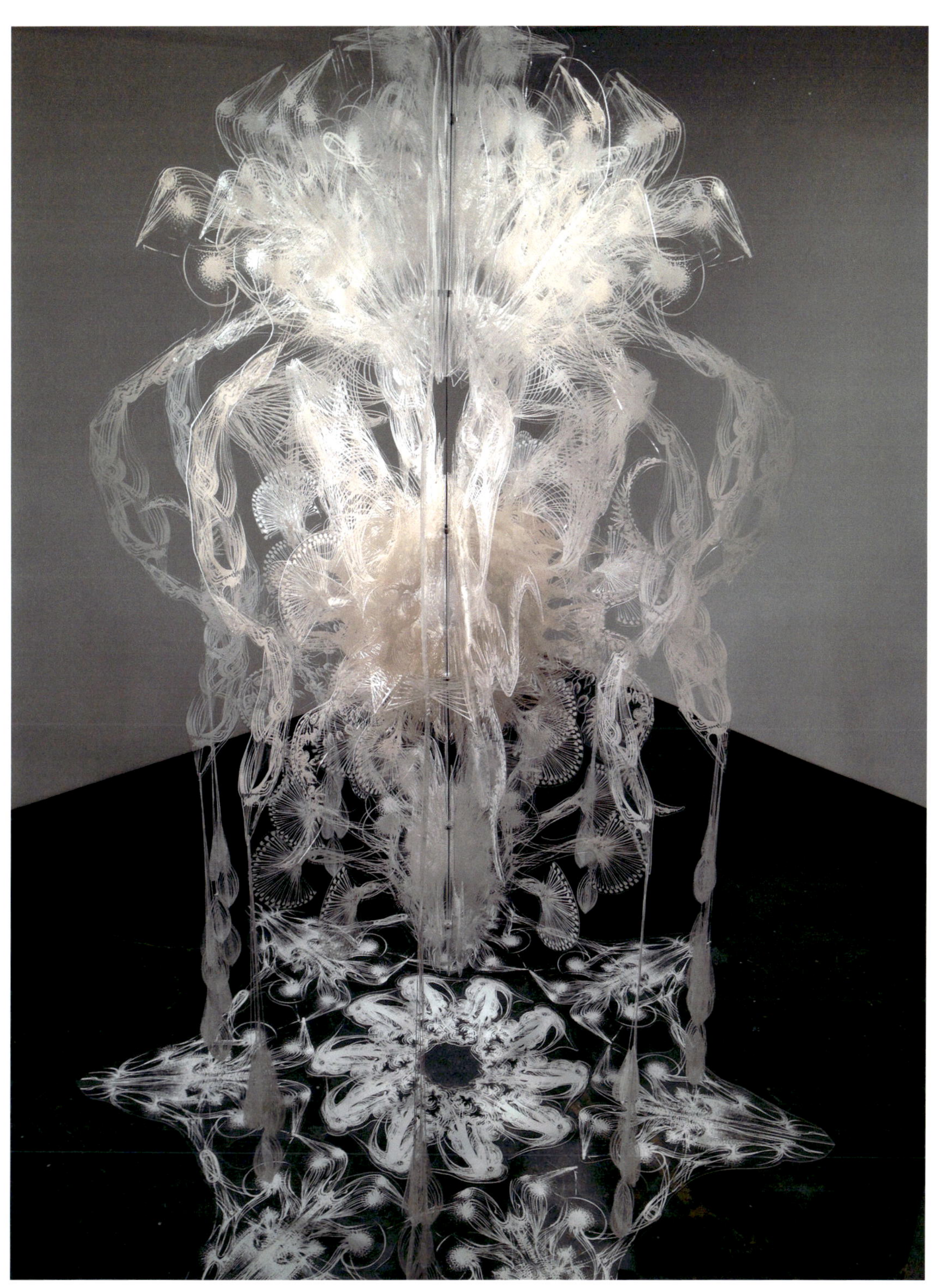

Susan Chrysler White, **Medusa**, 2013. Acrylic on plexiglass and stainless steel rods, 168 × 120 × 120 in. Courtesy Kim Foster Gallery, New York 

Paul Henry Ramirez, **Chunk 17** (detail), 2009. Acrylic on canvas, 72 × 72 in.
**Zero Point Zero**, performance in collaboration with choreographer Debra J. Fernandez, 2010. Costumes, props, and music for 20 dancers
Installation view: **BLACKOUT: A Centennial Commission by Paul Henry Ramirez**, Newark Museum, New Jersey, 2010
Courtesy of the artist

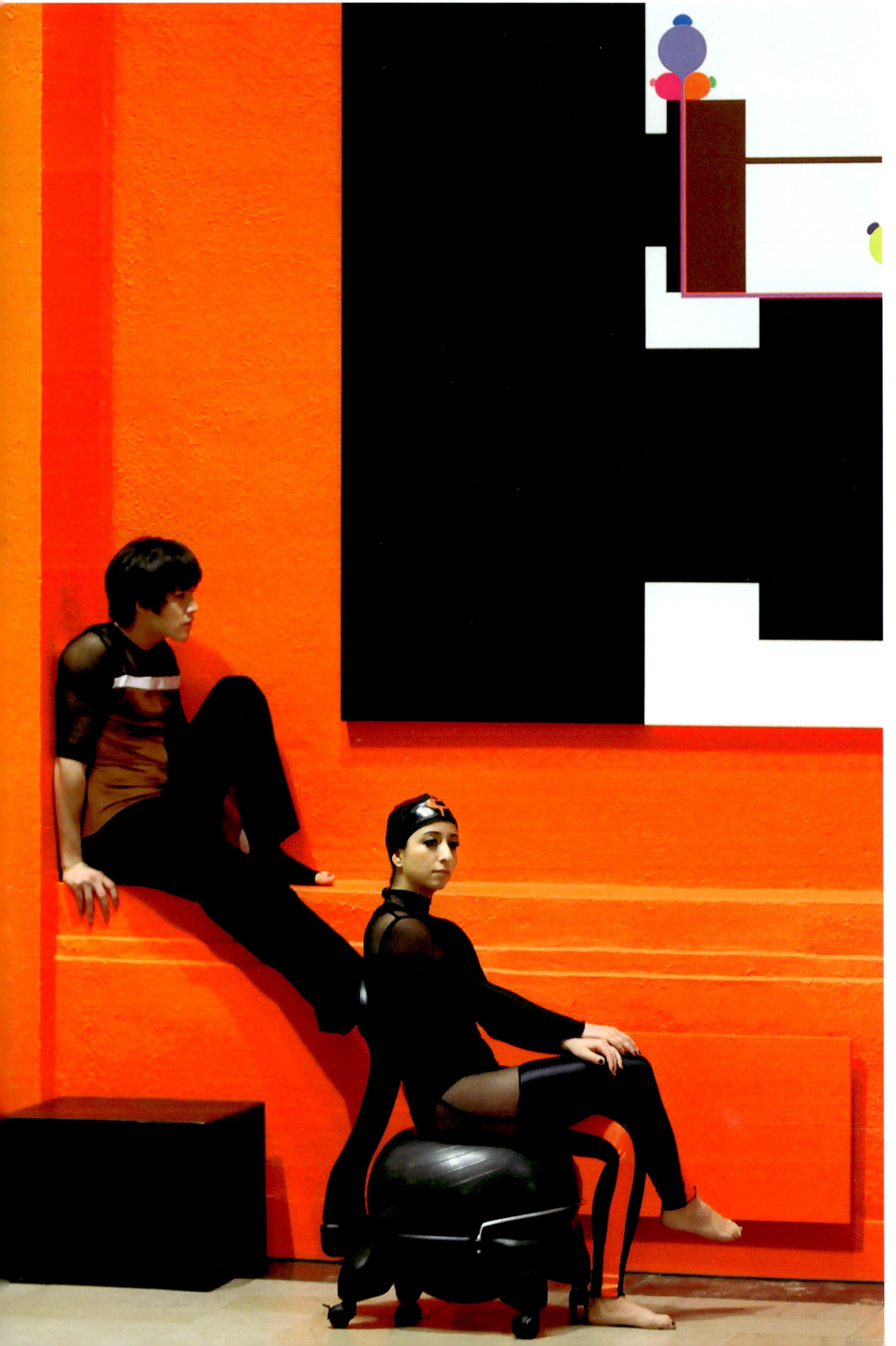

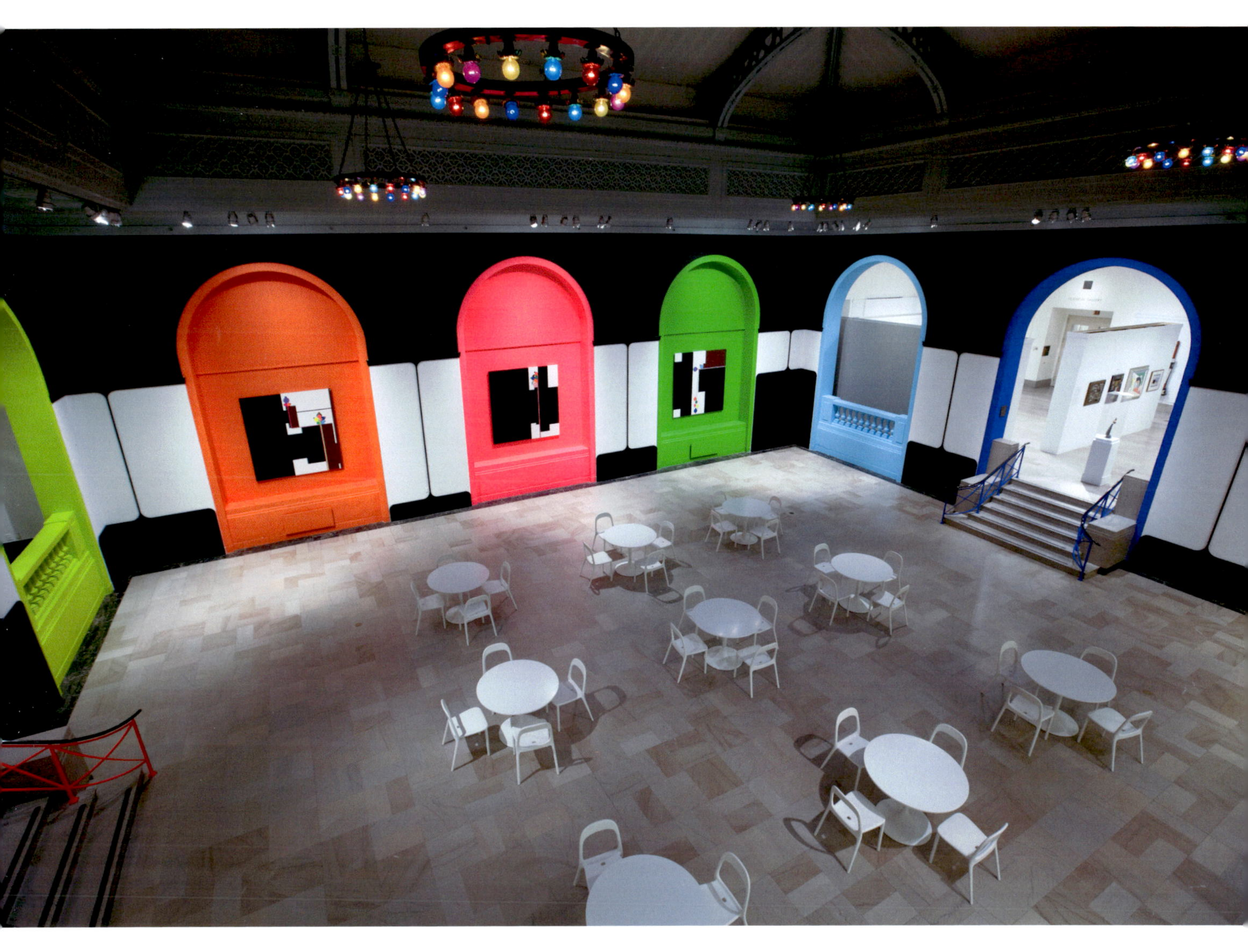

Paul Henry Ramirez, Engelhard Court featuring **CHUNK 17**, 2009; **CHUNK 16**, 2008; and **CHUNK 18**, 2009. Acrylic on canvas, 72 × 72 in. each
**CHUNK 18**, collection of the Newark Museum, New Jersey
Installation view: **BLACKOUT: A Centennial Commission by Paul Henry Ramirez**, Newark Museum, 2010
Wall painting, painted wood relief, furniture, and lighting, dimensions variable. Courtesy of the artist

Rex Ray, **Mylopronesta**, 2011. Oil, acrylic, and mixed media on linen, 55 × 55 in. Courtesy of the artist and Conduit Gallery, Dallas, Texas

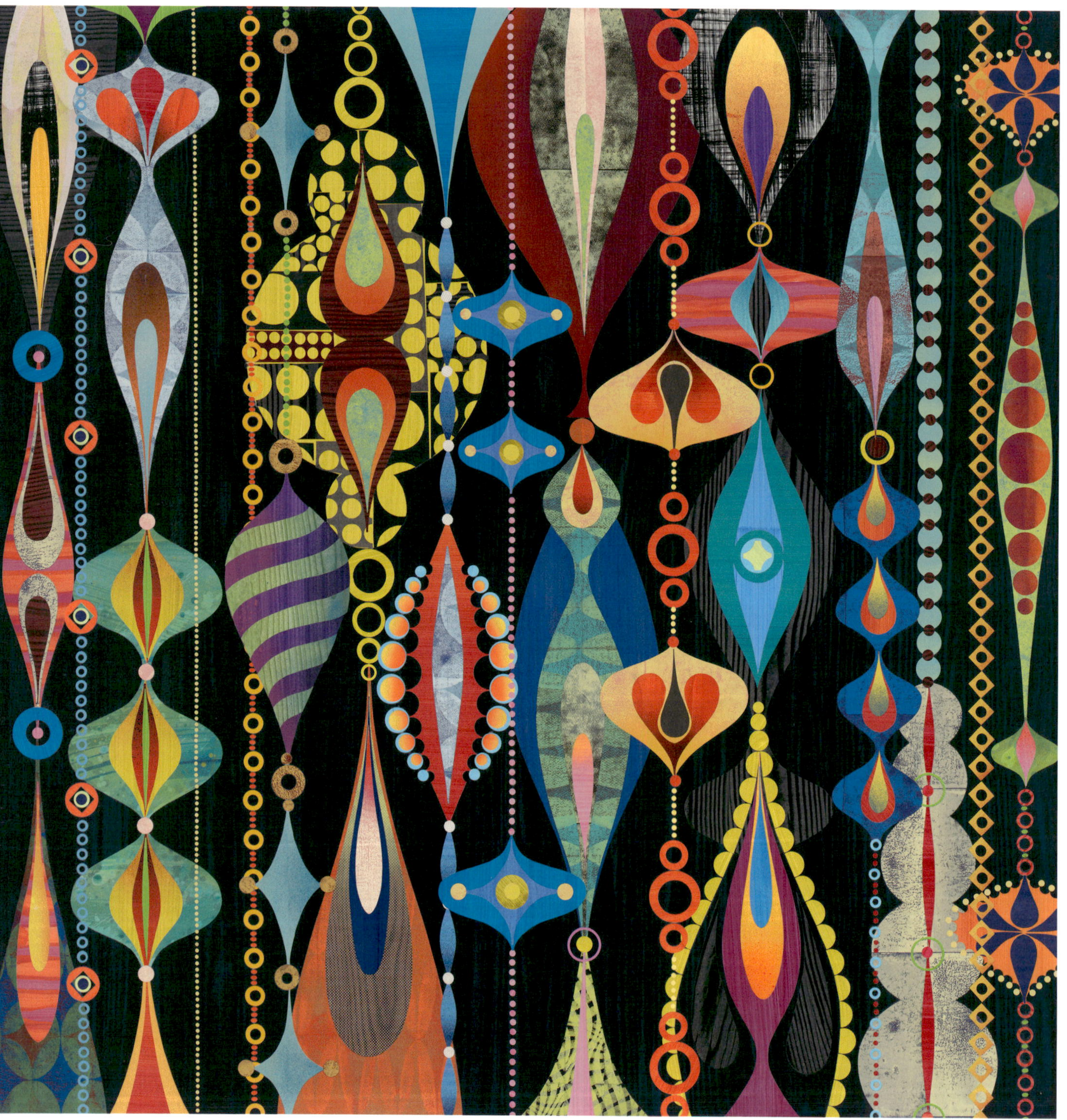

Rex Ray, **Lasalia**, 2007. Oil, acrylic, and mixed media on linen, 76 × 76 in. Courtesy of the artist and Conduit Gallery, Dallas, Texas

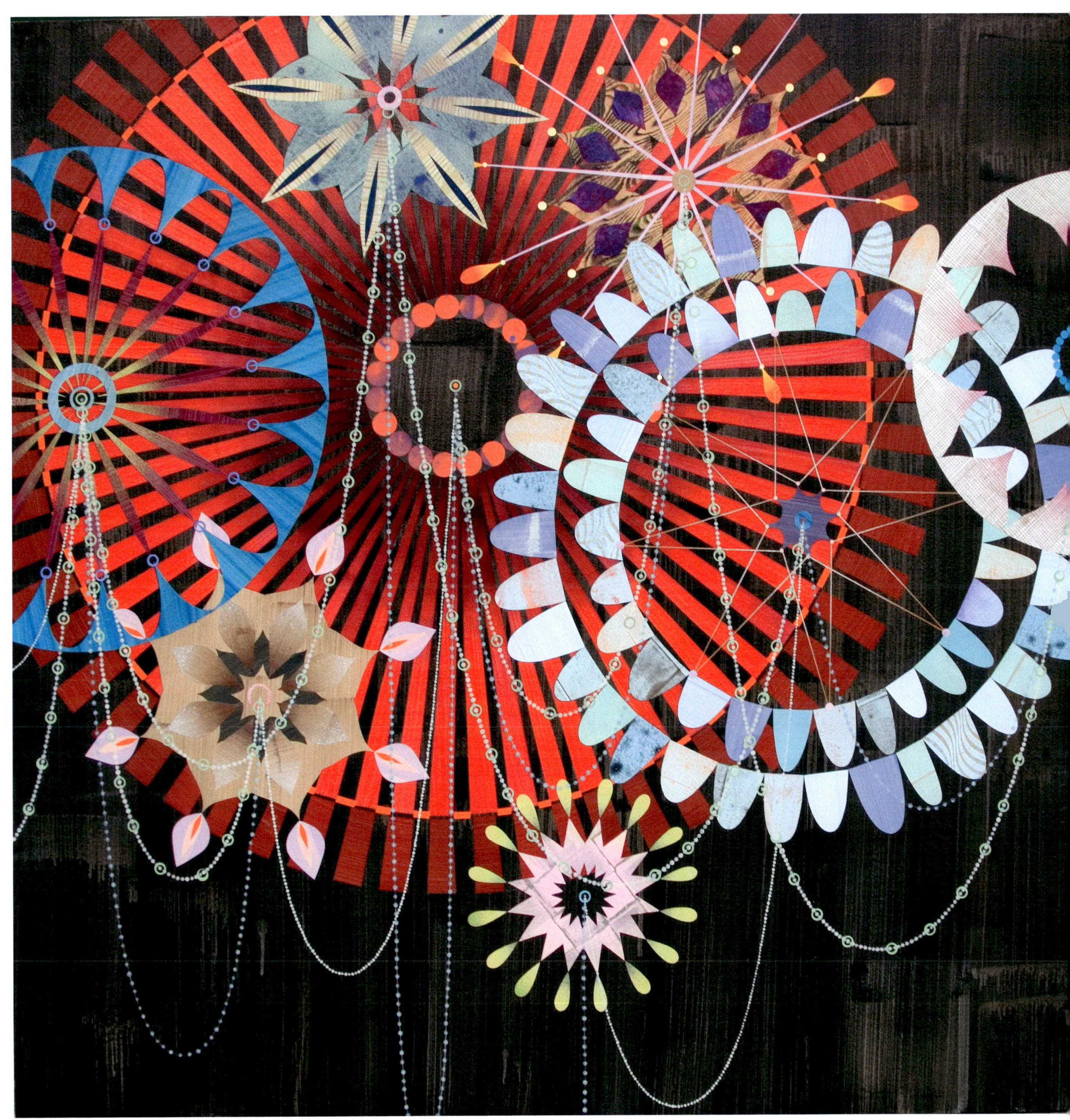

Rosalyn Schwartz, **Hannah and Her Brothers**, 2012. Mixed media on paper, 4 × 5 in. Courtesy of the artist

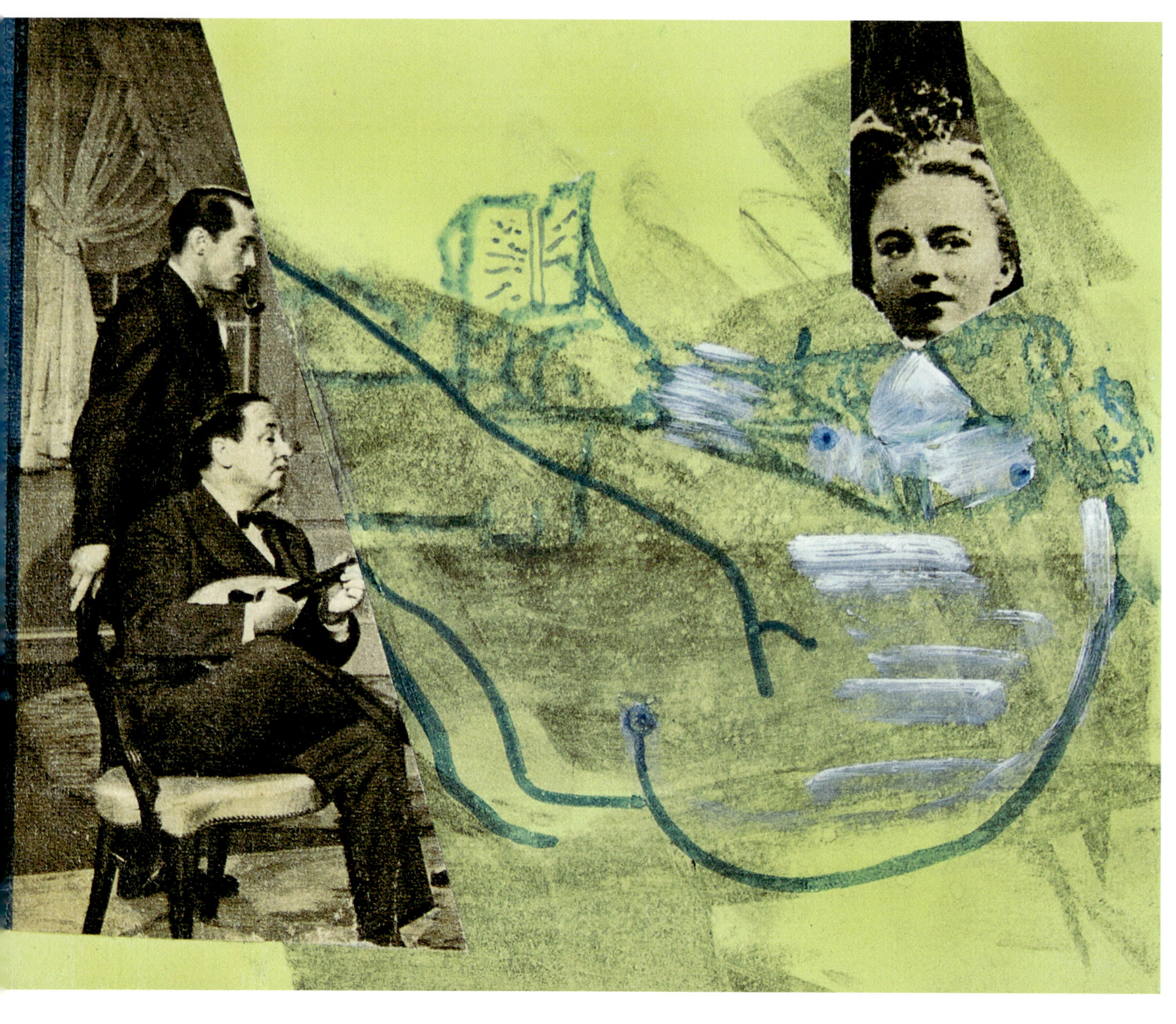

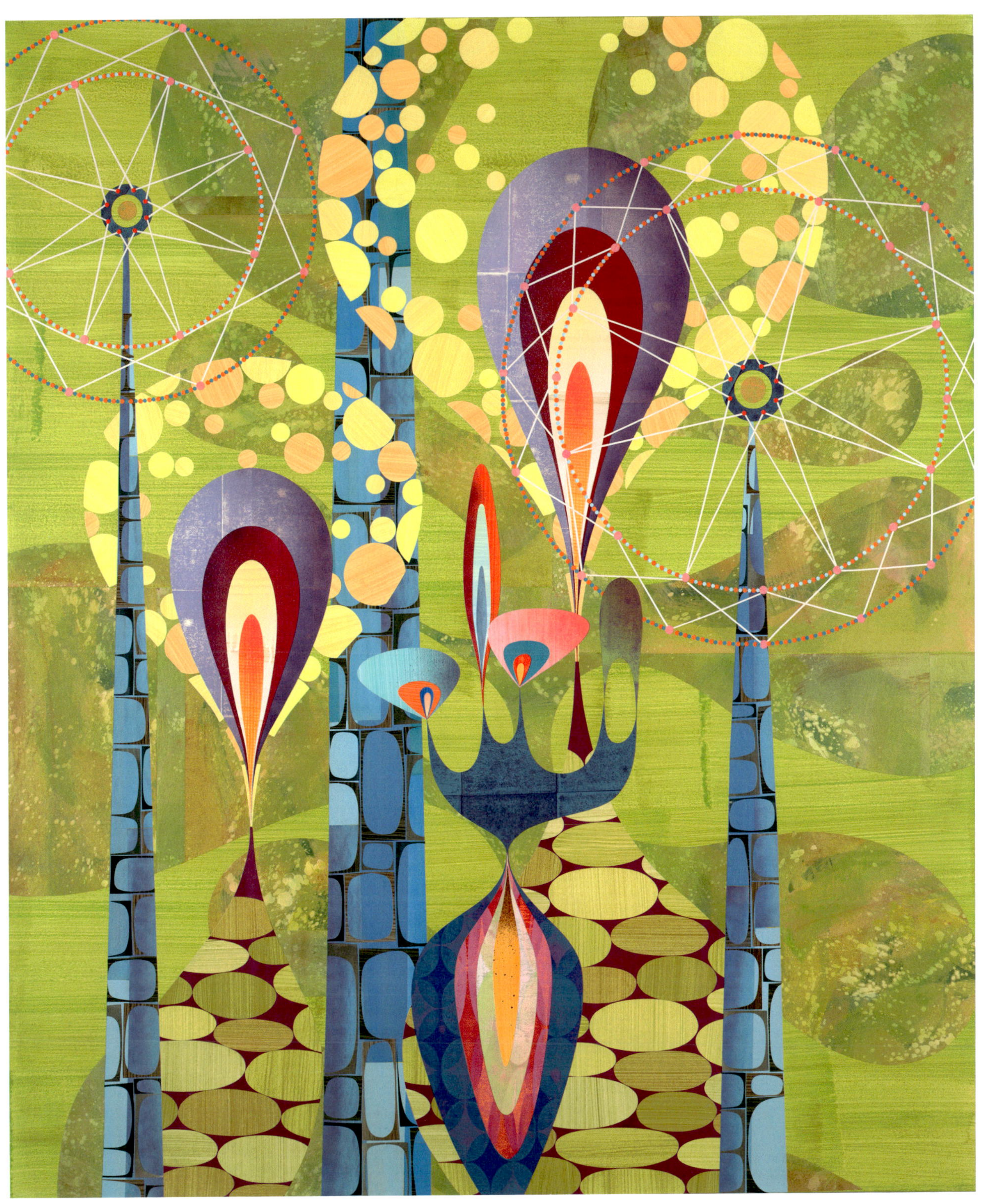

Rex Ray, **Erioderma**, 2009. Oil, acrylic, and mixed media on linen, 76 × 64 in. Courtesy of the artist and Turner Carroll Gallery, Santa Fe, New Mexico

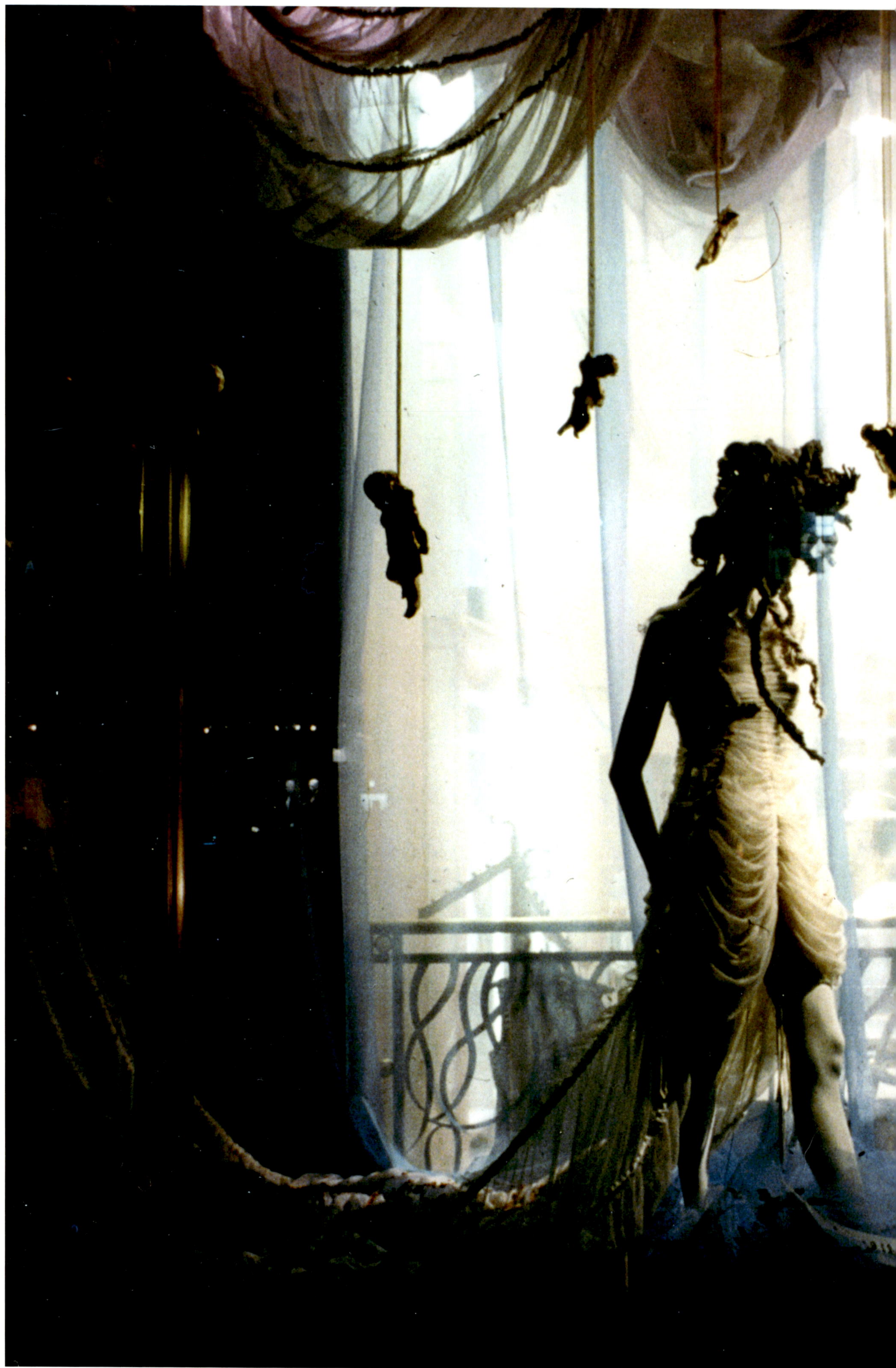

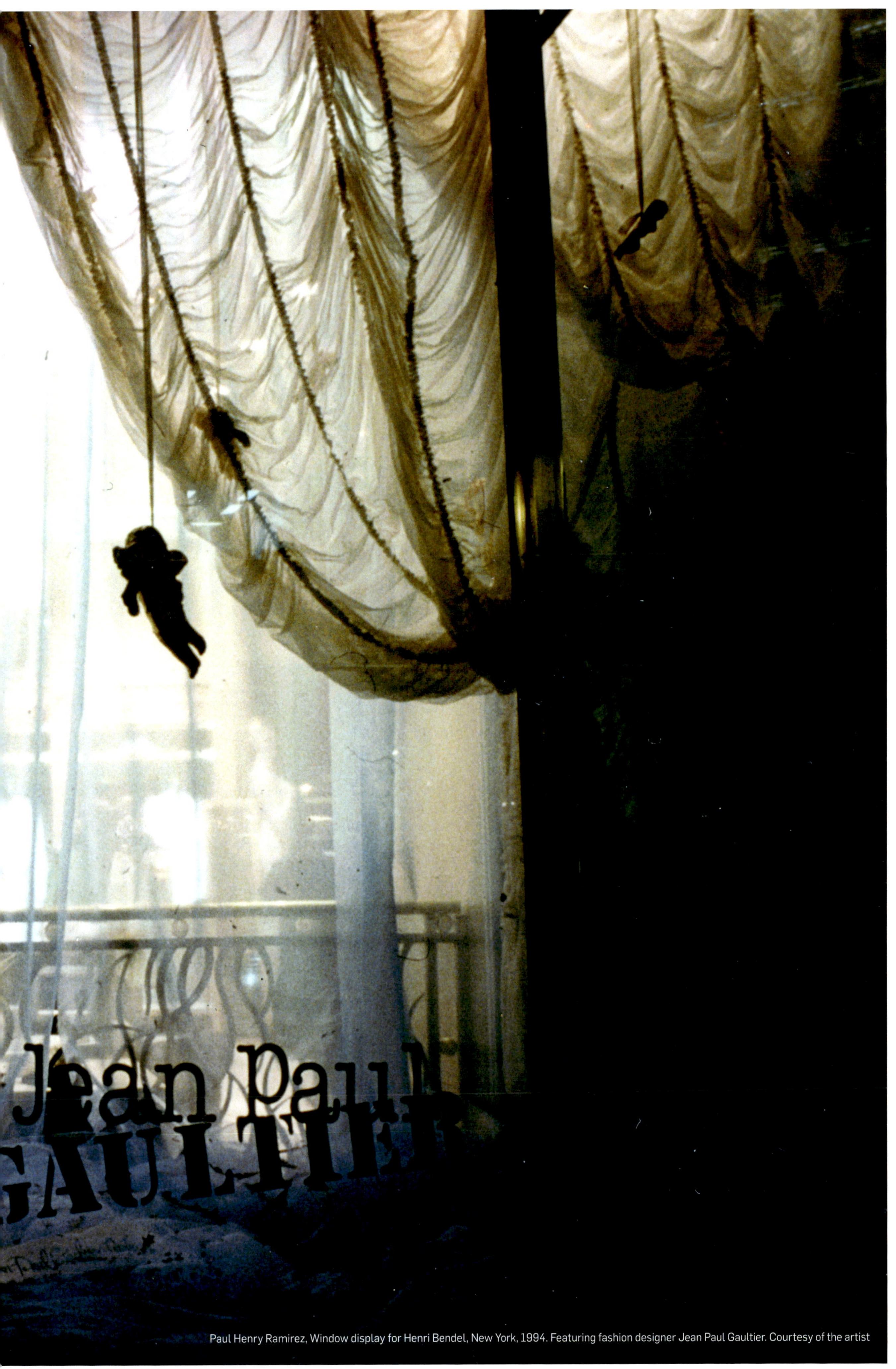


Paul Henry Ramirez, Window display for Henri Bendel, New York, 1994. Featuring fashion designer Jean Paul Gaultier. Courtesy of the artist

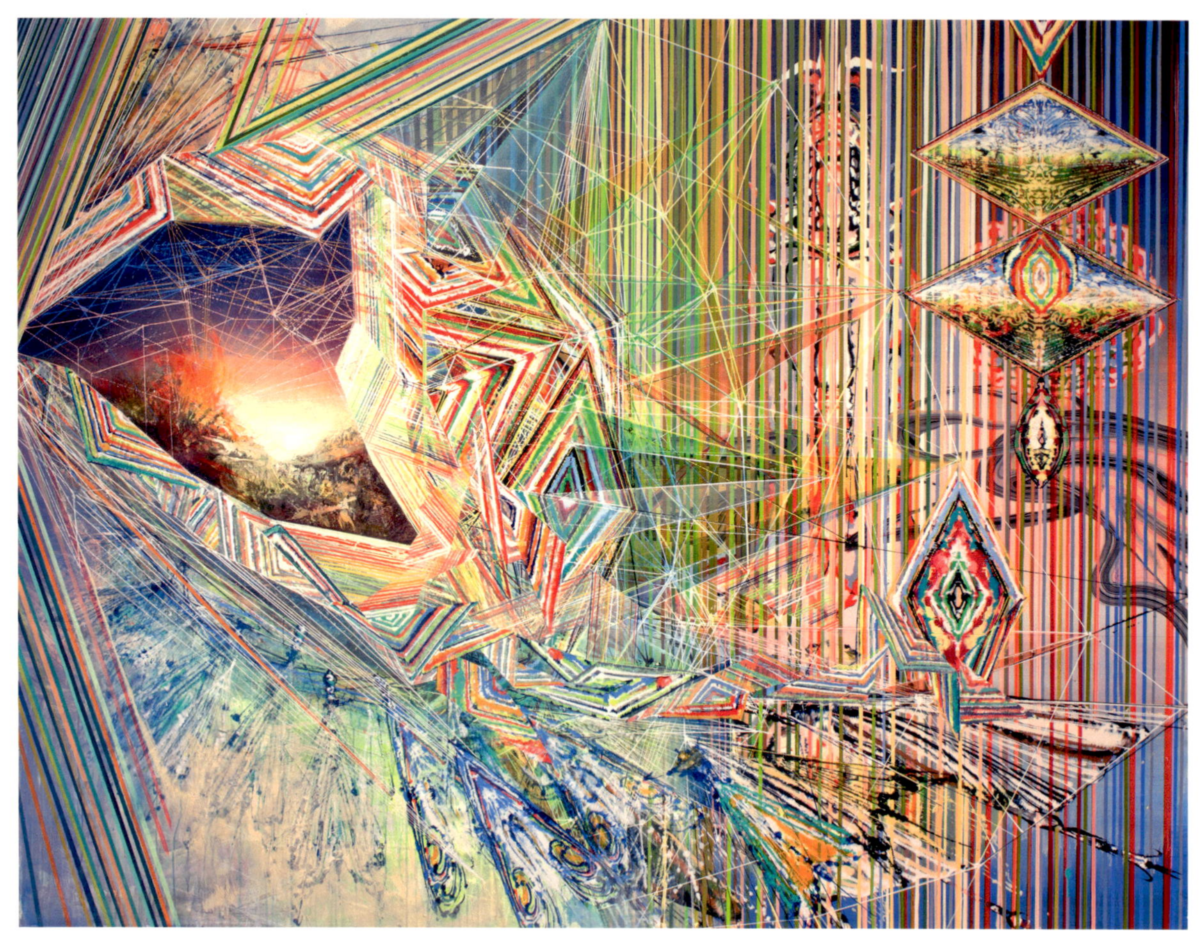

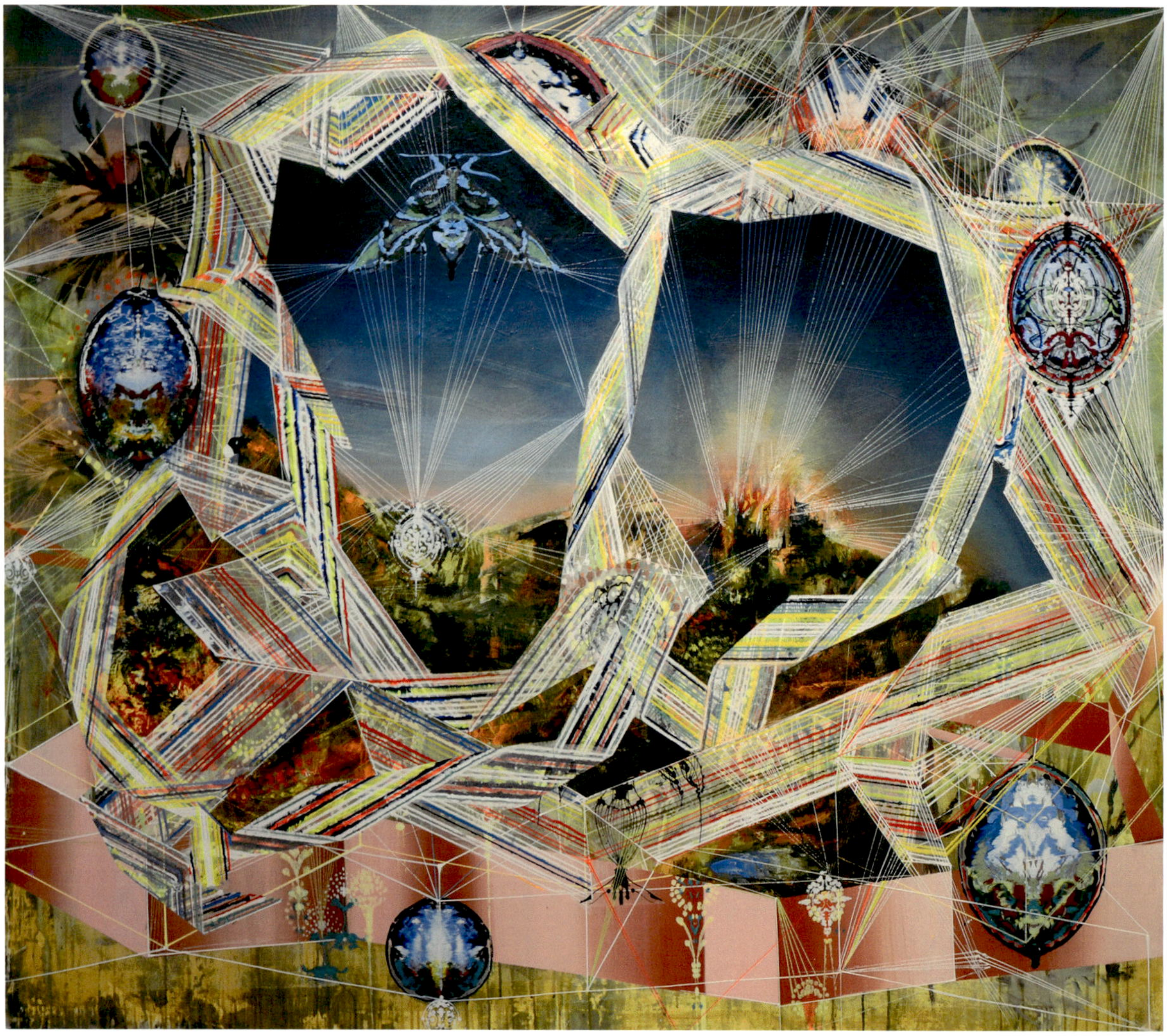

Susan Chrysler White, **Cradle**, 2010–13. Acrylic on canvas, 76 × 99 in. Courtesy of the artist

Susan Chrysler White, **Night Fires**, 2013. Acrylic on canvas, 68 × 74 in. Courtesy of the artist

Susan Chrysler White, Installation view: **Susan Chrysler White / Recent Work**, Sioux City Art Center, Iowa, 2013. Courtesy of the artist

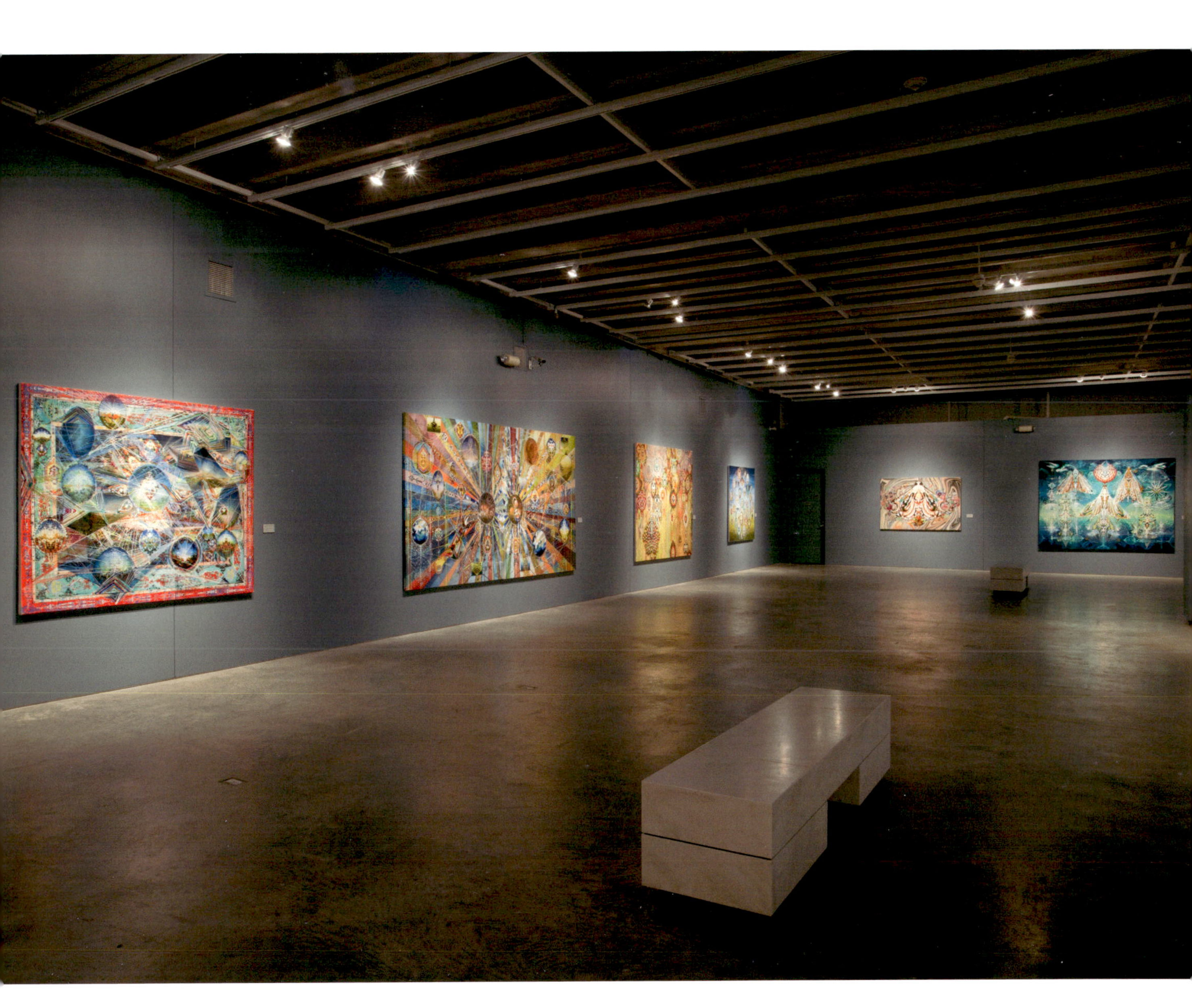

Rex Ray, **Pleopcialis**, 2010. Oil, acrylic, and mixed media on linen, 50 × 50 in. Courtesy of the artist and Gallery 16, San Francisco, California

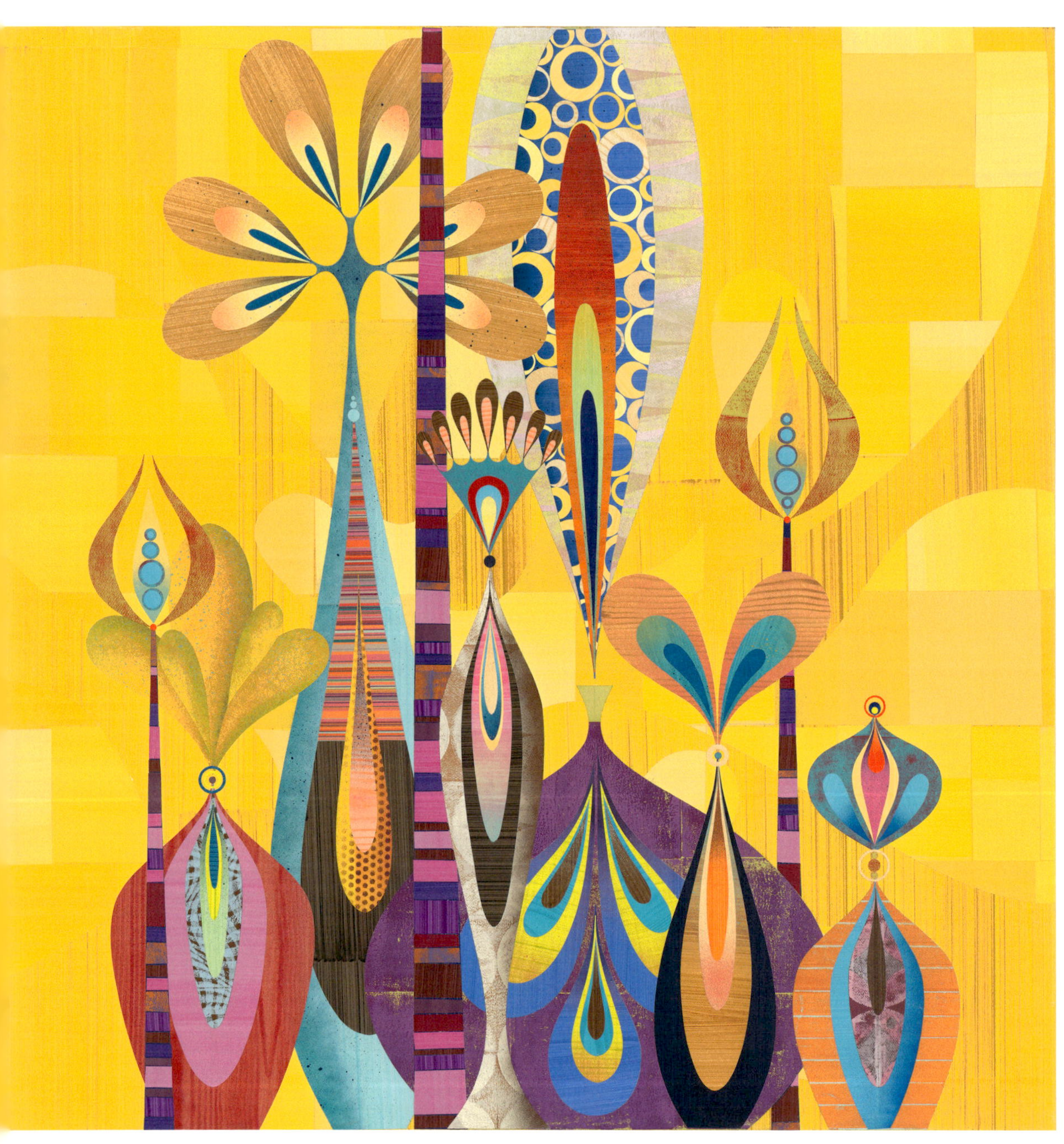

Paul Henry Ramirez, **Chunk 19**, 2009. Acrylic on canvas, 72 × 72 in. Courtesy of the artist

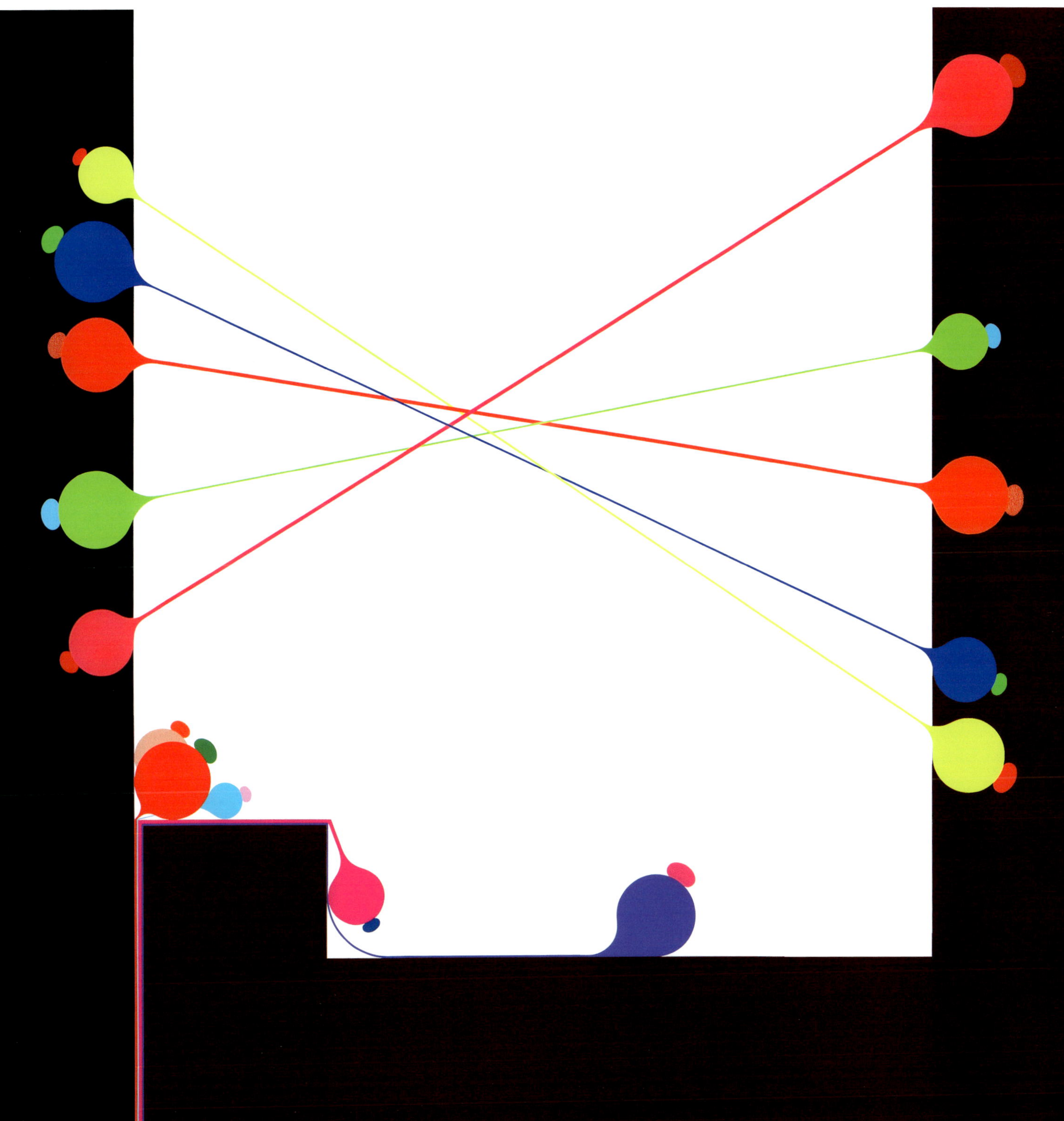

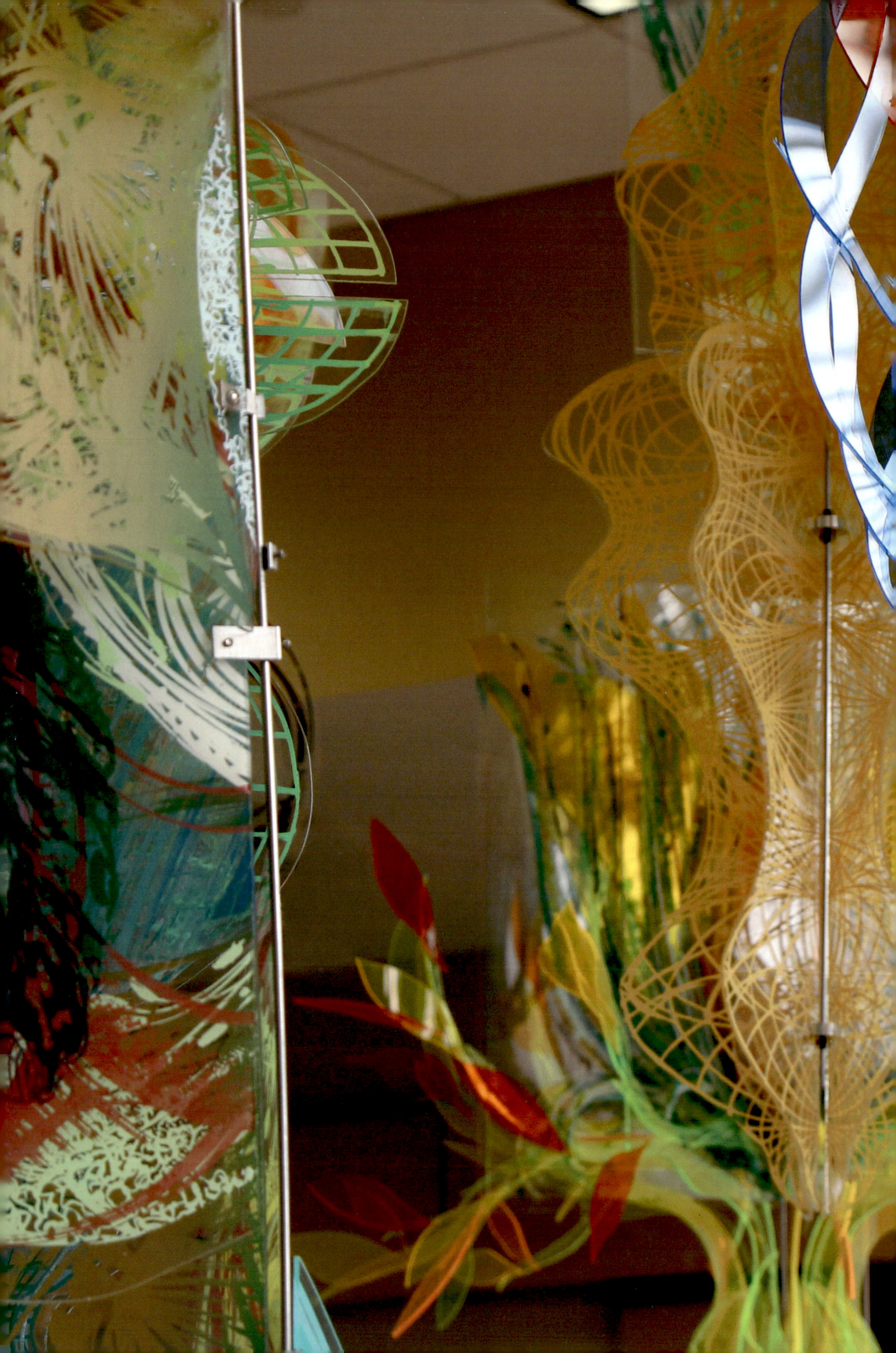

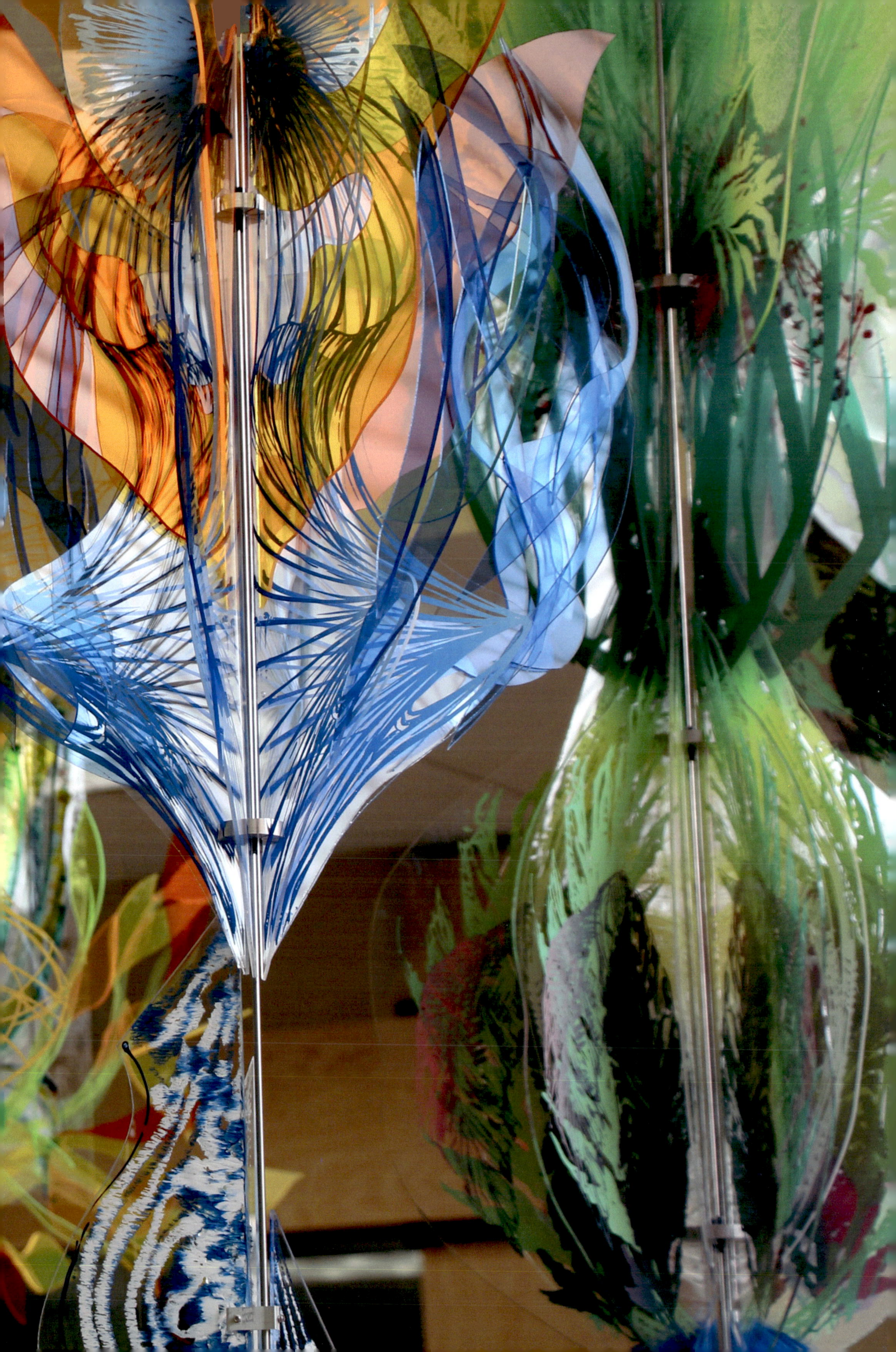

*Beauty Reigns: A Baroque Sensibility in Recent Painting* **provokes a number of thoughts, one of which is:** ***does beauty indeed reign?*** **The renegade critic Dave Hickey has been credited with retrieving beauty from the theoretical dustbin with the 1993 publication of** ***The Invisible Dragon: Four Essays on Beauty*****, predicting that beauty would be the defining aesthetic issue of the 1990s.**

# *Here's Lookin*

It was a challenge that other critics quickly accepted. Accordingly, beauty became topical, perhaps defining, the subject of heated debates, and a topic kicked about in innumerable lectures, panels, exhibitions, and publications, recalling the earlier "painting is dead" word-fights of the 1970s and 1980s.

Since the Enlightenment—or at least since Edmund Burke's *Philosophical Enquiry into the Origin of our Ideas of the Sublime and Beautiful* (1757) followed by Immanuel Kant's *Observations on the Feeling of the Beautiful and Sublime* (1764) and his *Critique of Judgment* (1790)—beauty and the sublime were the bedrock upon which aesthetics rested. As the twentieth century came and went, however, beauty was denounced and banished from the discourse. In a sweep of all that was considered retrograde, reactionary, and corrupt, it became the word none dared to speak. The 1970s and pluralism espoused an increasingly activist and socially engaged art, exploring gender, race, new technologies, and political and economic issues. Beauty was suspect, allied with the mechanisms of mass production and consumption, of capitalism and control, integral to the society of the spectacle. Eventually, the disdain for beauty culminated in the anti-aesthetics and cultural relativism of postmodernism.

Lilly Wei

# g at You

But too much might have been discarded, including pleasure. Certainly not everyone believed beauty, and with it formalism and retinal art, to be a pernicious tool wielded by an evil cabal for the subjugation of the masses. Those so-called masses, most uncooperatively, seem all too often to delight in beauty and in particular semblances of beauty that the art world often loathed, even as it claimed, in theory, that it sought a more democratized audience. But even worse, beauty, once synonymous with art, had come to seem bland, boring, of a certain age, and no longer desirable.

Postmodernism had signaled a preference for something less idealized, less academic and elitist, less bourgeois—although what could be more academic and elitist than some of its positions is hard to imagine. No more art as comfortable armchairs; no more beauty as truth. The results of this preference produced an aesthetic of the "abject" and the "end of pleasure," as Jeremy Gilbert-Rolfe states in *Beauty and the Contemporary Sublime* (1999). He argues for beauty but says that it is now to be found within the "delicate," the "fragile," and the "frivolous." All are associated with the feminine, all more or less disparaged in a culture founded on male precepts of authority. Because beauty declined to assure critics of its power, to assert that it had any power, it "scared people off" and "spooked the serious."

There also remains a puritanical streak in American culture that transforms all pleasures into guilt, a proclivity that suited the spiritual inclinations of modernism and its obsession with purity as well as the intellectual deconstructions and deliberations of postmodernism. But the mind should be intoxicated by every bouquet that art offers it, whether good or evil, by every issue that art is capable of raising, including the noxious and the scandalous. Art is not life; it is meant to entertain possibilities, to broaden and stimulate thought. After the previous culture wars, we might permit ourselves to revel in a little aesthetic ecstasy during what must by now be more heterodox, less culturally shackled times.

The contemporary art world has a short memory and an even shorter attention span. With the anti-aesthetic now in partial eclipse, beauty has been partially rehabilitated, and the critical penalty against it not so much rescinded as forgotten in the scrum of other issues clamoring for attention. As art reaches an increasingly diversified audience, it, too, adapts and diversifies. Indeed, art has been purely aesthetic only for brief intervals in its long history. It has been more often locked arm in arm with the political, the moral, and the religious, as inducement and inspiration.

Beauty, reclaiming some of its former roles, has been re-attached to the social, the political, and

Frank Stella (American, born 1936). ***Organdie***, 1998. Mixed media on canvas, 156 × 156 in. From the ***Imaginary Places*** series. Collection of the artist.



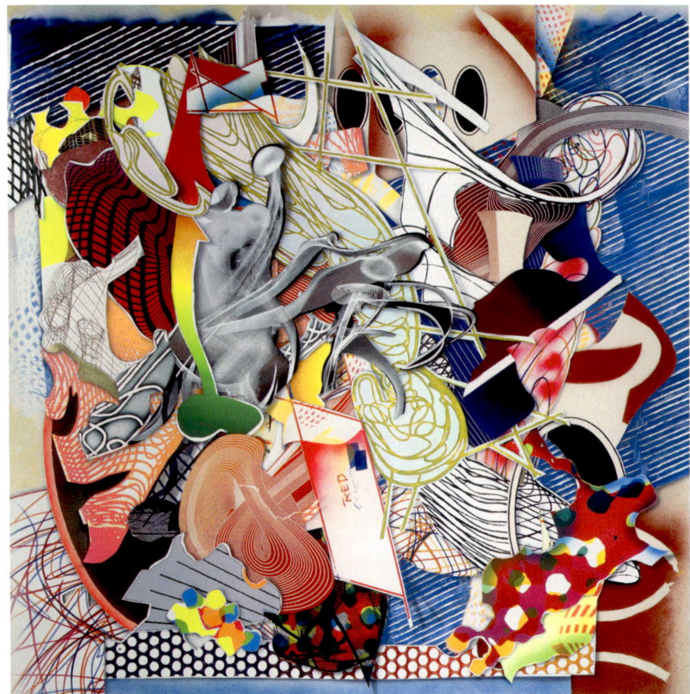


insofar as it still exists, the ineffable. To those considerations, we add the rather pressing considerations of the contemporary marketplace where beauty has pragmatic value: it sells. Beauty is not something we tire of; it is always sought, accompanied by a milling entourage of those who produce and present it, applaud and covet it.

Answering the first question, does beauty reign? —the answer is: sometimes. Assuming other guises, it is more inclusive in its designations, less condescending, less distant. Perhaps the one thing beauty is not is ironic, although the ironic might have its own beauty.

And what constitutes beauty now? What do we regard as beautiful? What was once thought objective, based on harmonious proportions and precise measurement, what was self-evident and absolute, is now undeniably less certain. Beauty is inconsistent, filtered through the subjective and a barrage of different cultural milieus, through intersecting, interacting global societies. Beauty, dusted off, rejuvenated, made more complex, is the richer for it.

Pleasure, we might agree, is what beauty should offer us, a pleasure that includes within it the perverse, even the transgressive. Within Paul McCarthy's debauched scenarios, for example, are passages of luminous beauty, made all the more so by the sharp contrast between the sordid and the ravishing. Beauty has been wrested, or rescued, from the old assumptions of what formalism was: from a code word for the reactionary, the discriminatory, and the racist; from aesthetic standards dictated by a dominant elite, as Harold Rosenberg once claimed. There is less need, I hope, to argue that art can have myriad functions and appearances. The pleasure that it gives should be capacious enough, cosmopolitan and canny enough to accommodate the needs and desires of today's audiences.

"Baroque" is the specific aesthetic of *Beauty Reigns: A Baroque Sensibility in Recent Painting* and it poses another question. What constitutes a baroque sensibility now? Baroque, historically, was not a term of praise, like the names of so many art movements. Derived, it is often said, from the contours of an irregular pearl, it connoted the rough, the imperfect, the irregular, and the anti-classical. Baroque departed from the order, serenity, and idealization of the Renaissance, itself modeled on Greek and Roman philosophies of the good, the beautiful, and the truthful, as understood by fifteenth- and sixteenth-century Italians.

Yet Baroque was exciting, dramatic, full of extreme movement and emotion, vividly colored. Its narratives were accessible, part of the offensive of the Counter Reformation in its attempt to stem the heresies of Luther and the other Protestant rebels. It offered the voluptuousness of the South against the mysticism of the North. It also offered illusions and lies.

The current baroque manifestations might be traced to the 1980s and 1990s, to artists such as Frank

Joseph Mallord William Turner (English, 1775–1851). ***Slave Ship (Slavers Throwing Overboard the Dead and Dying, Typhoon Coming On)***, 1840. Oil on canvas, 35¾ × 48¼ in. Museum of Fine Arts, Boston, Massachusetts; Henry Lillie Pierce Fund, 99.22. Photograph © 2014 Museum of Fine Arts, Boston.

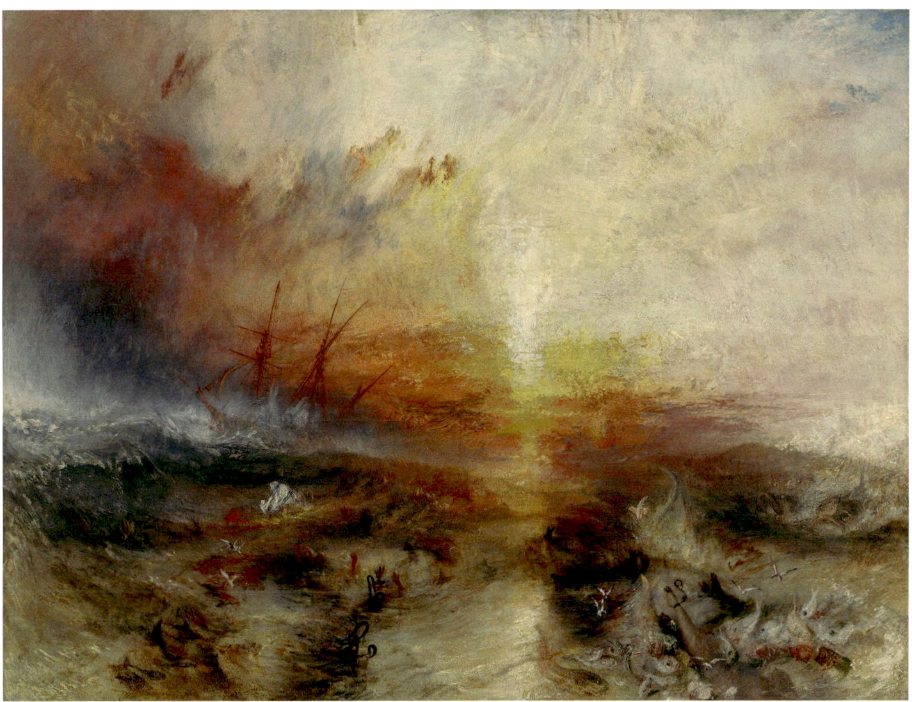

Stella, Frank Gehry, Jeff Koons, Julian Schnabel, Lisa Yuskavage, and Damien Hirst. It was a reaction against the overly conceptualized and conventional, introducing a more populist, less mediated interpretation emphasizing a syntax based on the vernacular. As in the original movement, anything defined as baroque luxuriates in theatricality and synesthesia, in fantasy and hyperbole, in the abundant use of materials and in overwhelming scale, in sensation and movement. It might be further characterized by traits of instability, mutability, and spectacle.

The sublime, on the other hand, has sometimes been considered the opposite of beauty and, in the traditional dichotomy, affiliated with the masculine, the immeasurable, the existential, and the profound. The Romantic sublime that once found its mirror in nature and in paintings by artists such as Caspar David Friedrich, J.M.W. Turner, and Thomas Cole was later summoned in earthworks by Robert Smithson, Michael Heizer, and Walter De Maria.

Today, the sublime appears to be migrating toward new technologies, cyberspace and virtual reality, toward mass media and installations. Technology, of late, has produced some of the most persuasive avatars of the sublime. The terror, awe, and exaltation that nature once inspired (and still does) can now be mimed through technical means. Olafur Eliasson's astonishing imitation of the sun in his *weather project* at Tate Modern's Turbine Hall in 2003 was a superb instance of the contemporary sublime. So was James Turrell's transformation of the Guggenheim's atrium during the summer of 2013. Less high-tech but equally poetic was the sprawling, enigmatic, muddied ruin of an outdoor installation by Pierre Huyghe at Documenta 13 in 2012.

It seems harder for painting to express the sublime, after we have seen what new technologies can summon up at a click of a mouse. But painting, the more or less hand-made, still has its allure, its very specific beauty. As it moves outside its prescribed stance of disinterestedness and becomes engaged, it assumes a more complex role in the world.

Social content and beauty in art are not mutually exclusive and together can tease out a deeper, detailed, more nuanced pleasure. *Guernica* (1937), after all, provides as much, if not more, aesthetic gratification as it does political agency. Arthur Danto, in his book, *The Abuse of Beauty*, ends with the notion that beauty is an option for art but a necessity for life "as we would want to live it."

What does beauty promise us in *Beauty Reigns*? It promises first and foremost a sumptuous giddiness of imagery with paintings that look so juicy that if we squeezed them, color might drip out. Their baroque tendencies are a tribute to abundance, to the distinctive styles of thirteen artists, inspired by many different sources, intents, and narratives. These artists are also connected by a sense of beauty that is not about impossible perfection but finds its bliss in the idiosyncratic, in the charisma and egalitarianism of

Robert Smithson (American, 1938–1973). ***Spiral Jetty***, 1970. Mud, salt crystals, rocks, and water. 1500 ft. long and 15 ft. wide. Great Salt Lake, Utah. DIA Center for the Arts, New York.

Courtesy of James Cohan Gallery, New York/Shanghai.
Photograph by Gianfranco Gorgoni.

Olafur Eliasson (Danish-Icelandic, born 1967). ***The weather project***, 2003. Mono-frequency lights, projection foil, haze machines, mirror foil, aluminium, and scaffolding, $87\frac{5}{8} \times 73\frac{3}{16} \times 509\frac{13}{16}$ ft.
Installation view: Turbine Hall, Tate Modern, London, Great Britain.
Courtesy of the artist; neugerriemschneider, Berlin; and Tanya Bonakdar Gallery, New York.
Photograph courtesy of Studio Olafur Eliasson.


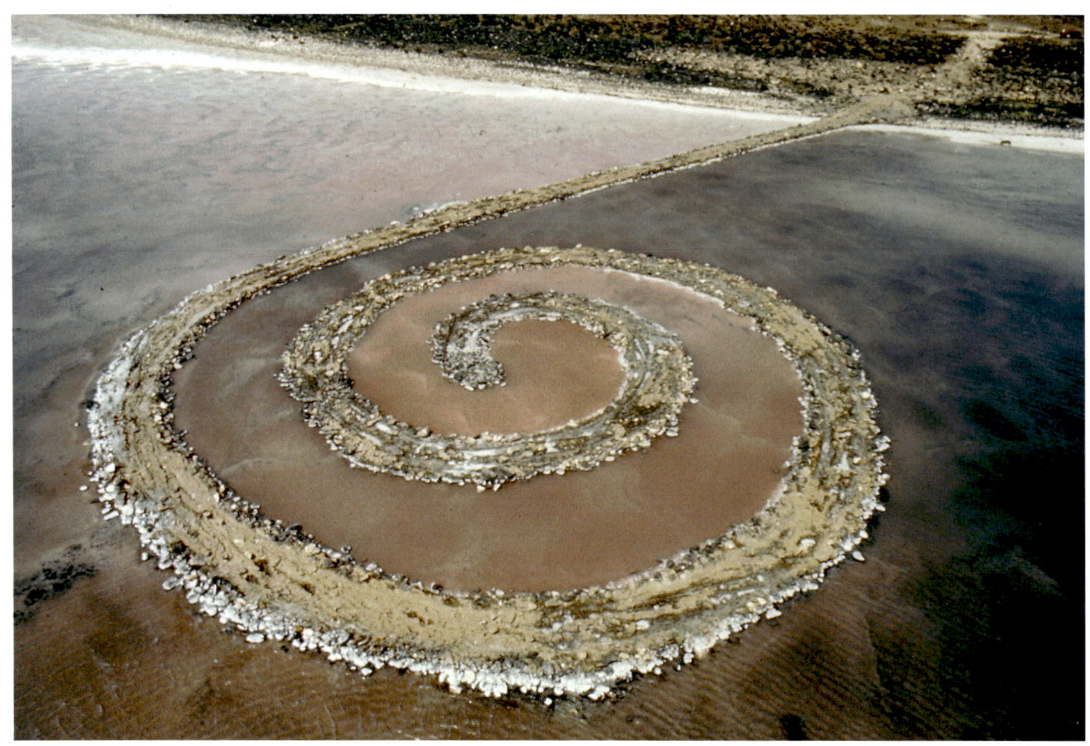

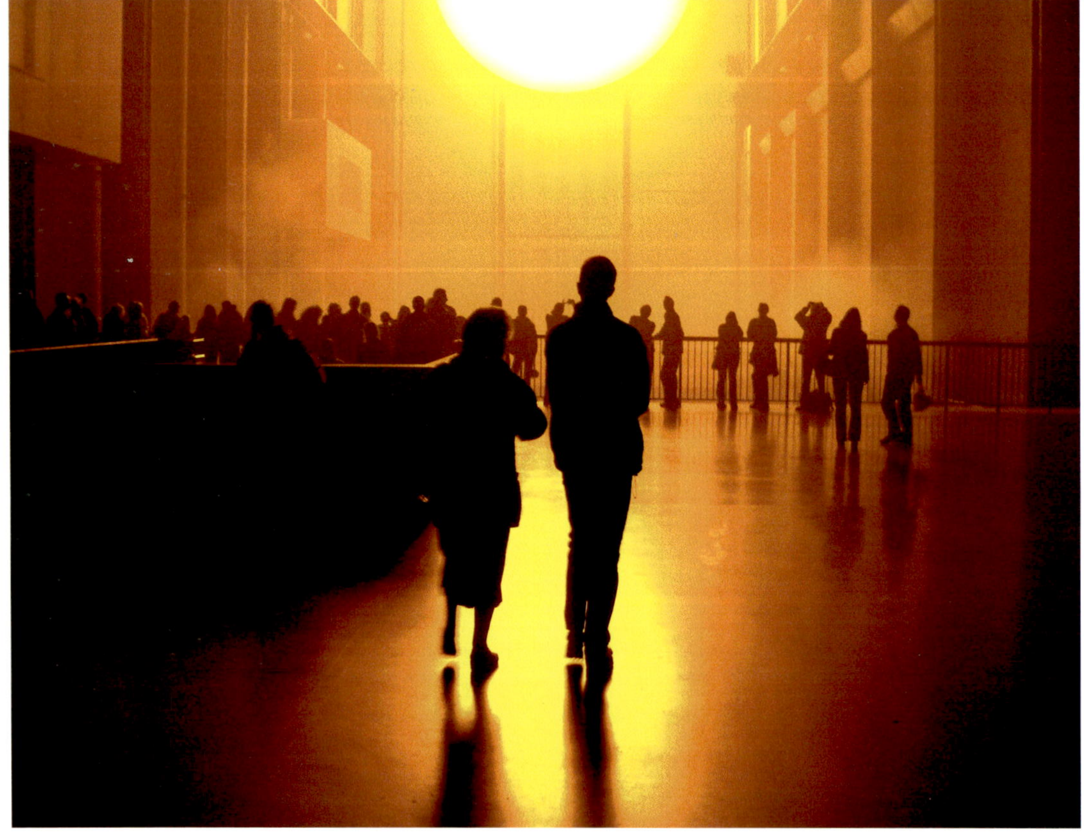

Beatriz Milhazes. **Popeye**, 2008. Acrylic on canvas, 78¾ × 54¾ in.
Courtesy of the artist and James Cohan Gallery, New York.

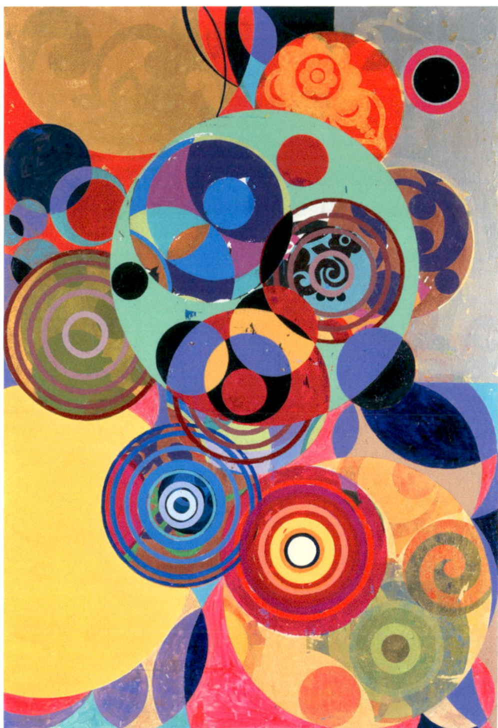

Kamrooz Aram. ***Generation After Generation, Revolution After Revelation*** (detail), 2010. Oil on canvas, 108 × 60 in.
Courtesy of the artist and Green Art Gallery, Dubai, United Arab Emirates.

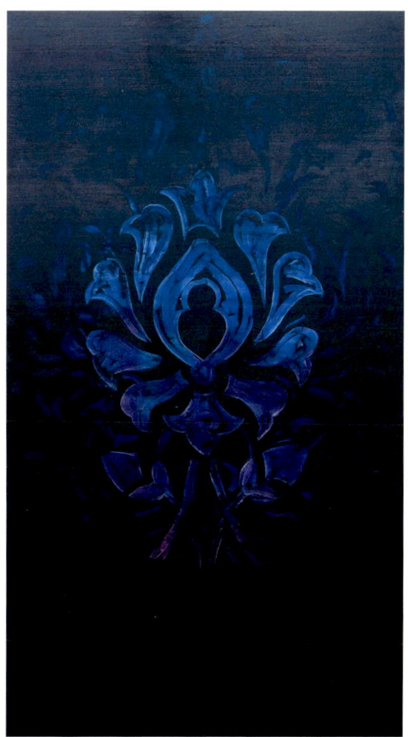

pop imagery, and a broader-based, less buttoned-up, less categorical picture of reality in which design, architecture, and the decorative arts make a significant contribution.

With the exception of Beatriz Milhazes, these artists currently work in the United States although several were born elsewhere. For the most part, they offer up seemingly light-hearted dissections of American culture bounced off other aesthetic heritages. Content is pegged to a fluid, globally sourced lexicon of images, mapping multiple visual systems that startle us into delight. I say seemingly light-hearted because the underside of spectacle is problematical, and the narratives presented here are often intentionally difficult to pin down and not without critical intent.

They are often not narratives at all but liminal images that, on the one hand, convey a tumbled, extravagant zest for life, and on the other, a disquieting panorama of the course of empire gone amok. They are all meticulously executed, tightly controlled, densely focused. In the bonanza of its offerings, *Beauty Reigns* also reexamines the decorative impulse and hails design as its "significant other."

It is an homage to craft as much as concept that, detail by detail, transforms color, shape, repetition, and rhythm into the pleasurable, ravishing, unembarrassed, unrepentant embodiments of beauty. In *The Picture of Dorian Gray* (1890), Oscar Wilde's protagonist said "It is only shallow people who do not judge by appearances. The true mystery of the world is the visible, not the invisible."

These thirteen artists might be considered abstract artists or they might not, a designation that either way no longer stirs passions, part of the contemporary urge to combine, proliferate, complicate, and innovate.

Kamrooz Aram is known for multiple bodies of work from drawings, paintings, and collages to mixed-media installations. Born in Iran but raised in America, his dual heritage is reflected in the richness of his visual vocabulary, inspired by the traditional patterns and decorative motifs of the Middle East in confrontation with the tropes of Western modernism and contemporary art. Aram's use of resplendent ornamentation and brilliant bursts of color is visually seductive as well as critically acute, challenging the problematical distinctions between East and West and investigating the different readings and complex functions of motifs across cultures, influenced by Edward Said's seminal discourse on Orientalism. Aram's images highlight and question how identities are constructed and culture transmitted, how tradition intersects with the present.

Jiha Moon is another artist who is bicultural, born in South Korea and based in Atlanta. Her very colorful, very lyrical paintings are characterized by

Jiha Moon. ***Migration***, 2011. Ink, acrylic, hanji paper, embroidery patches, and spray paint on hanji paper, 42 × 62 in.
Courtesy of the artist and RYAN LEE, New York.

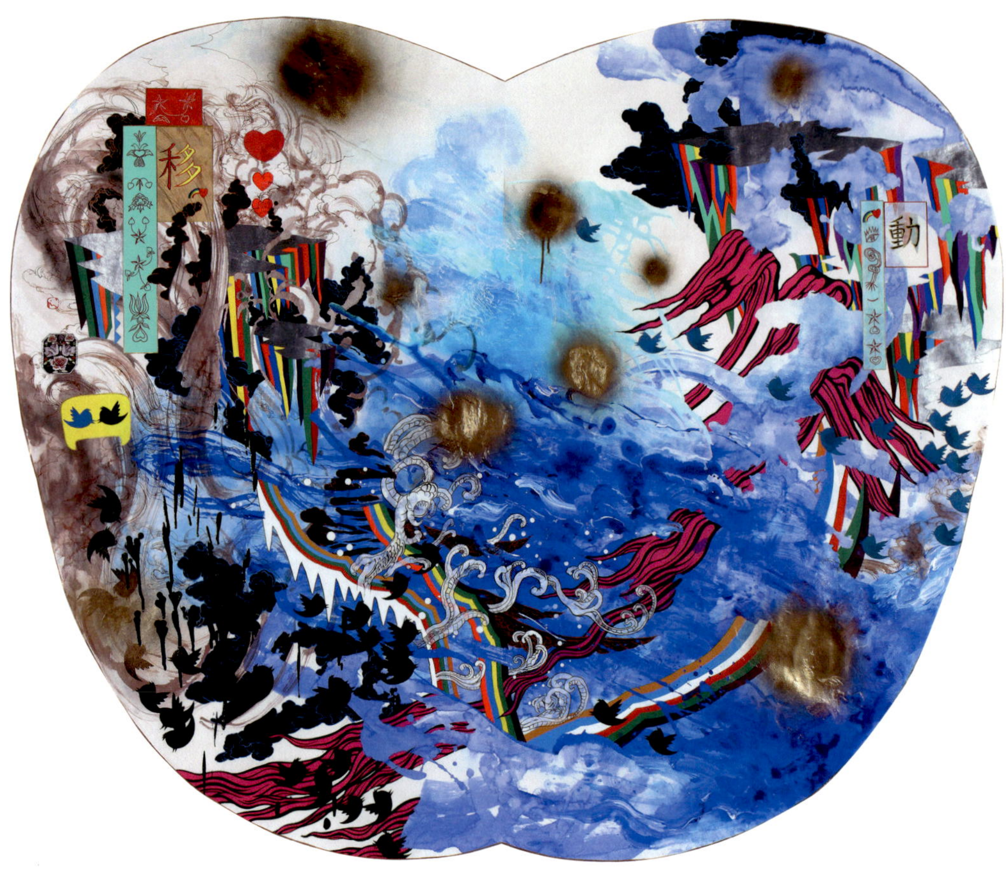


lush brushstrokes anchored by expert drawing and delicate traceries, by the abstract and the figurative. The result is both beautiful and abject, their seduction quotient enhanced by contrast and by the tension of opposition. Her sources, too, are varied: Baroque or Buddhist clouds drift by, as well as clusters of lines and shapes that recall Tang dynasty landscapes or European surrealism, emoji and Internet icons, Lewis Carroll's Alice, and folk art of all kinds.

It is Moon's version of cross-pollination of cultures, disciplines, and art-historical periods, although she avoids pop images that have become too much of a cliché. She works primarily on *hanji*, a Korean mulberry paper, and at times places inserts to extend the picture plane. She also collages fabrics, embroidery, etchings, and woodblock prints into her paintings, analogous to cut-and-paste computer commands and the importation of images from the web. She crams information into her imagined realm, as packed as a populous Asian city.

Rex Ray, Fausto Fernandez, and Jose Alvarez (D.O.P.A.), the first two Americans and based in California, and the third from Venezuela and based in Fort Lauderdale, Florida, are equally extravagant in terms of materials and sources. Ray emphasizes graphic design and, like Moon, incorporates collage and mixed media. His brilliantly colored, geometrically based abstract forms are built up to create jeweled fantasias of enormous appeal. Fernandez, another mixed media and collage artist who also works frequently on public art projects, constructs his intricate paintings from what he calls "instructional materials" such as maps, sewing patterns, and architectural blueprints that are the schematics of lived life and its intertwined and proliferating connections. Alvarez, whose delightful, delicate images often float in front of a measureless ground, which he further explores in his videos, also plays with a wide array of matter such as mica, enamel, feathers, porcupine quills, sequins, organdy, and other materials. His sources are astrophysics, science fiction, mathematical configurations, anthropology, and other sciences.

Admired for her spirited, brilliantly colored paintings, Brazilian artist Beatriz Milhazes has been greatly influenced by P&D (Pattern and Decoration), modernist abstraction, and the art of her native country. Captivatingly bold, repetitive, rhythmic, and hedonistic, the distressed look of her surfaces is in part

Rex Ray. ***Untitled*** (detail), 2009. Oil, acrylic, and mixed media on linen, 76 × 76 in.
Courtesy of the artist.

Jose Alvarez (D.O.P.A.). ***The Promise Land***, 2013. Acrylic, ink, colored pencil, feathers, quills, crystals, flocking, and mica with resin on wood panel, 90 × 72 in.
Collection of Beth Rudin DeWoody. Courtesy of the artist and Gavlak Gallery, Palm Beach, Florida.

Fausto Fernandez. ***Broken Down and Simplified***, 2012. Collage, acrylic, and spray paint on canvas, 84 × 48 in.
Courtesy of the artist.

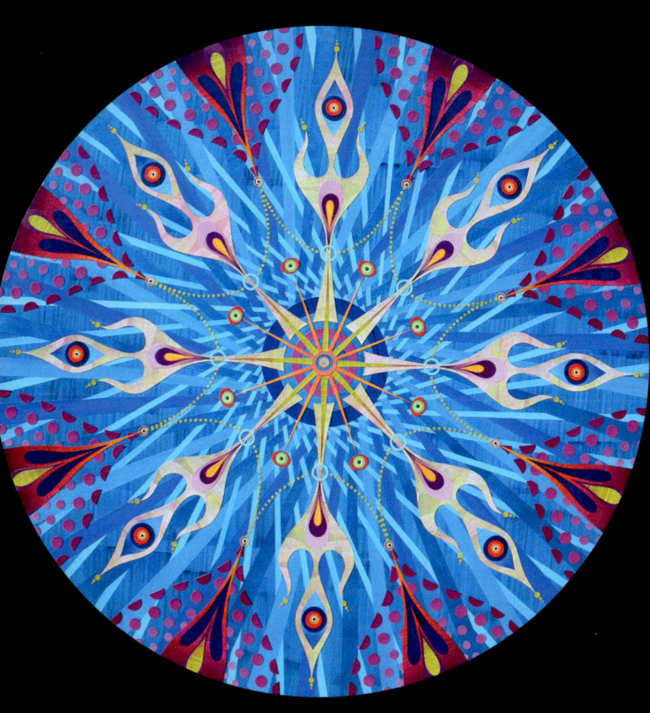

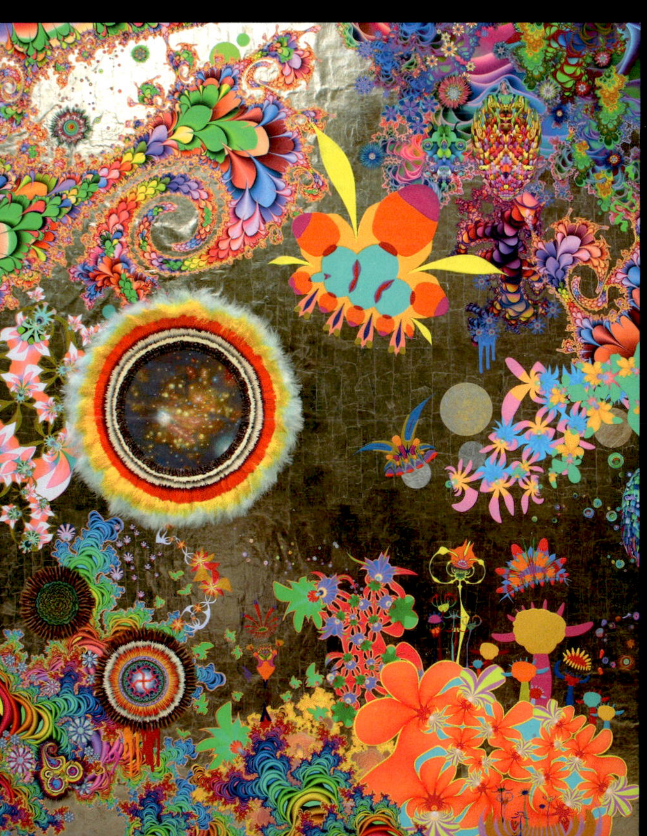

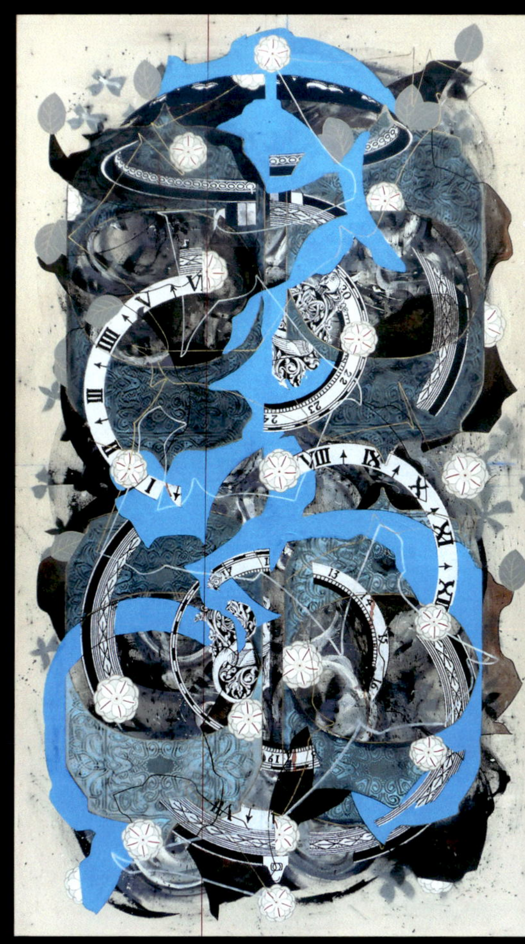

Nancy Lorenz. **Custom screen for Chanel**, New Bond Street, London, Great Britain, 2013. Moon gold leaf, white gold leaf, mother-of-pearl, and lacquer on panels, 122⅝ × 330⅜ in.
Courtesy of the artist and Peter Marino Architect, New York.

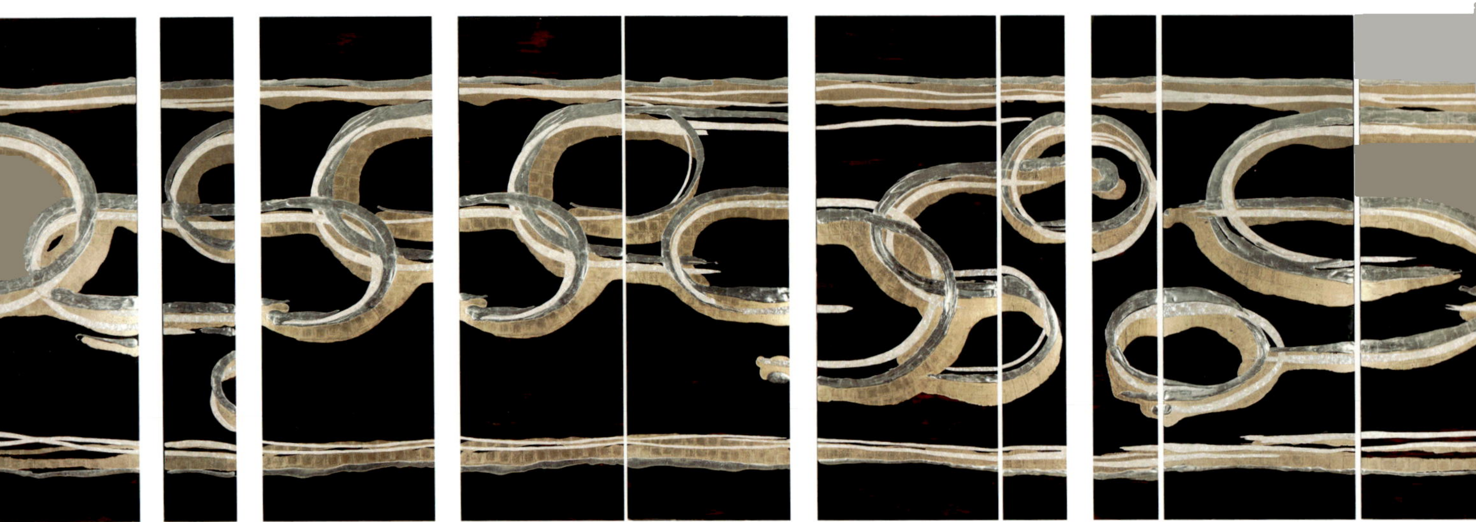

created by collage, pigment, and her signature technique of decalcomania in which she paints on sheets of plastic, glues them to the surface of her paintings, and then rips them off. Milhazes's work owes much to the legacy of *tropicália*, a widespread Brazilian movement that pervaded all forms of the country's creative endeavors in the 1960s, from art to theater to poetry, and especially music.

*Tropicália* forged an alliance between high and low, between popular culture, including the folkloric, and the avant-garde, reconciling traditional Brazilian artistic forms and international modernism. In the course of that seminal decade in Brazil, abstraction became increasingly political, its ostensibly neutral vocabulary an encryption protesting the repressive policies of Latin America's military dictatorships. Non-objective abstraction was linked to the progressive, opposing mainstream political and cultural establishments, a language that vaulted national borders, its legacy still reverberant.

Nancy Lorenz, based in New York, is also not averse to cultural synthesis. She, however, reverses the direction of the influence from East to West, combining modernist styles with a deep love for traditional Japanese art and craftsmanship. She lived in Tokyo for five years as a teenager and was smitten with the country, its culture, its ancient rituals, and its refinement. Beauty in Japan was elegant, subtle, and prized. There was little difference between fine arts and design; a gilded screen was as revered as a painted hanging scroll.

Lorenz found the Japanese pride in execution profoundly sympathetic, and, combining it with the grand gestures of Abstract Expressionism, developed a signature style executed in mother-of-pearl inlay, lacquer, and gold leaf. Her gleaming vision is far from abject, far from the street detritus so critical to so much contemporary art. Her vision of the world is more rarefied and courtly, where a canonical beauty is not questioned.

Also based in Manhattan, Ryan McGinness's projects are another exemplar of hybridization, most emphatically that of cross-breeding fine arts with the logos and imagery of commerce, pillaging art history as well as advertising and design. From this, he shapes a flamboyant, assertive, constantly morphing and jubilant language of pictograms—we might say a kind of graphic logorrhea that could be called "designer Dada," with more than a vestige of the surreal.

His productions increasingly sophisticated, McGinness, another cosmopolite of the global market and its signs, has often downplayed the presence of an embedded narrative in his works. He has said that he aspires to beauty, but beyond the first impression of the rich, vividly colored surfaces that suggest tapestries, wallpaper, signs, posters, and billboards of mass-market brands, his specific figures are not always pretty, he has said. Nor are they meant to be pretty.

Ryan McGinness. ***Submit to the Universe***, 2008. Acrylic on canvas, 96 × 96 in. Private collection.
Courtesy of Ryan McGinness Studios, Inc./Art Resource, NY.


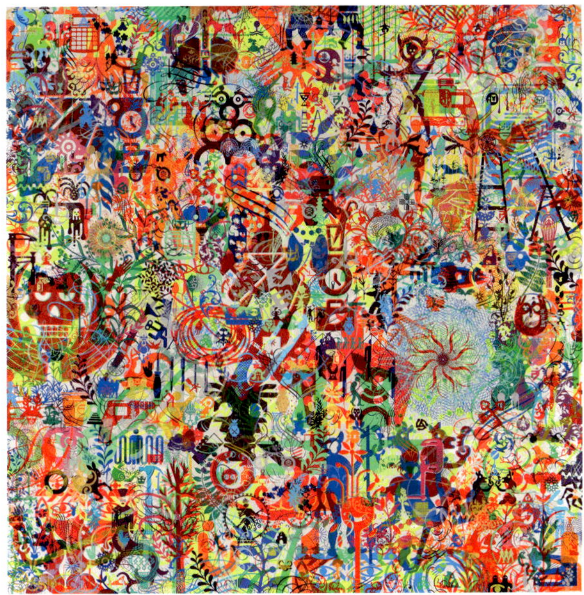

Annette Davidek. ***Untitled***, 2004. Oil on birch panel, 38 × 32 in.
Courtesy of the artist and Littlejohn Contemporary, New York.

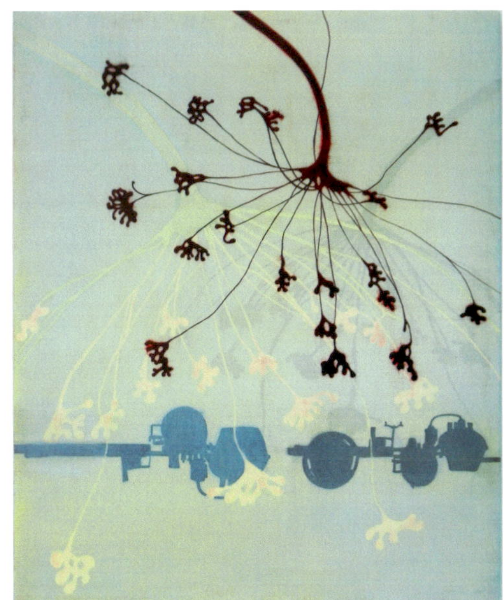

Subversion is on his mind, as his evocative titles imply. His content is not as detached, not as cool or mediated, when closely viewed.

New York artist Annette Davidek focuses on organic motifs taken from diagrams of plants, other life forms, and technological drawings. While abstract, her lilting images suggest roots, branches, the human circulatory system, atoms, and so on, all bio-networks in flux. She applies thin layers of oil paint onto birch panels to create a translucency that appears to be liquid, a radiant solution in which her delicate lines and forms are suspended, with background images that hover like ghosts, fluorescent colors juxtaposed with silhouetted shapes. A tribute to nature, to light, and to beauty, her work functions as a kind of contemporary icon with nature as its saint.

Based in Iowa City, Susan Chrysler White is another painter enamored of the organic. Her densely configured abstractions are also inspired by nature, her repetitions and accumulations referring to the macrocosm of environmental systems and their disorders, the sublime of nature. Like several of the other artists, she uses collage, affixing pieces of cut-up or torn glassine paper overlaid with built-up layers of poured or pressed acrylic and enamel paint onto her canvases. Made without brushes, her work shows that the element of chance is important to her process. She addresses the concept of the decorative as an expression that can also have psychological and philosophical reverberations, slipping botanized images of the Buddha and the Virgin into her paintings as another way to blend nature and the spiritual.

Charles Burwell, who lives and works in Philadelphia, is greatly invested in process and in the ways in which paintings are constructed. His emphasis on an inflected formality is shared with the others. He derives inspiration from artists who are masters of touch and mark, such as Mark Tobey, Cy Twombly, and Agnes Martin. Line is his preference, as well as the meticulous building up of surfaces one layer at a time.

His forms, as an evolving, personalized lexicon, are geometric and organic. They are taken from nature and the industrial, from disciplines such as the natural sciences and archaeology. His newest endeavors depend upon simplification and an increasing ambiguity of imagery, although a tantalizing familiarity remains. In addition to traditional oil and acrylic, he has been experimenting with digital technology. Burwell, in his own way, plays old against new, high against low, fine arts against the decorative.

Paul Henry Ramirez, currently living in New Jersey, is perhaps best known for his site-specific installations, transforming a room or a gallery into an enchanted realm. His version of the baroque appropriates architectural structure and real space as a theatre for his exuberant, partly abstract, partly figurative wall paintings. His candy-colored biomorphic shapes accompanied by fine-line filigree and

Susan Chrysler White. ***Kabuki***, 2012. Acrylic and glassine on canvas, 30 × 30 in.
Courtesy of the artist.

Charles Burwell. ***First One, Then Another***, 20
Acrylic on panel, 24 × 24 in.
Courtesy of Bridgette Mayer Gallery, Philadelphia, Pe

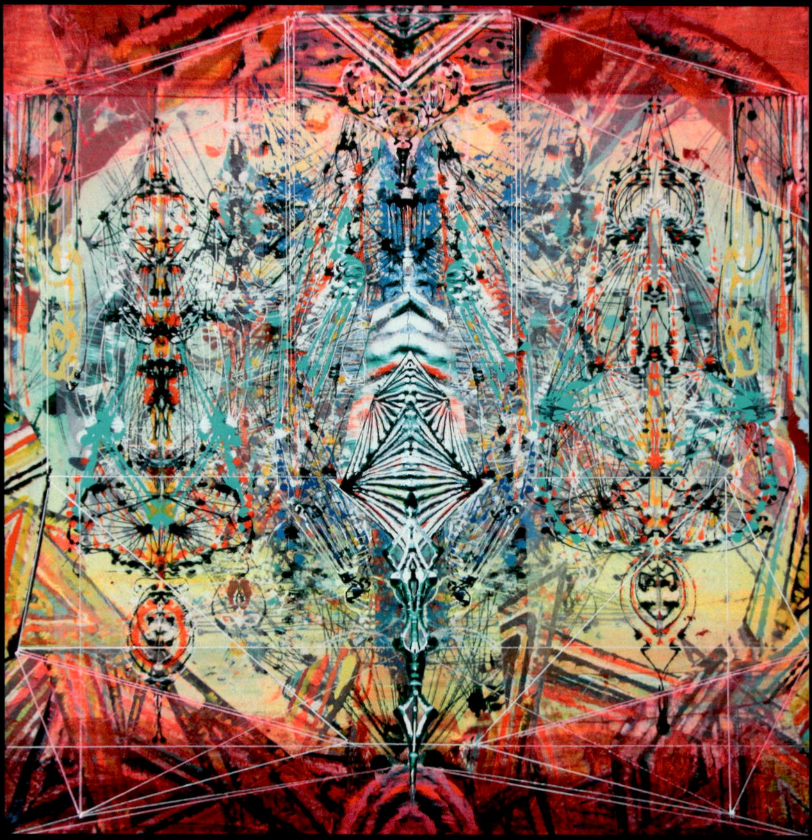

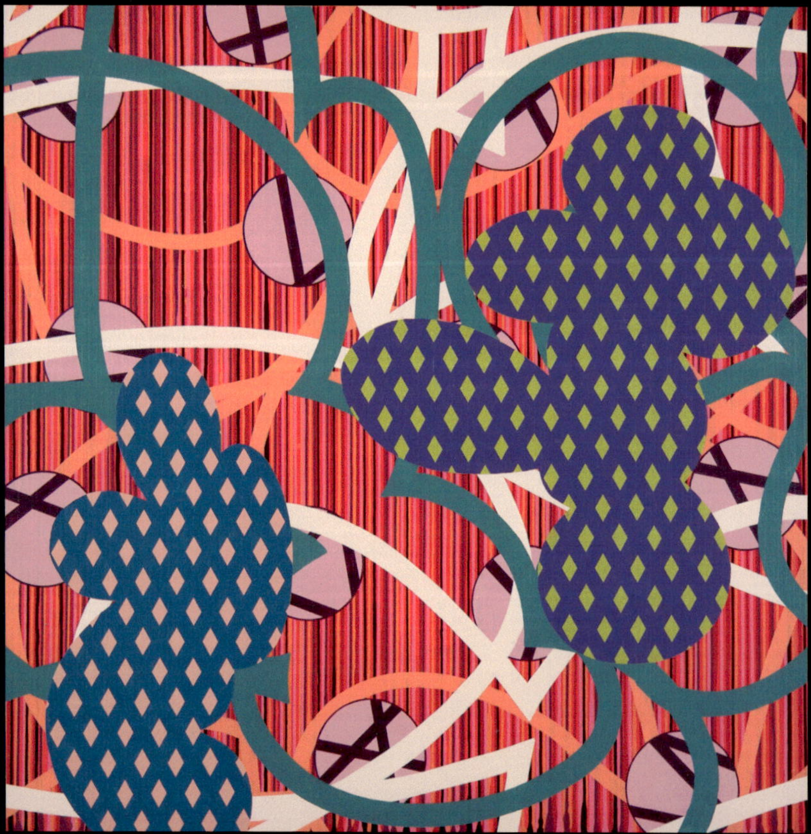

Paul Henry Ramirez. ***SPIN (pink)***, 2009. Screenprint on linen with wall-mounted rotating armature, 44 × 44 in.
Collection of the Tarble Arts Center, Eastern Illinois University, Charleston, Illinois; and the Smithsonian American Art Museum, Washington, DC. Installation view: Tarble Arts Center, 2012. Courtesy of the artist.

Rosalyn Schwartz. ***Rococo Nightmare***, 2012. Mixed media on paper, 11 × 8 in.
Courtesy of the artist.

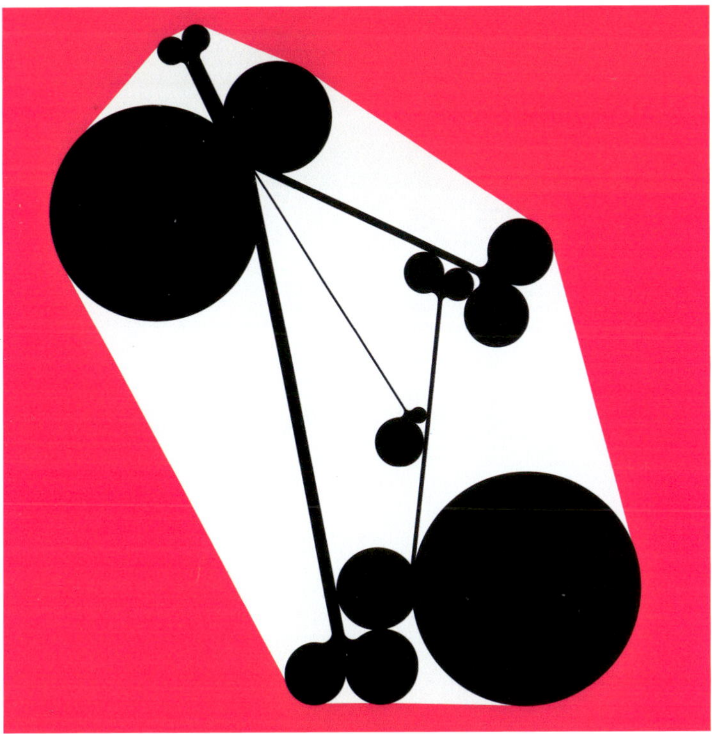

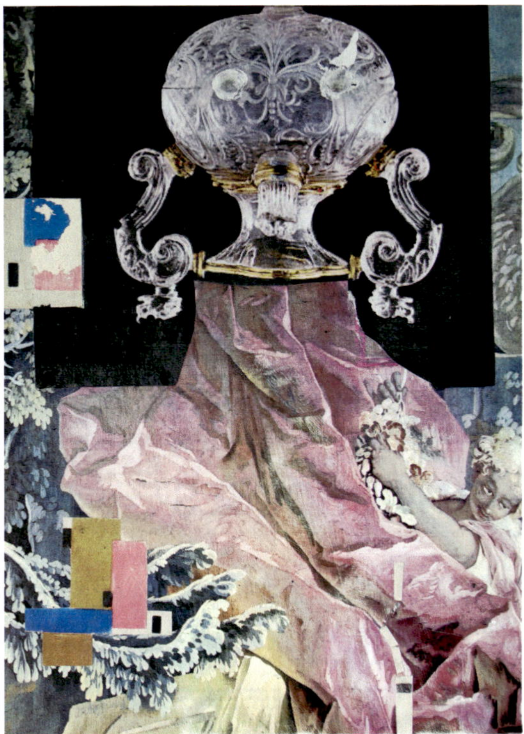

flourishes—trumpet their resemblance to male and female body parts. Their cheeky adolescent eroticism alternates between titillating and more abstract readings that owe much to modernist geometries, mid-century graphics, Color Field, and Pop art in which a circle is indeed also a breast. A formalist and designer, Ramirez jauntily walks the precarious line between disciplines, expertly balancing the serious and the playful, his hijinks a pleasure to behold.

Based in Urbana, Illinois, Rosalyn Schwartz is a passionate advocate for beauty. Her imagination is ecstatic, decadent, and intent on seduction. Her paintings are reveries and romances haunted by the dream of beauty. While her notion of beauty is steeped in pleasure, she knows that it is unstable, transient, and bittersweet. Intensely emotional and personal, Schwartz's paintings focus on cherished objects and memorabilia, recalling the history of fine art and the decorative arts. She merges the patterns and motifs of interior design with abstract configurations and lushly bravura brushwork. She is one of the most painterly of the participating artists. Schwartz also explores the conflicts inherent in our notions of beauty, acknowledging beauty's promises and potency as well as its weaknesses and betrayals.

Is everything beauty? Even in a relativist period—which ours is (and hard-won)—the answer may still be a resounding "no." But to fix any one standard for the judgment of beauty is not possible, so what defines beauty depends upon audiences that will have their own very emphatic notions of what that is. Those notions will not include everything and will not be the same.

The crucial issue is that these audiences remain diverse, their points of view acknowledged without imposing hierarchies, without censorship. Their experiences of art and beauty will therefore remain keen and undiluted because the art that they are seeing is unmediated. As Dave Hickey so sweepingly and optimistically says at the conclusion of *The Invisible Dragon*, "Nothing redeems but beauty, its generous permission, its glorious celebration of all that has previously been uncelebrated."

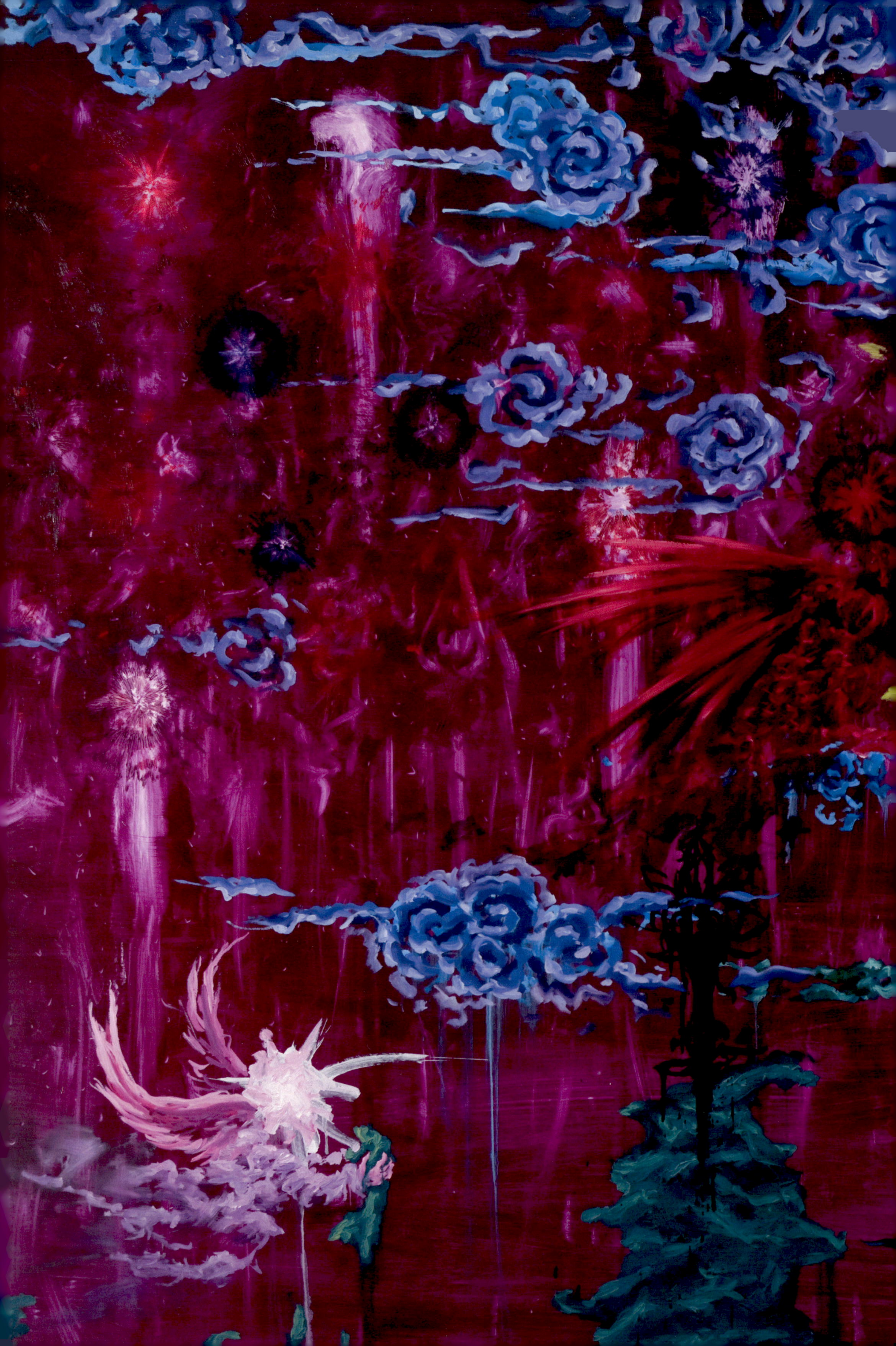

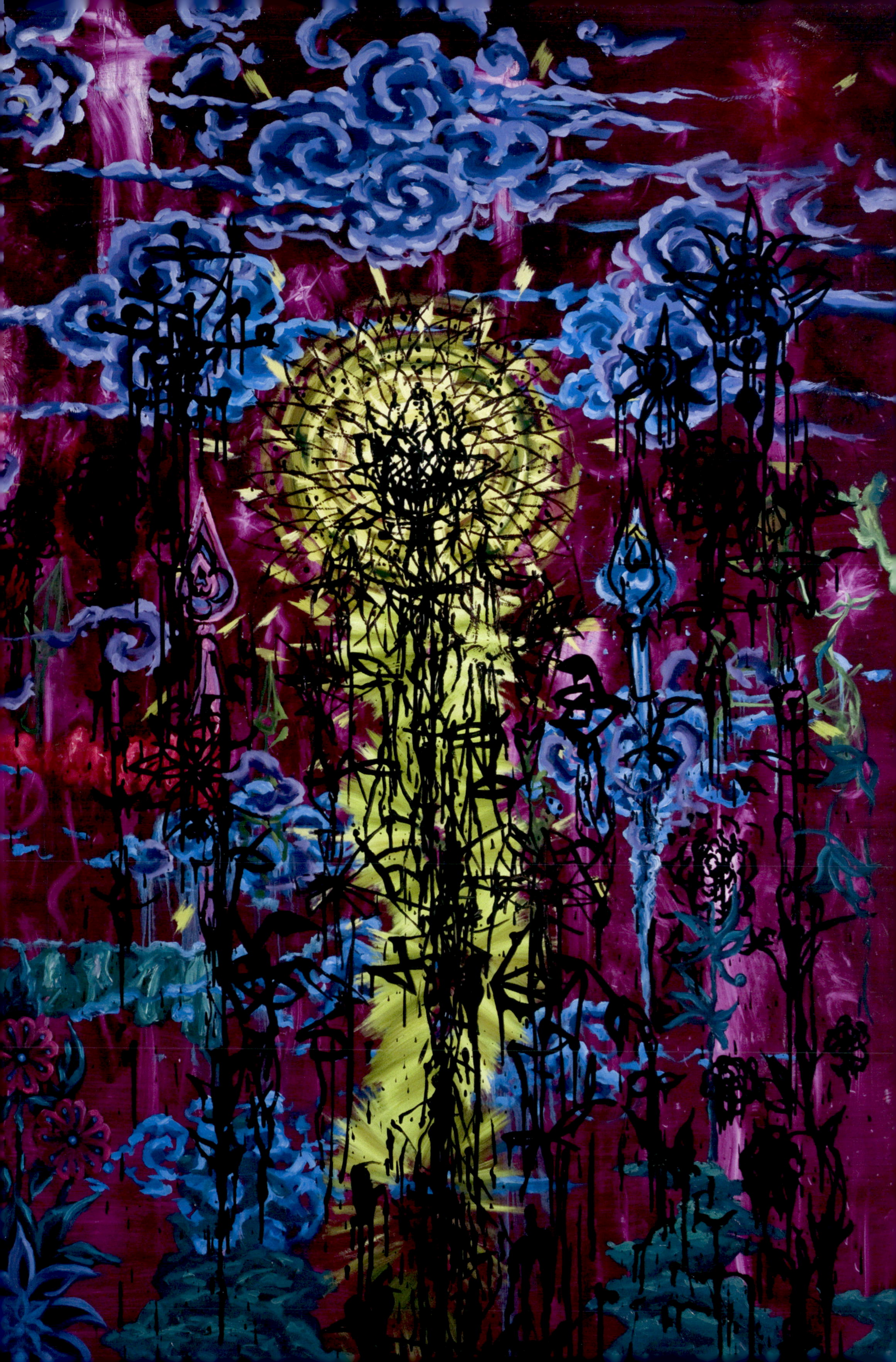

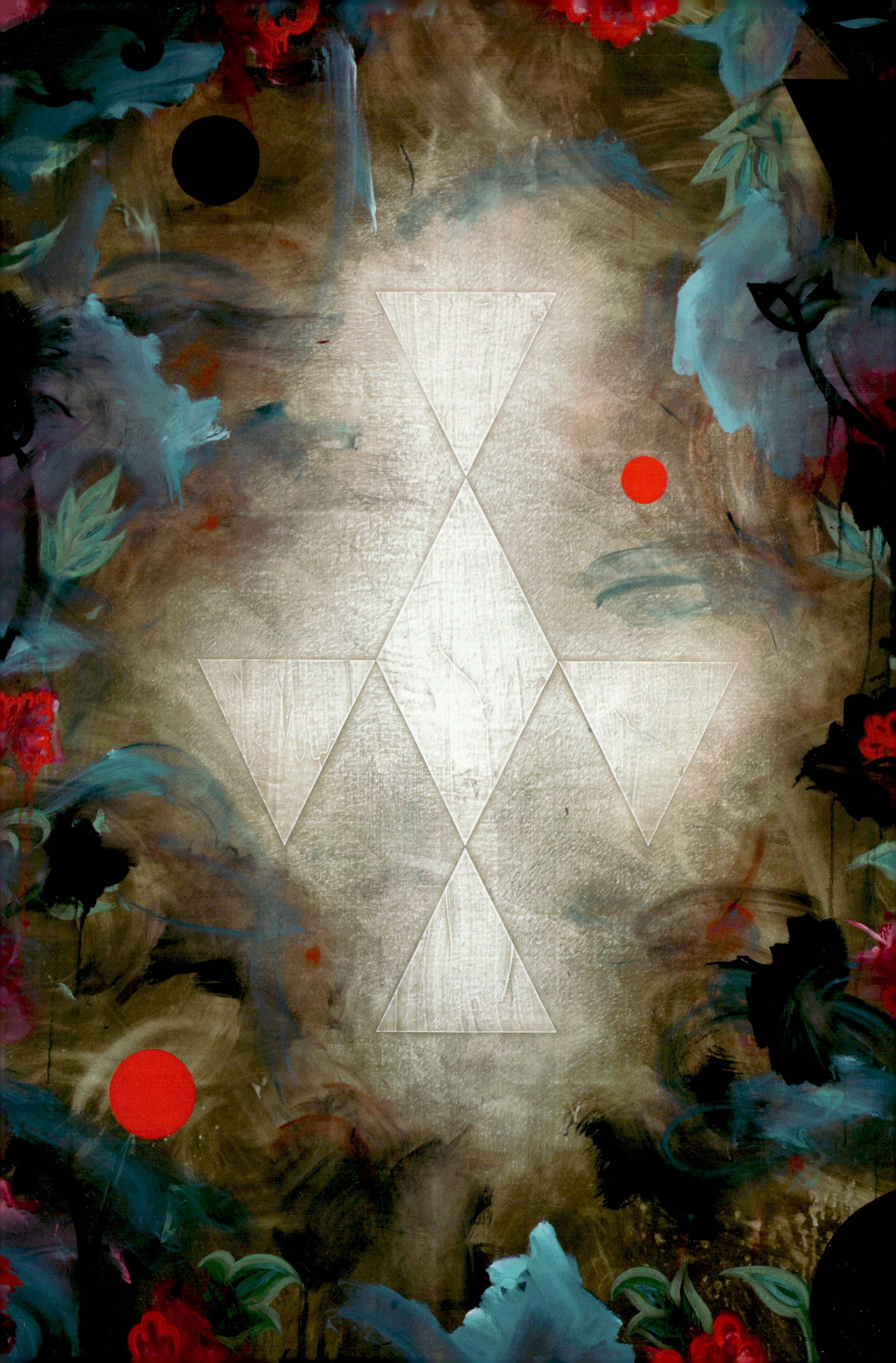

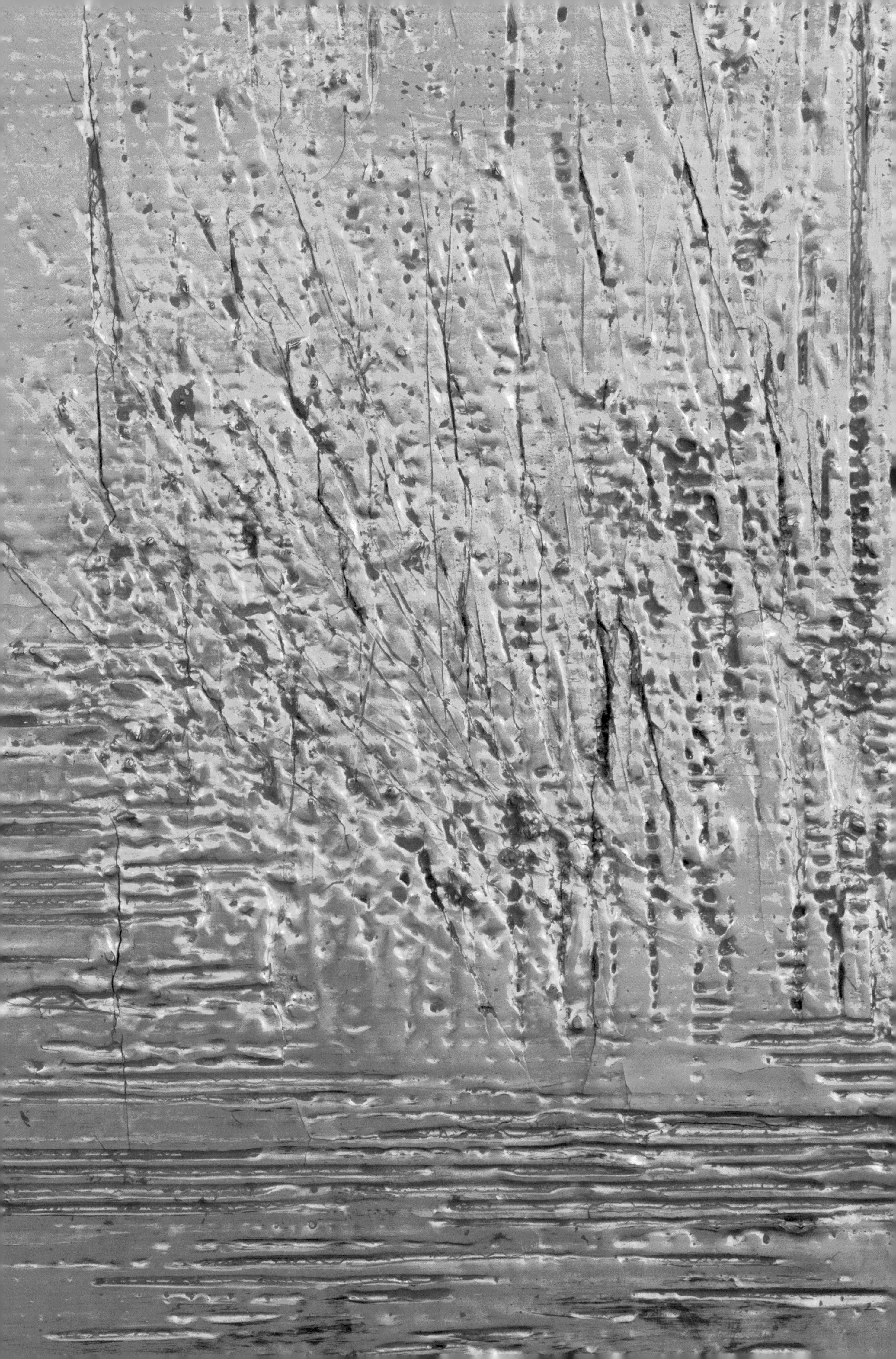

*Beauty Reigns: A Baroque Sensibility in Recent Painting* is published on the occasion of an exhibition of the same title, presented at the McNay Art Museum, San Antonio, Texas, June 11-August 17, 2014. This exhibition was organized by the McNay Art Museum.


Library of Congress Cataloging-in-Publication Data
Beauty reigns : a baroque sensibility in recent painting / René Paul Barilleaux, Lilly Wei, Stephen Westfall.
pages cm
"Beauty Reigns: A Baroque Sensibility in Recent Painting is published on the occasion of an exhibition of the same title, presented at the McNay Art Museum, San Antonio, Texas, June 11–August 17, 2014."
ISBN 978-0-615-86451-8 (alk. paper)
1. Painting, Abstract—Exhibitions. I. Barilleaux, René Paul. II. Wei, Lilly. III. Westfall, Stephen. IV. McNay Art Museum.
ND196.A2B43 2014
759.07'074764351—dc23 2013050221

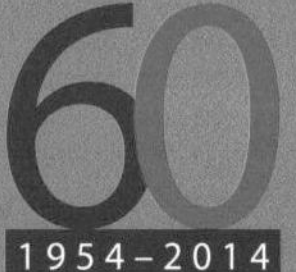


Published by the McNay Art Museum
www.mcnayart.org

theMcNay
McNay Art Museum

Distributed by D.A.P./Distributed Art Publishers
www.artbook.com

Photography credits:
Front endsheet and inside cover spread and pages 2–3, 32, 36–37, 47, 50, 53, 135 (bottom): Warren Flagler
Pages 1, 139 (left): Jeffery Surges
Pages 4, 60–61: Erma Estwick
Pages 5, 62–63 (top and bottom): Max Yawney
Pages 6-7: Peter Halmagyi
Pages 8–9, 12, 38, 48–49, 142: Jason Mandella
Page 33: Jessica Lin Cox
Pages 54, 58, 68 (top and bottom), 75, 137 (right): Greg Davidek
Page 55: Sarah Shreves
Pages 56, 65, 72–73: Keith Barraclough
Pages 57, 70, 133, 136, 140–141, 143: Adam Reich
Pages 66-67: Ian Lefebvre
Page 76: Alex Wagner
Page 77: Tom Fecht
Pages 86–87: Cormac Regan
Page 94: Serge Hasenböhler
Page 95 (top and middle): Claire Schneider
Page 95 (bottom): Roy Porello
Page 96: Anton Perich
Pages 98, 101 (top), 106–107: Megan Roche
Page 99: Jill Tobin
Page 101 (bottom): Jeff Bruce
Pages 102–103: Marty Snortum
Pages 104, 118: Maggie Day
Pages 108, 125: Charlotte Raymond
Page 111, 139 (right): William Arnold
Pages 112–113: Antonio Petracca
Page 115: Raymond Adams
Page 120–121: Paul Henry Ramirez
Pages 122 (top), 123: Justin Meyer
Page 122 (bottom): Sharon Conklin

Front endsheet and inside cover spread: Jose Alvarez (D.O.P.A.), *We Came From the Stars* (detail), 2011; Acrylic, enamel, ink, colored pencil, organdy, feathers, quills, crystals, and mixed media on ultrachrome prints, 72 × 176 in. Collection of the McNay Art Museum; Museum Purchase with funds from the McNay Contemporary Collectors Forum.
Back endsheet and inside cover spread: Rex Ray, *Discolaria* (detail), 2009; Oil, acrylic, and mixed media on linen, 108 × 304 in. Courtesy of the artist and Gallery 16, San Francisco, California.
Page 1: Paul Henry Ramirez, *CHUNK 2* (detail), 2007; Acrylic on canvas, 66 × 66 in. Courtesy of the artist.
Page 2: Jose Alvarez (D.O.P.A.), *Untitled #3* (detail), 2009; Collage, flocking, and crystals on paper, 20 × 13 in. Collection of Bill Mercur; Courtesy of the artist and Gavlak Gallery, Palm Beach, Florida.
Page 3: Jose Alvarez (D.O.P.A.), *Living One's Life as a Work of Art* (detail), 2012; Feathers, ink, colored pencil, crystals, quills, handmade paper, and collage on paper, 19 × 13 in. Collection of Graham and Candace Walsh; Courtesy of the artist and Gavlak Gallery, Palm Beach, Florida.
Page 4: Nancy Lorenz, *Silver Cloud and Black Moon Screen* (detail), 2012; Silver leaf, mother-of-pearl, red clay, and black clay on panels, 72 × 78 in. Courtesy of the artist and PDX Contemporary Art, Portland, Oregon.
Page 5: Annette Davidek, *Untitled* (detail), 2008; Oil on birch panel, 48 × 42 in. Courtesy of the artist and Littlejohn Contemporary, New York.
Pages 6–7: Nancy Lorenz, *Water Study* (detail), 2005; Gold leaf, silver leaf, mother-of-pearl, and pigment on panel, 168 × 840 in. Beverly Hilton Hotel, Beverly Hills, California; Courtesy of the artist and Beverly Hilton Hotel.
Pages 8–9: Kamrooz Aram, *Untitled (Palimpsest #3)* (detail), 2013; Oil, wax, and oil pastel on canvas, 84 × 72 in. Collection of HH Sh Zayed bin Sultan bin Khalifa Al Nahyan, Abu Dhabi, United Arab Emirates; Courtesy of the artist and Green Art Gallery, Dubai, United Arab Emirates.
Page 12: Kamrooz Aram, *Backdrop for a Spirited Decline (Palimpsest #18)* (detail), 2013; Oil, wax, and oil pastel on canvas, 60 × 54 in. Courtesy of the artist and Green Art Gallery, Dubai, United Arab Emirates.
Pages 18–19: Nancy Lorenz, *Skies and Beyond* (detail), 2012; Palladium leaf, black clay, and gesso on panel, on nappa box, 7¾ × 11 × 4 in. From the Bottega Veneta series; Courtesy of the artist and Bottega Veneta, Milan, Italy.
Page 62: Annette Davidek, *Untitled* (detail), 2012; Oil on birch panel, 48 × 42 in. Courtesy of the artist and Littlejohn Contemporary, New York.
Pages 126–127: Susan Chrysler White, *Baroque Garden* (detail), 2013; Acrylic on plexiglass with stainless steel, 180 × 300 × 258 in. Courtesy of the artist.
Pages 140–141: Kamrooz Aram, *Untitled*, 2009; Oil on canvas, 85 × 108 in. Courtesy of the artist and Green Art Gallery, Dubai, United Arab Emirates.
Page 142: Kamrooz Aram, *Untitled (Angelus Novus)* (detail), 2013; Oil on canvas, 84 × 66 in. Courtesy of the artist and Green Art Gallery, Dubai, United Arab Emirates.
Page 143: Nancy Lorenz, *Red Gold, Cardboard I* (detail), 2013; Red gold leaf, gesso, clay, and cardboard on panel, 24 × 18 in. Courtesy of the artist and Morgan Lehman Gallery, New York.



Produced by Marquand Books, Inc., Seattle
www.marquand.com

Designed by Jeff Wincapaw
Typset in Flama and Adobe Text Pro and Flama by Brynn Warriner
Edited by Marcia Goren Weser
Proofread by Craig Bunch, Diana George, and Althea Ruoppo
Color management by iocolor, Seattle, Washington
Printed and bound in China by Artron Color Printing Co., Ltd.

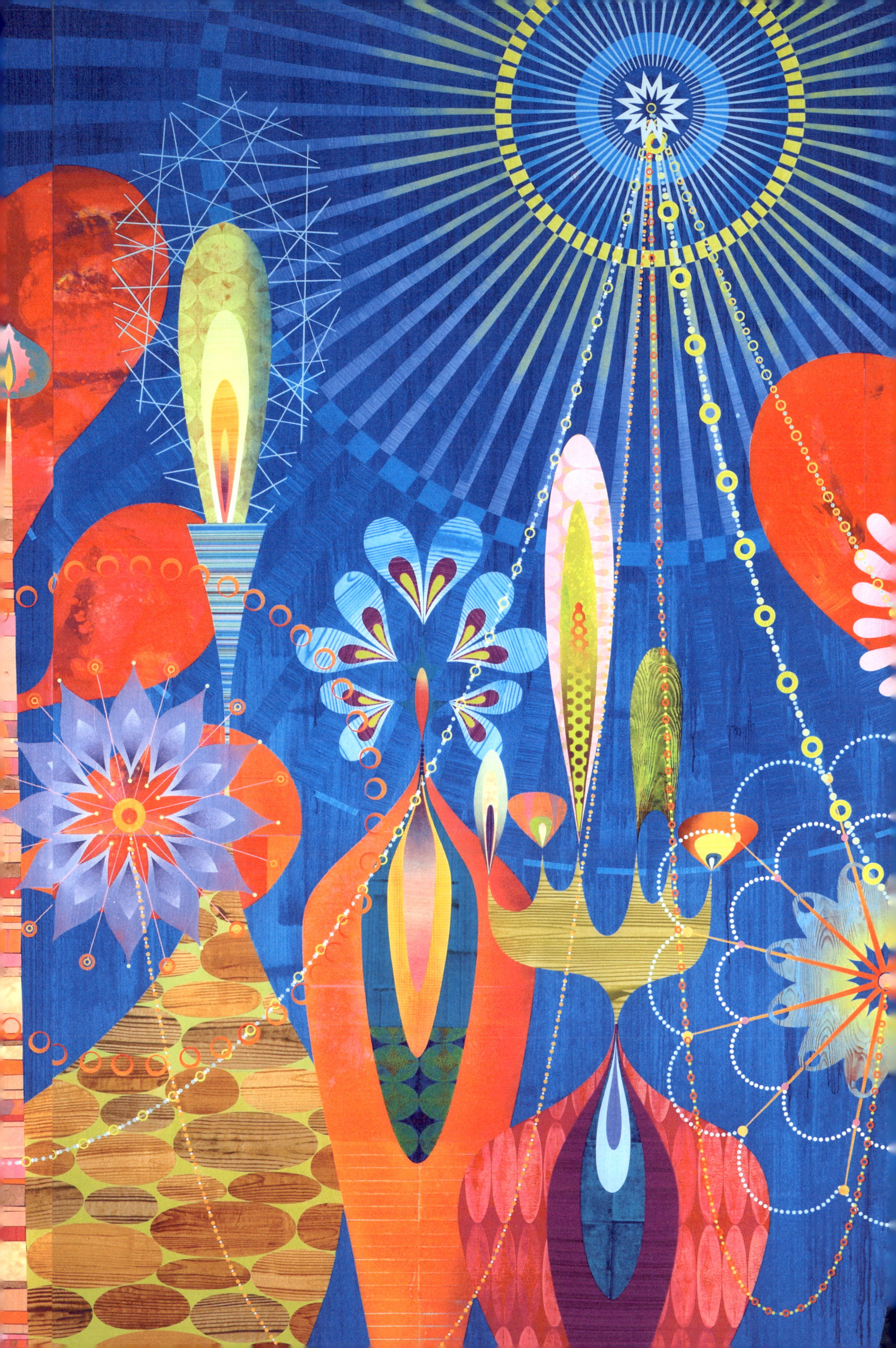

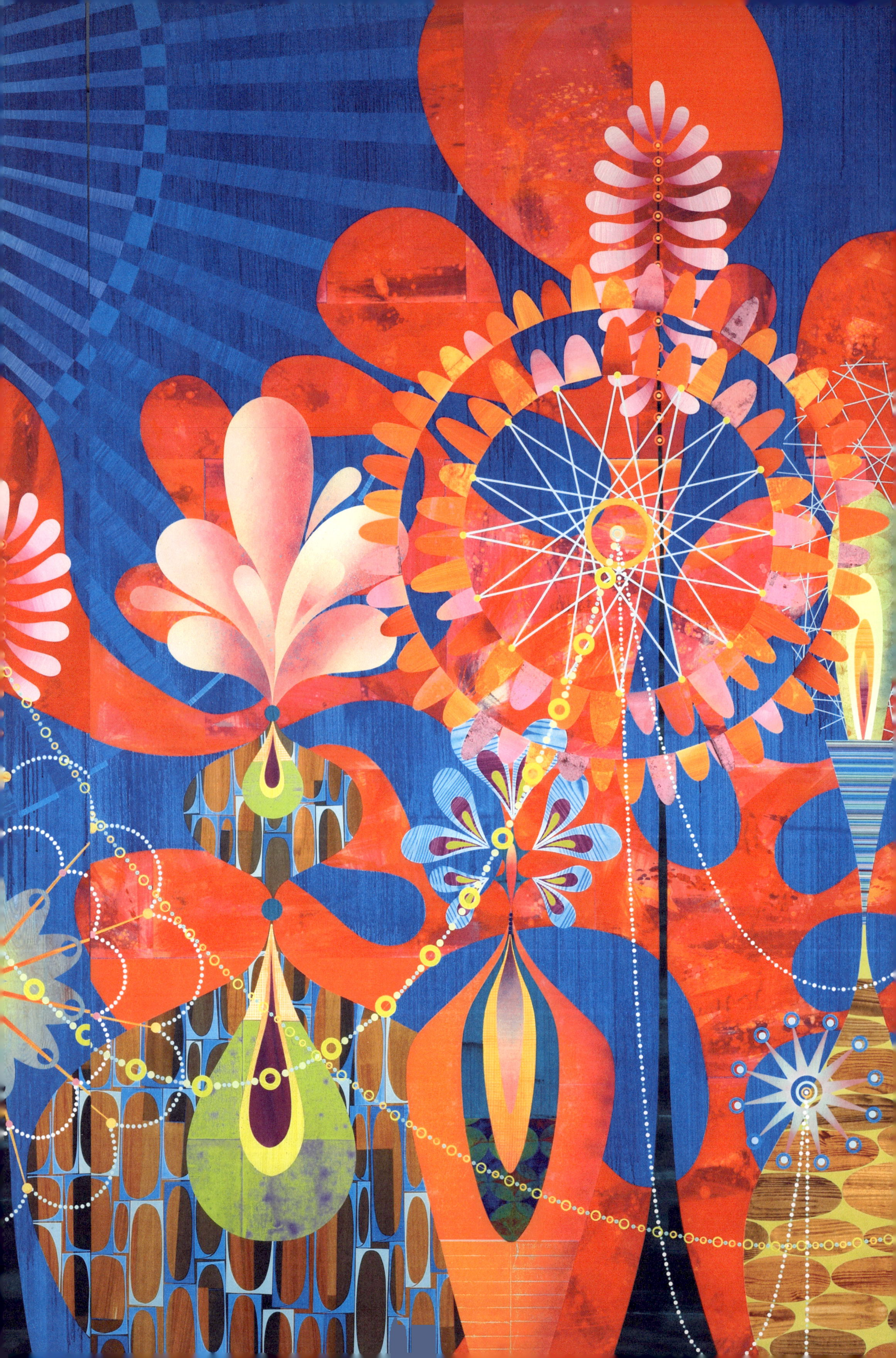